Worker Absenteeism
and Sick Pay

Absenteeism is the single most important cause of lost labour time, yet it has received much less scholarly attention than more dramatic forms of industrial disruption, such as strikes. Arguing that any explanation of absence rates must take into account the interests of employers and employees alike, this book constructs a model of the markets for absence and sick pay. These are not independent, since sick pay affects workers' incentives to be absent, and absences affect employers' willingness to provide sick pay. The book reviews the available empirical evidence relating to both markets, stressing the importance of careful identification of the effect of the price of absence on demand, since this is a crucial quantity for firms' policies. It concludes by discussing the implications of the model for human resources management, and for the role of the state in sick pay provision.

JOHN TREBLE retired recently as Professor of Economics at Swansea University. He has previously taught and held visiting posts in the United Kingdom, North America, Europe and Australia. His work is mainly in labour economics, with some forays into economic history. Professor Treble was the founder of Britain's national labour economics conference, now called the Work and Pensions Economics Group, and served a full term on the founding Committee of the European Society of Labour Economists.

TIM BARMBY has held the Jaffrey Chair of Political Economy at the University of Aberdeen since 2004, before which he was Professor of Economics at Durham University. His main academic interest is in the empirical analysis of the incentive effects of labour contracts. He has worked with John Treble on the economic analysis of absenteeism for more than twenty-five years.

Worker Absenteeism and Sick Pay

JOHN TREBLE AND TIM BARMBY

CAMBRIDGE
UNIVERSITY PRESS

Shaftesbury Road, Cambridge CB2 8EA, United Kingdom

One Liberty Plaza, 20th Floor, New York, NY 10006, USA

477 Williamstown Road, Port Melbourne, VIC 3207, Australia

314–321, 3rd Floor, Plot 3, Splendor Forum, Jasola District Centre, New Delhi – 110025, India

103 Penang Road, #05–06/07, Visioncrest Commercial, Singapore 238467

Cambridge University Press is part of Cambridge University Press & Assessment, a department of the University of Cambridge.

We share the University's mission to contribute to society through the pursuit of education, learning and research at the highest international levels of excellence.

www.cambridge.org
Information on this title: www.cambridge.org/9780521806954

First published 2011

A catalogue record for this publication is available from the British Library

Library of Congress Cataloging-in-Publication data
Treble, John.
    Worker absenteeism and sick pay / by John Treble and Tim Barmby.
        p. cm.
    ISBN 978-0-521-80695-4 (Hardback)
    1. Sick leave. 2. Absenteeism (Labor) I. Barmby, Tim. II. Title.
    HD5115.5.T69 2011
    331.25′762—dc22

ISBN   978-0-521-80695-4   Hardback

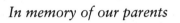
In memory of our parents

Note on cover illustration

The cover illustration shows a limestone ostrakon with a register of workmen's absences from Deir el-Medina, Egypt (19th Dynasty, around 1250 BC). The ostrakon is held at the British Museum: "This *ostrakon* seems to be a workman's register for 280 days of Year 40 of the reign of Ramesses II (about 1279–1213 BC). A list of forty names is arranged in columns of hieratic script on the right-hand edge of each side. To the left are dates written in black in a horizontal line. The reasons for absences are written above the dates in red ink. They are varied and give us a fascinating insight into some aspects of life in ancient Egypt. Illness figures prominently; a couple of examples of illnesses of the eyes are mentioned. One workman functioned as a doctor and was often away attending on others. Absences due to deaths of relatives are recorded, as are also references to purifications, perhaps relating to childbirth. Frequently a day missed is down to a man 'being with his boss'; other sources show that workmen did frequently do work for their superiors. Occasionally a man is away 'building his house', or at 'his festival', and there are even examples of drinking, in particular 'drinking with Khonsu'."

Contact John Treble at j.g.treble@swansea.ac.uk

Contents

Figures

Tables

Preface

This book has been a long time in the making, and we have many people and organisations to thank for support of many different kinds. The unwitting provider of many of the ideas in the book was a frozen chicken factory in Aldershot, which employed the youthful John Treble for a few weeks in 1967. During a labour economics class at the University of Hull in the early 1980s a third-year undergraduate student (whose name is now lost in the mists of time) asked an innocent question about prices and incentives, which provided the initial impetus for all our work on absenteeism. Our ideas about the empirical matters were given a considerable boost by a large British firm in the fast-moving consumer goods sector, which not only gave us access to its personnel and pay records but also paid for research assistance for two years. A second British firm, in the financial sector, was similarly generous with data, and also provided financial support, as did the Economic and Social Research Council (ESRC). The ESRC and the Leverhulme Trust have supported this work with several grants of varying sizes. Empirical work using French data was supported by the British Council and the French Ministry for Foreign Affairs under the Alliance programme.

As important as money in enabling an enterprise such as this is finding time in which to do it. Once again, several organisations have given us space to develop ideas at some length. The ESRC and the Leverhulme Trust, again; la Fondation des Treilles; ERMES and LEM at Université de Paris II (Panthéon-Assas); the Institute for Labour Research at the University of Essex; the Centre for Labour Economics at Århus Universitet; the Tinbergen Institute; and the economics departments at Vrije Universitet, Amsterdam, Universität München, Universität Hannover, the University of Arizona and Curtin University. Thanks must also go to Per Johansson for organising a workshop on absence in Uppsala at which the demand and supply idea was first tried out.

Many friends (some of whom have also been colleagues and co-authors) have been generous with their time, their creativity and the frankness of their criticism. They include: Rick Audas, Felix Bellaby, Chris Bojke, Sarah Bridges, Sarah Brown, Frank den Butter, Melvyn Coles, Peter Dolton (who also suggested the cover image), Martin Dufwenberg, Barbara Eberth, Marco Ercolani, Price Fishback, Edwin van Gameren, Knut Gerlach, Donna Gilleskie, Wolter Hassink, Peter Kenyon, Joseph Lanfranchi, Makram Larguem, Ada Ma, Mike Nolan, Ron Oaxaca, Chris Orme, John Sessions, Suzyrman Sibly, Ali Skalli, John Skåtun, Gesine Stephan, Rado Vadovic, Simon Vicary and Rainer Winkelmann. To these should be added seminar participants at conferences and economics departments too numerous to list, even if we had kept a record. Denise Drummond very kindly and carefully checked the Index.

Special mention must be made of Joseph Lanfranchi, Gauthier Lanot and Ron Oaxaca, who found time to read the entire manuscript. The final version has benefited greatly from their efforts, but they should not be blamed for any remaining errors, inaccuracies or omissions.

1 | *Introduction*

Ever since the first worker was employed, employers have concerned themselves with worker discipline. Workers agree to work but, having agreed, are unable or unwilling to supply their labour as reliably as the employer would wish. Ultimately, discipline can be enforced by sacking offending workers, but this is not necessarily the most profitable solution. Bryson (2007), for instance, observes that

[Elizabethan] actors were subjected to rigorous contractual obligations, with graduated penalties for missing rehearsals, being drunk or tardy, failing to be 'ready apparelled' at the right moment, or – strikingly – for wearing any stage costumes outside the playhouse. Costumes were extremely valuable, so the fine was a decidedly whopping (and thus probably never imposed) £40. But even the most minor infractions, like tardiness, could cost an actor two days' pay.

On the other hand, Stone's (1950) account of work patterns in an Elizabethan coal mine between 1580 and 1582 indicates that efforts by the employer to control absence were non-existent:

[T]he Sheffield accounts . . . offer a very different explanation than that of the ruthless employer sacking and hiring his workmen at will. Rather. . . the miner worked when and as long as he thought fit and the employer was obliged to content himself with methodically recording the rate of absenteeism. Involuntary absenteeism as shown in the accounts was extremely rare, though some of the unexplained short-time weeks may have been caused by illness. The only recorded illness was in the second week in August 1580, when production was halved, the marginal explanation being that the 'collyers were syck'. A fortnight later, the full output per shift was again being performed so that the malady could not have been serious. During the whole three and a half years only one industrial accident took place when one of the pickmen, Handcock, was hurt in the third week of June 1582 and was away for a total of seven weeks, no effort being made to replace him during this time. There can be no doubt, however, that in the vast majority of cases absenteeism at Sheffield was voluntary. One of the pickmen was continually taking a day or two off during

1

the week, thus breaking the regular production schedule of the pit. The bank-man, as the foreman, was more responsible, but on one occasion at least all work had to stop for three days, because 'Copeley the barrower went forth'. Furthermore, the whole gang irregularly took itself off for celebrations, or for recuperation from such festivities. Sheffield fair day in November 1581 they took off. Again in May 1581, the entry runs: 'Monday after the fair day, they wrought not.' They took off the day before St James's Day, and Easter Saturday in different years, quite unexpectedly. Sometimes it is merely recorded 'the collyers was away besides' or some such phrase. All this was over and above the regular fixed holidays which they unfailingly allocated to themselves on the saints' days of the old pre-Reformation calendar. [. . .] In fact. . .they had between a month and five weeks' regular holiday every year – which is hardly what one has been led to expect of a defenceless working class freshly subjected to the full pressure of unbridled capitalism.

Taken with Sundays, this reduced the days in the year available for work to about 280, while normal interruptions due to other causes whittled down the figure still further. Damp in the mine, flooding and over-production all played their part, and in actual fact the days' work done were as follows:

1579 July–December, six months	83 days (flooding and damp)
1580 January–December, twelve months	256 days (12 days' flooding)
1581 January–December, twelve months	256½ days
1582 January–December, twelve months	227 days (24 days laid off)

Of course no payments were made when no work was done, and as a result the yearly earnings for a typical year 1580 were very small. The barrower and the two pickmen in continual employment each earned £6, and the bankman earned – officially and on his own reckoning – £9. The pickmen's and bar-rower's actual average weekly wage was therefore far below starvation level.

Although the accounts for maintenance and new mining show that the miners earned substantial sums from time to time doing extra work about the mine, yet even these do not suffice to compensate for the poverty of the annual wage. It seems therefore almost certain that economic factors as well as super-stition drove the miners to this insistence upon what were by sixteenth-century standards wholly extravagant holidays. They must have been cottagers with casual employment on their own gardens or about the Earl's park. While there is no shred of evidence in the accounts to support this suggestion, it is difficult to see what other explanation is possible for the situation as it has been described.

The work contract in this Elizabethan coal mine was very simple. It seems to have specified six working days per week, except when certain specified religious holidays occurred. No sick pay was paid, and, despite the fact that the total pay was 'far below starvation level', voluntary absence was frequent, apparently organised and unpunished by any sort of disciplinary procedure. Stone does not report what the daily hours may have been, but it appears that subsistence was ensured by small-scale agriculture independently of this employment. Compare this with the typical worker in a developed economy at the start of the twenty-first century, whose single source of income is a five-day week; who will be paid during holiday leave; who will have some insurance against loss of income due to sickness; and whose absences are monitored and, if not satisfactorily explained, will trigger managerial action, usually disciplinary in nature. Furthermore, many employers have arrangements in place to enable absent workers' tasks to be covered in some way.

The study of worker absence over the last century or so has been dominated by the idea that absence is a problem of worker discipline. Many commentators take as given the proposition that low absence rates are good absence rates, while conceding that eliminating absence altogether is an impossibility. One theme of this book is that these ideas are misleading and, if they are used as the basis for human resources (HR) practice, can lead to policies that encourage inefficiency.

Since we are economists, our arguments use the tools of economics. These enable us to extend our purview beyond the existing literature's stress on absence as a problem in the psychological make-up or social circumstances of workers. We accept that these are important, but just as important, if firms' and governments' policies are to be well founded, are the interests of firms and governments. Taking these interests into account leads to more acute insights than are available when only the behaviour of workers is considered.

The Elizabethan coal mine gives an idea of what absence behaviour would be like without cover arrangements, managerial control, holiday entitlements and sick pay. Work still got done, but it was interrupted either by individual absence[1] or by coordinated group absence. It is also important to note one advantage of this arrangement from the employer's point of view: the mine could be closed when it was

---

[1] It would be interesting to know what their co-workers thought of Copeley the barrower when he 'went forth' and of the disruption caused by the pickman's absences. It is possible that they were able to reduce the cost of regular disruption by covering the pickman's work. Another possibility is that they were laid off, and could use their time more or less equally productively elsewhere.

unworkable, without any remuneration being due to disappointed workers. Under these work arrangements, disruptions could occur either because the capital was available unreliably, or because labour was available unreliably. Modern firms often insure workers against capital disruption, by paying them when machines fail, or negotiating terms for a layoff.

The coal mine described in Stone's article was a capital asset, which would remain unproductive unless it had labour input. The available work force clearly had outside activities, which they could exploit. Whatever the pickman was doing on the days when he failed to show up, he presumably thought he was devoting time to the most profitable activity available to him. The view of absence that we put forward in this book differs little from this. The theoretical models described here are an attempt to analyse the important considerations for firms confronted with workers whose attendance may be unreliable. We also examine the considerations surrounding the attendance decisions of workers, and particularly the effect of different contracts on those decisions.

While we ourselves are economists, and we use the methods of economics in our approach, we have attempted to make this book accessible to non-economists. The text has technical aspects, but throughout we have endeavoured to give sufficient non-technical explanation so that non-specialists should be able to follow the arguments. In particular, we believe that there are important messages in it for human resources practitioners, other managers and policy-makers. In particular, Chapter 8 pulls together the main messages of our argument for managers, and Chapter 9 attempts to outline how it might influence the thinking of policy-makers. We also hope that researchers in other disciplines will find food for thought in these pages, although we would not expect (nor do we think it desirable) that they would adopt our way of thinking about absenteeism unreservedly.

One of our main criteria is to provide a coherent framework within which to conduct analysis of these issues. This has taken a surprisingly long time to emerge. Early attempts to analyse absenteeism failed to be coherent at all. The difficulties can be illustrated with two early discussions of absence and alcohol by eminent economists.

In 1919 Irving Fisher (cited by Benge, 1923) took a normative view:

Another force for prohibition is the force of industrialism and of the modern desire for efficiency both on the part of industries and on the part of individuals. Industry is applying modern science. From two to four glasses of beer will reduce the output of typesetters by 8 per cent. These and other experiments demonstrate that we will increase, by enforcing prohibition, the economic productivity of this nation from 10 to 20 per cent, and will add to the national output of the US between 7 to 15 billion dollars' worth of product, every year, reckoned at the moderate level of prices. These forces, the ideals of work, the requirements of modern industrial competition, the findings of modern science and the ideals of morality in American life are the forces which have put over prohibition, and it must be on these forces that we shall depend to enforce prohibition.

In the same year Paul Douglas published the first survey of the absenteeism literature (Douglas, 1919). In discussing the relationship between alcohol and absenteeism, he says:

(l) *Liquor.* The influence of liquor in causing absenteeism cannot be accurately measured. The majority of employment managers, however, state that from their observation, drinking men are absent far more frequently than abstainers. It is also true that shipyards in dry states have somewhat better attendance records than those in wet states. Although the whole matter is one on which no absolute statement can be made, it seems reasonably certain, all other things being equal, that complete prohibition will bring with it a decided improvement in working attendance.

(m) *Wage income higher than standard of living.* When a workman receives more money than he wishes to spend or save, he will stop working and thus bring his income down to his standard of living. If . . . real wages increase faster than the standard of living, absenteeism necessarily results. This was the situation created in several war industries where wages increased faster than the wants of the worker. It was undoubtedly a factor in certain sections of the shipbuilding and munition industries. A higher standard of living, therefore, decreases absenteeism as indeed does an increase in prices. It should be clearly realized that the term 'higher standard of living' carries with it no ethical implications.

It might perhaps more accurately be called 'more expensive standard of living'. The new wants which go to form it may be vicious. The Hawaiian planters are said to prefer dissolute laborers, addicted to drinking and gambling, to sober men, because they work harder and more constantly to satisfy their wants. From the standpoint of human values, therefore, absenteeism with all its waste may be far more profitable than some additional wants. Those who believe that progress consists in the multiplication of wants would do well to consider the qualitative as well as the quantitative aspects of the standard of living.

One central point that Douglas seems to be making is that drunks are more unreliable (or more given to absenteeism) than more sober types. When he discusses 'standard of living', though, he argues (or, at least, relays a rumour about pineapple growers) that, because drunks require a larger income to maintain their habit, they are more reliable at work than sober types. Douglas's confusion here arises partly from the idea (which has now largely been jettisoned by labour economists) that 'standard of living' is somehow exogenous to the labour market. According to this view, people have a target income and stop working when they reach it[2] – an assumption that was made unnecessary by Robbins' (1930) exposition of the roots of labour supply in choice theory, which explains exactly how an increase in the wage rate can generate a lower supply of labour, when workers view their welfare as dependent on their total income and available non-work time. Robbins' argument, which has recently been clarified by Sorauren (2008), relies on the now commonplace prediction of choice theory that an increase in a wage rate has two effects. It changes wealth as well as relative values. While the latter change has a predictable effect, the former does not, so the total impact is unpredictable. This model is now a key part of every course in microeconomics, but in 1919, when Douglas was writing, it was certainly not a familiar part of economists' analyses of the labour market.

A second issue raised by Douglas's remarks is not so easily disposed of. It is claimed not only that 'dissolute workers. . .work harder', but also that they work 'more constantly'. The 'constancy' of work (or of other kinds of productive inputs) has not been the subject of much economic theorising. Indeed, we believe that one of the chief contributions of this book is to point out the inadequacy of deterministic models in explanations of absenteeism. Such models may have some power in explaining average effects, but they fail when asked to deal with questions associated with contracting between firms and workers, which must necessarily take into account the facts that illness is to be expected, that it has negative impacts on the worker as well as on the employer and that these impacts are at least partially ameliorable, by the use of substitute inputs or by insurance.

---

[2] This idea has resurfaced in the 'behavioural economics' literature. See, especially, Camerer *et al.* (1997) and the riposte by Farber (2005).

The above quotation by Douglas begins with the remark that '[t]he influence of liquor in causing absenteeism cannot be accurately measured'. Recent work using theoretical ideas and empirical techniques similar to those described in this book is beginning to make this remark seem like an untruth (Johannsson, Böckerman and Uutela, 2009). We believe that this is evidence of the progress that the use of economic concepts can make in the understanding of absence. In particular, this book argues that absenteeism cannot be fully understood without appeal to the idea of a market.

We refer to the decisions of employers as 'supply-side' decisions and of workers as 'demand-side' decisions. Workers demand absence from time to time, even though they are parties to a contract according to which they undertake to attend. The extent to which workers will do this depends not only on their contract, their sense of responsibility, commitment, honour, and other socio-psychological factors, but also on how they value time spent other than at work. This varies considerably, and often in an unpredictable way. Sickness, sick children, jury service, pastimes and a whole host of possibly unpredictable[3] events can change a worker's valuation of time spent at work relative to time spent elsewhere. This idea is a key part of the book. If a worker's valuation of time spent in different activities did not change, the problem of labour supply would be simple. A job offer specifying a particular work pattern would either be acceptable or not. If it were not acceptable, it would be rejected. If it were acceptable, there is no reason why the worker would not abide by it.[4] Uncertainty is an inalienable part of any explanation of absence rates.

The idea that there is a 'supply' of absence is harder to swallow. It becomes easier to accept, perhaps, once it is made clear that 'supply' is a technical term used by economists to mean not just an amount of something offered by a supplier – economists call that 'quantity

---

[3] Unpredictable, or simply unusual. One of us, John Treble, can remember being required to take time off from work so that his co-workers could watch the live television broadcast of Princess Anne's wedding. Although their relative valuation of time had changed so much that it would have been unwise for the manager to try to enforce their contract, Treble's had not changed at all, so he got a good deal out of it.

[4] There is an argument due to Reza (1975) and Dunn and Youngblood (1986) that workers sign a contract for more hours than they would ideally like, and then take absences to compensate for the difference. We do not find this argument very convincing for a number of reasons, which are discussed in Chapter 3.

supplied' – but the relationship between quantity supplied and price. When we speak of the 'supply of absence' in the following pages, we mean that employers will generally tolerate a particular level of absence among their workers. (They would rather not have to, but they do because they know that without such tolerance employing workers would be very expensive.) The extent to which they will do so depends on how costly absence is to them, and how costly it is for them to monitor and control it. A firm's 'supply of absence' is the relationship between different levels of absence and the marginal cost to the firm of each of them.

Sickness is a source of uncertainty for workers. An employer who can help them handle that uncertainty will generally be able to pay lower wages than one who cannot, since risk-averse workers will be prepared to accept lower wages in return for reduced uncertainty. The costs to employers of providing such services depend on many things, but one thing is sure: these costs will not be the same for all employers. A market supply curve will thus be generated.

It would be naïve, though, to claim that the market for absence can be studied in isolation. Apart from the obvious fact that absence is a labour market phenomenon and cannot be studied separately from the labour market as a whole, the argument in the last paragraph suggests that employers might also supply certain kinds of insurance, so that the markets for these kinds of insurance become entangled with the study of absence as well.

While absenteeism seems to have become a major concern for employers sometime around the end of the nineteenth century, it was not until the middle of the twentieth that the insurance aspects became matters of managerial and regulatory concern. The US debates have been described and discussed in detail by Murray (2007), although, rather frustratingly, he ends his narrative before the post-war adoption by some US states of state-administered insurance against loss of income due to sickness. In most European countries, systems similar to the one initiated in 1883 by Count Otto von Bismarck in Germany were adopted, and in many of them these remain the basis for modern arrangements. A striking exception is the United Kingdom, where the state withdrew from its administrative role during the 1980s, and from most of its regulatory role in the early 1990s.

What kind of protections can employers give to workers against the uncertain consequences of illness? There are essentially three: they can provide job security, they can provide full or partial replacement income, or they can provide insurance against the extra costs of illness. The extent to which employers provide these things varies enormously between different economies, and in many economies it is heavily influenced by government provision or regulation. In England and Wales, for instance, job protection is governed largely by case law (employers are expected to handle dismissals due to illness in a 'fair and reasonable' manner). Replacement income is practically unregulated, although it is subject to small statutory minimum amounts. Health care is provided by a national health service, funded largely from general taxation. In the United States, on the other hand, federal law prohibits the dismissal of workers for taking small amounts of absence for reasons related to their own or their family's health. Replacement income is not federally regulated, although five states have sick pay arrangements funded from hypothecated tax receipts. Health plans are often provided by employers, but provision is by no means universal.

The reasons for the widely different mixes of private as opposed to public provision of the two insurances mentioned in the last paragraph are not well understood. The debate about the public provision of health care is moribund in Britain, since a consensus exists in that country that the National Health Service, while imperfect, is better than the alternatives (or, at least, that sticking with it is better than switching to any alternative). The debate in the United States rages, since there is a widespread suspicion that the current arrangements are not sustainable, allied to an equally widespread and deep suspicion of government intervention in markets. The final chapter of this book is an attempt to open a debate about the provision of sick pay, on the basis of the claim that, if experience rating were to be adopted by firms providing it, the classic problems raised by asymmetric information in insurance markets need not arise.

The idea of absence as the outcome of a market process is central to this book. Although it is no more than an idea, it has important practical implications. In particular, it invites reconsideration of the idea of absenteeism as an avoidable cost. The total costs of absence are themselves complex, and very hard to measure. In Britain, the Confederation of British Industry (CBI) attempts to do this every year, and regularly comes up with a figure well in excess of £10 billion. However, these estimates can be taken seriously only as an indication of the order of magnitude of the total costs. Because it would be unwise for a firm to try to impose zero levels of absence, there is no suggestion that there is a free lunch worth £10 billion that can be consumed whenever managers can summon up the energy to do so. In fact, absence control is an expensive business. Even the unsophisticated Elizabethan way of keeping track of and recording worker attendance would have taken some time, which the foreman could have used doing more valuable things had his workforce not been so fickle. In modern developed countries, those same tasks involve the installation and maintenance of time-keeping equipment, setting up and maintaining computer-based records, calculating the effect of absence on pay, keeping the relevant government administrative departments informed and handling disputes when things go wrong with any of these things. One British firm that we have studied in detail employs one full-time clerical worker in each of its plants simply to handle the day-to-day administration of its absence records and their interface with the firm's pay systems. In addition to this, the attendance system needs to be maintained, and its use, development and application needs to be guided and supervised by managers.

One of our own studies (discussed in more detail in Chapter 6) has developed an alternative approach to the measurement of absence costs. It suggests that the balance between the gain from managerial effort put into absenteeism reduction by our sample of French firms and the costs of that effort is well struck. Apparently, there is little in the way of free lunches to be had for French managers, given the technology that they are operating and the regulatory framework within which they work. As far as we can tell, they do a good job of identifying and acting on opportunities for absence reduction that cost less than they return.

The supply side of our models is dominated by the idea that not all production processes are equally disrupted by absence. In particular, teamwork makes absences costly, because an absence affects the productivity of an entire team; similarly, capital use makes absences costly, because the equipment falls idle as well as the worker. Once again, the detail of these arguments is complex, and their appearance in the actual world of work is not easy to disentangle from other differences between firms. If team work is more expensive, it will be worthwhile for firms that cannot avoid it to make adjustments to hiring practices, pay and conditions in an effort to reduce the expense. This means that any relationship that one might try to observe between the extent of team working and the cost of absence will be obscured by the other differences between firms (such as choice of technology) that are correlated with the extent of teamwork. That such a relationship exists is one of the results of the French study referred to above.

This diversity between firms in the costs they may incur through uncontrolled absenteeism is echoed by a similar diversity on the demand side. The idea introduced above that absence must be due to variations in workers' valuations of time at work relative to time elsewhere carries no implication that the *pattern* of these changes is the same for all workers. Some workers are more prone to sickness than others. Some workers have children whose care takes a greater priority than work if they are sick. Some pastimes depend on suitable weather conditions to be enjoyable. For example, people who like to climb frozen waterfalls are probably more likely to be absent from work on days when waterfalls are frozen than when they are not. It would have been a brave employer who tried to enforce attendance on the day of Princess Diana's funeral in Britain in 1997.[5]

On both sides of the 'market for absenteeism', then, there is diversity. Firms differ according to the costs that they incur if absence is allowed to go unchecked; and workers differ according to the way in which their relative valuations of time in or out of work vary. Clearly, the 'market' would work better if workers were to be matched to jobs in such a way that workers who find it cheap to provide reliable labour supply were to be employed in jobs in which unreliable workers are costly. This idea is explored in detail in Chapter 4, but it should not really be very surprising. People with child care responsibilities (who are usually women) are more likely to take part-time jobs than those who do not. Relationships between household circumstances and labour market behaviour have become a major part of empirical research in labour economics in recent years. In many countries (but not Britain), labour market regulators recognise this by including the sickness of immediate family members as a legitimate cause of worker absence. In Scandinavia and elsewhere in Europe, this is manifest as part of the state sick pay provision. In the United States, it appears as part of federal job protection legislation.

---

[5] This remark does not, of course, apply to the employers of workers involved in the conduct and reporting of the funeral itself.

The idea that workers sort between firms in a consistent way according to the costs and benefits of reliable labour supply is central to the arguments in this book. It has deep implications for the interpretation of data relating to absenteeism, and has been a constant theme in our empirical work. It also has implications for the design of sick pay schemes.

The first part of this book is positive, in the sense that it describes a model of the market for absence, and provides empirical evidence intended to make that model seem more convincing than some of the alternative ideas that have been presented. It tries to be a description of the world as it is. The last part discusses the implications of the model for human resources management, and for the role of the state in sick pay provision.

In the light of our evidence that managers (in France at least) do a pretty good job of managing absence, it is probably presumptuous of us to try to lecture managers on how to manage. However, we hope that the view of the absence market taken here will encourage HR managers to think beyond the rather limited advice available from professional associations. In the United Kingdom (the country we know best), this advice is based almost wholly on the idea that absence management is exclusively concerned with the control of worker behaviour. So that records must be kept, there have to be incentive schemes and disciplinary procedures, all of which must accord with the law. British managers actually have quite a lot more freedom than managers elsewhere in the incentive schemes that they can offer, since sick pay is only minimally regulated by the British government.

We are not foolish enough to think that these activities are not useful, but we do believe that there are broader horizons to be viewed. Consider, for instance, the pervasive idea that there exists a 'best practice' rate of absence, which for some commentators constitutes a benchmark against which management performance in absence control may be judged. According to the view put forward here, this is not correct. First, as we have argued above, different kinds of work organisation incur different absence costs. For example, firms that use teamwork a lot will benefit more from a reduction in absence rates than those that do not. This means that the 'benchmark' should probably be different for firms with more extensive teamwork than other firms. Second, the costs of absence can be controlled in ways other than by reducing absence rates themselves. The use of covering staff, such as supply teachers and nurses, or temporary agency staff, is one way of reducing the disruption caused by absence. Some firms employ more staff than they strictly need, or encourage a broadening of skill mixes, so that the role of absent workers can be filled internally. A fuller discussion of the possibilities is presented in Chapter 8, but the point to be stressed is that managers should not have absence control as a goal at all. What they should be concentrating on, rather, is control of the *costs* of absence, which is a much broader and more subtle remit.

What should the role of the state be in the provision of sick pay? The debate over this question began in Bismarck's day, and continues still. Modern developed economies show a wide diversity of practice, in which Sweden's (generous and controversial) and the United States' (patchy and controversial) arrangements stand out. Since the early 1990s Britain has had virtually no state intervention in this market, while in many continental European countries generous levels of sick pay are provided by the state. In our final chapter, we use the model developed in the earlier part of the book to argue that market solutions to this problem are available.

Before launching into our book, which is an exposition of work that has developed within the economics profession, it is worthwhile stopping briefly to consider how the models described herein relate to literature in other disciplines. Much of the management literature on absenteeism is informed by the model published in 1978 by Steers and Rhodes. This is despite the fact that the model seems to have little empirical validity, except to the extent that the structure proposed is itself based on a reading of the empirical evidence available at the time the paper was written. The model is presented as a chart indicating linkages between various possible influences on the decision to attend. Some of these are one-way, such as the linkage between 'Personal characteristics' and 'Ability to attend'. Others involve feedback, so that 'Attendance motivation' feeds into 'Employee attendance' which feeds into 'Pressure to attend', which feeds back into 'Attendance motivation'. Such a chart could always be represented as a system of simultaneous equations, in which the left-hand-side variables represent all the concepts with arrows pointing towards them in the chart, with the right-hand-side variables representing the concepts from which the arrows emanate.

The way in which the model is written down is not a problem. The real problem (this is borne out by subsequent research in which the model is investigated) is that many of the concepts are too vague to be very useful in practice. Let us take one that appears comparatively clear: 'Employee attendance'. Much ink has been spilled over how to measure this,[6] and yet compared with 'Pressure to attend' or 'Ability to attend' it seems like a fairly straightforward concept. Attempts to calibrate the model and check how well it fits the data are many, but get lost in a welter of different techniques for putting the ideas into operation (Harrison and Martocchio, 1998). One recent attempt took seriously a suggestion by Harrison and Martocchio that time aggregation might help; that smoothed data would help improve the fit of the model. Steel, Rentsch and Van Scotter (2007) end their paper with the following summary:

The Steers and Rhodes (1978) model of employee attendance was published more than a quarter century ago. The model has stood the test of time as an important integrative framework for the absenteeism literature. Surprisingly, however, there have been few attempts to test the model comprehensively. . .

Previous tests of this model managed to explain as much as 16% of the variance in an absenteeism criterion (Brooke & Price, 1989) and as little as 3% (Lee, 1989). The current study's findings may help to explain some of the inconsistency in previous empirical findings. Our data suggest that absence timeframes (i.e., data cumulation intervals) may be systematically affecting validational outcomes. Results from our predictive analysis showed that the Steers and Rhodes model explained increasingly more criterion variance as absence criteria covering longer periods were introduced. For instance, the model explained only 9% of the variance in a 3-month absence criterion, but this increased to 17% of the variance in a 60-month measure of absenteeism.

In this book we offer a different 'integrative framework' from the Steers–Rhodes model. It is 'different' rather than 'new' because all we have done is take the conventional toolkit of economics and see how it can be used in the analysis of absence. In particular, we use the ideas of supply, demand and price; the idea of assignment within markets; the principal–agent model; and some parts of the literature on optimal insurance. Using conventional economic ideas, in turn,

---

[6] Chadwick-Jones (1981) gives an early summary of these difficulties.

provides access to the arsenal of econometric tools that have been developed to calibrate and test economic models. We regard our attempts as very promising, although we remain frustrated at the difficulties we have experienced in extracting meaningful data from conventional sources. The work we have done owes a lot to the insight of Steve Allen, whose papers from the early 1980s were the first to use a market approach to the problem of absence (Allen, 1981a, 1981b, 1983, 1984). In turn, his work was based largely on Sherwin Rosen's hedonic model of markets (Rosen, 1974), which we have amplified in a number of ways. We have added models of what lies behind workers' indifference maps, and models of firms' motivations. The indifference maps, together with the idea of price, stand in for the Steers–Rhodes concepts of 'Personal characteristics', 'Attendance motivation' and 'Ability to attend', while firms' motivations do not seem to be explicitly addressed in the literature in the Steers–Rhodes tradition.

There is, really, only one idea in this book. It is that reorienting the focus of absenteeism research and practice away from a focus on the worker, towards a focus on the bargain that workers (perhaps by way of an intermediating union) make with their employers, frees up many research possibilities that have been blocked by the concentration on the Steers–Rhodes framework. Perhaps the most significant such opportunity that we unlock in these pages is the relationship between absence and sick pay. In addition, the use of conventional economic and econometric methods allows the problem of identification to be tackled in a way that is many miles from the seemingly endless debates about the definition of variables that characterise the Steers–Rhodes exchanges. In turn, we are able to say things about the economic costs of absence that that literature has been unable to address meaningfully, and also to shed light on the issues surrounding the provision and design of sick pay that, as far as we are aware, have not been raised beforehand, let alone addressed.

Mention of 'sick pay' prompts a note on language. This book is written in English English rather than any other flavour. This means that we spell 'flavour' and 'labour' with a 'u' rather than without, and when 'dependent' is a noun we spell it 'dependant'. More importantly, talk about 'sick pay' in North America and you are doomed to plunge your audience into a morass of incomprehension. This is because the US and Canadian systems are based on different laws and institutions from those used in Europe. These differences, which are discussed in more detail in Chapter 9, become particularly acute when sick pay is mentioned, because North Americans think first of 'sick leave' and then 'paid sick leave' rather than 'sick pay'. From the point of view of economic analysis, the difference between paid sick leave and sick pay, European-style, is only a difference in the structure of constraints, and it would be tedious to repeat 'sick pay or paid sick leave' when we mean both. We therefore use the term 'sick pay' to refer to any remuneration for contractual hours not attended, ostensibly for reasons of sickness. This includes both sick pay and paid sick leave. When the distinction between the two is important, we specifically make it, or it will be obvious from the context.

The book begins with three chapters on theory, followed by three chapters on empirical matters and two chapters on policy. Chapter 10 contains a summary of the entire book.

2 | *The supply of absence and the provision of sick pay*

Why are hours fixed?

A job advertisement makes an initial offer of terms for a contract. A typical job advertisement describes the job, and something about the qualities and qualifications of the candidates that the advertiser thinks are suitable to fill it. Apart from legally required statements about avoiding discrimination in the selection process, the only other things an advertisement usually contains are statements about pay, other remuneration, hours of work and holiday (or vacation) allowances. These statements may be vague ('generous remuneration package', 'full-time') or they may be precise, but advertisements that omit them altogether are rare. More often than not, firms are concerned that the people they employ work for a specified number of hours per week, for a specified number of weeks per year. In addition, many contracts specify when in the week those hours will be, although the question of when in the year the weeks will be is usually subject to negotiation. These are the aspects of the work contract that create the concept of absenteeism.

Indeed, one could argue that firms are primarily responsible for creating their own absence problems, because they insist that workers turn up to work at specified times. If firms did not do this, they could not complain that the workers are violating their contracts when they do not turn up when required to do so by their contract.

Not all contracts specify times of work precisely, and some not at all. The typical British university lecturer's contract specifies something along the lines of 'hours commensurate with proper performance of the duties of the post', while the Elizabethan coal mine mentioned in Chapter 1 seems to have left its workers entirely unfettered. These differences in work contracts beg the question of why they exist. Why is it that some workers are required to turn up at particular times, and can therefore be absent, while other employers do not seem to care too much whether their workers are at work or not?

We distinguish two ways in which contractual hours can be fixed. An employer might require attendance for a certain total number of hours, or at specific times. Some contracts with flexible working time combine these two: workers may be required to put in a given total number of hours and be present at work during some specified core hours. By contrast, some jobs impose few (if any) constraints. Our own work as university teachers and researchers requires that we turn up to give lectures and run seminars at specific times and places, but does not impose any constraints on the amount of time we devote to other activities, or when this time is spent. As a result, some academics acquire a reputation for working strange hours, and their offices are always accessible. Absenteeism among coal miners in Britain seems only to have been perceived as a problem towards the end of the nineteenth century, when mechanisation developed. Before this, miners had pretty much free choice of how many shifts they would work in a week, but, once a shift had started, it would usually be completed, because mine shaft lifts would be dedicated to raising coal rather than men while the shift was in progress.

The apparently straightforward question of why firms fix hours instantly becomes rather more complex, and three strands of the literature deal with three different aspects of it: fixing total time; fixing total time per worker; and fixing specific hours.

Leontief (1946) observes that, for many commodities traded in competitive markets, it is sufficient for the seller to name an offer price, leaving it up to buyers to decide how much is to be bought at that price. Labour bargains do not seem to work like this. Instead, the bargaining is over the total quantity of employment as well as the wage. Leontief argues that this is a manifestation of monopoly power. A monopolist (or monopsonist) can 'improve' on the bargain made when price alone is fixed in a sale contract, by making a take-it-or-leave-it offer of a fixed quantity at a particular price. If a price alone is specified, the seller of labour is left free to determine hours, and will choose them to maximise their own welfare. If the monopsonist specifies both price and quantity, the seller can be forced to accept a situation in which they are only just as well off as they are without a trade at all. This outcome is efficient, but the monopolist is able to extract all the surplus.

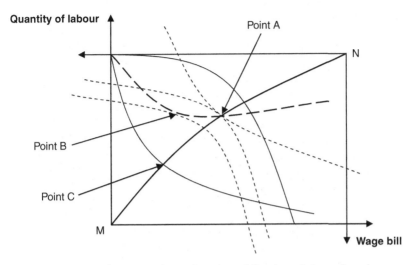

Figure 2.1 Leontief's monopoly explanation of fixed total time of work

The point is illustrated in Figure 2.1, where the initial endowment of goods[1] is assumed to be in the top left-hand corner. The traders are called M, whose origin is at the bottom left, and N, whose origin is at top right. M initially has labour but no wages; N initially has wages but no labour. The contract curve is the heavy solid line. It represents the set of efficient bargains. Any point off this curve can be improved on by making both parties better off. At points on the curve it is not possible to redistribute without making at least one of the parties worse off. The heavy dashed line is M's offer curve, representing the hours that M would choose at a range of different prices. The remaining curves are all indifference curves. The indifference curves through the initial endowment are shown solid and others dotted. The first fundamental theorem of welfare economics says that there will be a price at which the parties can trade to some point on the contract curve (point A). However, if one of the parties has market power they can block this allocation to an extent limited only by the other party's incentive to trade at all. If N is the monopolist, they will set a price that maximises their own utility subject to the other party's offer

---

[1] Leontief calls his goods A and B. They are measured on the vertical and horizontal axes, respectively. Hall and Lilien (1979) interpret them as the wage bill and the quantity of labour.

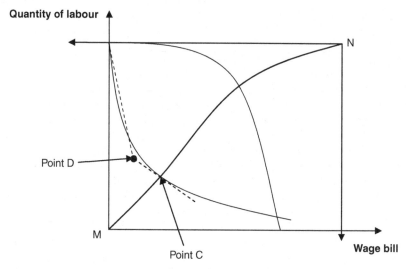

Figure 2.2 A two-part wage structure to extract surplus

curve (point B). This implies that N sets the price while M decides how much to buy at that price. Leontief's point is that, for the monopolist, even better is to make an offer in which the offered price is conditional on accepting a particular quantity. This offer maximises N's utility subject to M being no worse off than at the endowment point, and is represented by point C. Not only is point C preferred by N to point B, it is also efficient. Thus, by specifying quantity as a condition of trade, the monopolist is able to engineer an efficient redistribution in their own favour. Intuitively, the monopolist is able to wield more market power by specifying both dimensions of the bargain than they can do by specifying only one. If price only is specified, the monopolist is relinquishing part of their power to the seller of labour for no good reason.

Hall and Lilien (1979) point out that offering a wage/hours package is not the only way in which an employer with monopoly power can enforce an equilibrium such as point C. It is possible to achieve the same outcome with a non-linear compensation schedule. What is required is an arrangement such that the marginal wage rate is equal to the slope of the firm's indifference curve (or isoprofit line) at point C. There are many ways in which this could be done. In Figure 2.2 a two-part schedule is indicated, in which a low wage is paid for an initial fixed number of hours to take the allocation to point D;

paying a higher wage with no hours stipulated would then lead the seller to choose point C.

The idea that hours constraints on workers serve to enable employers to extract more from them than they otherwise could is not the only possible explanation. Another is that employers may wish to make tied offers of hourly wage and work week if production or other costs vary with shift length or with days worked, or, indeed, if the productivity of individual workers depends on the behaviour of other workers. Such cost differences could arise from fixed costs of shift changeover, hiring and training, or from a non-constant marginal product as an individual worker puts in more hours per week.

Very early in the study of fatigue effects, the idea that there may be large variations in worker productivity through the day was questioned by Vernon (1921), who reports a number of studies of manual labour. Vernon identifies three influences on the rate of output during a day: 'practice-efficiency', 'fatigue' and an 'end-spurt' effect. Vernon summarises the results of several British and US studies as follows:

(I)t may be said that with few exceptions the hourly output in the afternoon spell is as great as that in the morning spell, provided that the hours of work do not exceed 10 per day. We must not conclude, however, that such a result indicates no fatigue in the workers. We saw that in the morning spell the workers generally failed to produce their full output owing to lack of practice-efficiency, and they very seldom improved their output by an end-spurt. In the afternoon spell, on the other hand, they benefited by much of the practice-efficiency acquired in the morning, and they sometimes showed an end-spurt. Hence it follows that there was a sufficient fatigue effect in the afternoon to neutralise the access of productivity produced by the operation of these two factors.

This point of view is reinforced by a study of men employed in heavy manual work, loading iron barrows with iron ore, limestone or coke using shovels, and then wheeling the barrows twenty or thirty yards so that they could be emptied (by a machine) into a blast furnace. Twelve men per shift were observed continuously for five months. Figure 2.3 reproduces Vernon's figure 8, in which he summarises his data. The curves show the average charging rates across the entire five months for men on the afternoon and night shifts.[2] Each shift was interrupted halfway through by a break, and within each of the four resulting

---

[2] He does not say why the morning shift has been omitted.

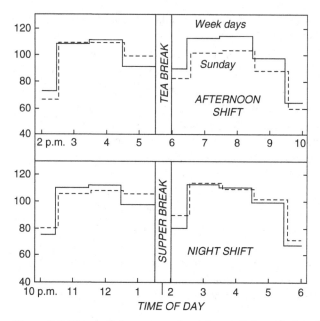

Figure 2.3 Vernon's data on productivity variations during the day

work spells the inverted-U pattern created by practice-efficiency and fatigue is apparent, but there is little sign of great differences in productivity between the two halves of each shift or between afternoon and night work. There is also a little natural experiment reported in this diagram, since on Sundays the mornings and afternoons were worked by the same people, who therefore would have worked for sixteen hours continuously. The top panel of the diagram, therefore, compares weekday workers (who started work at 2 p.m.) with Sunday workers, who started at 6 a.m. Vernon interprets the lower output on Sunday afternoon as a genuine fatigue effect, rather than anything specific to do with Sunday work, since the night shift on Sundays shows little different average productivity from weekday shifts, while, during the last quarter of their sixteen-hour shift, the double-shift barrow men were clearly barrowing less.

Barzel (1973) offers an analysis of the joint determination of daily wages and hours of work, when there are productivity differences through the day of the kind described by Vernon. His analysis assumes a pattern of daily productivity in which productivity rises at the start of the day and then turns down as fatigue sets in. The argument can readily be adapted to the bimodal pattern recorded by Vernon, at the

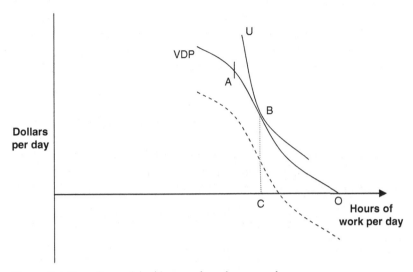

Figure 2.4 Barzel's model of hours of work per worker

cost of some added complexity.[3] The departure point is the observation that the standard depiction of wage rates as being equal for all hours worked leads to the indeterminacy of hours. If productivity varies through the day, and workers are paid their marginal product, the workers' budget constraints are non-linear. A practice-efficiency effect at the start of each day and a fatigue effect at the end will generate a unimodal pattern of output per hour, and, as long as output per hour remains positive, total output per day will be increasing in hours worked. Assuming a constant output price yields what Barzel calls the value of daily product (VDP) curve, shown in Figure 2.4. Ignoring the possibility of multiple equilibria, desired hours for an individual with tastes represented by the indifference curve labelled U are given by the distance OC. The daily pay for these hours is BC, and, clearly, in this model daily pay (and hence the average hourly wage) and hours will be positively correlated. The average hourly wage is not generally equal to the marginal hourly wage. In fact, for hours less than those offered when the equilibrium is at point A, marginal hourly wages are greater than average hourly wages.

Barzel uses the non-linearity of VDP to argue that firms will offer a package contract specifying daily (but not hourly) wages and a fixed

---

[3] Bimodality may be used to explain why many employers offer two kinds of contracts: full-time and part-time.

number of hours. It is possible to compute average hourly wages, but, unless the optimal point happens to be at A in the figure, marginal and average hours will not be equal. At point B, marginal wages are greater than average wages, which explains why overtime rates typically exceed rates for basic hours.

In this model, heterogeneity of tastes generates heterogeneity of desired hours, and, as long as there is sufficient diversity across firms in offered hours/wage packages, every worker should attain their desired combination. The curve labelled VDP illustrates the impact on the model of the introduction of costs that are not related to the intensity of work. These might include the cost of training, or of travel to work. They do not, of course, change the essential message of Barzel's paper, which is that the average wage and the marginal wage may differ at the efficient hours contract.

There are, then, two distinct explanations in the economic literature as to why firms seek to fix contractually the quantity of labour traded: a monopsonistic firm can gain by fixing total labour supply (while at the same time generating an efficient outcome); and average costs can be reduced by offering labour contracts to individual workers that jointly specify fixed daily wages and working hours. Neither of these arguments has anything to say about why a firm would insist on a worker attending at specific hours. That there is great variation across occupations in the extent to which firms insist on specific hours is clear from the following examples.

New York City taxi drivers. A large proportion of taxi drivers in New York rent their cabs from a garage, pay for their own petrol and keep all fare receipts. They are free to work what hours they will (up to a regulated limit of twelve hours a day) subject to the availability of a cab, which is guaranteed for them during a specified time slot.

Coal mining in County Durham, England. During the late nineteenth century these mines were worked by the bord-and-pillar system, which involved a set of discrete workplaces. Hewers, in pairs called 'mates' or 'marras', were assigned responsibility from time to time for a workplace, and once this assignment was made had an exclusive property right to it. The two members of a pair would not work together, though. Instead, they would alternate shifts, so that both daily shifts were covered. The main difference between this system and the New York taxi drivers is that the coal miners did not receive the sales price of their product directly, receiving instead a piece rate that was linked to the sales price under the terms of an agreement that applied to the whole coalfield.

A frozen chicken plant in Aldershot, England, 1967.[4] Chickens arrived in crates at the start of a production line, were slaughtered and processed on the line and then frozen, ninety minutes after first being hung. Each stage on the line, except for plucking, which was done by a machine, required the input of a given minimum number of operatives. Thus, for the line to work at full capacity, four chicken hangers were required, two slaughterers, three de-neckers and four gutters. Work contracts specified eight-hour shifts, with one half-hour break after four hours and shorter breaks mid-morning and mid-afternoon. Start times, finish times and all breaks were coordinated according to the progress of the line. Chicken hanger shifts started at 7:30, freezer operators at 9:00. Pay was for time spent working. Workers who were more than fifteen minutes late for their shift were sent home for the rest of the day. If the line broke down, the production manager would decide whether or not to continue paying the workers.

University lecturers in Britain. The usual contract for university lecturers imposes very few constraints on the time that lecturers should work. However, they do usually include a clause that requires the worker to undertake such duties as the head of department may direct. In practice, this means that some activities are time-constrained, such as giving lectures or attending committees. Other activities are required to have time devoted to them – such as office hours for students – but when and how much are at the discretion of the worker.[5] However, a large part of the work activities of academic staff is not required to be done at any particular time, nor in any particular place.

These examples point to some aspects of work that determine whether or not work time is controlled. Taxi drivers' work is organised in such a way as to be almost purely individualistic. Their output is produced in a way that is largely independent of the effort of others.

[4] This example is based on the personal experience of one of the authors (John Treble).

[5] While he was a professor at Stanford, Thorsten Veblen reputedly changed his posted office hours from '10–11, MWF' to '10–10:05, Mondays'. See www.stanfordalumni.org/news/magazine/1997/sepoct/articles/veblen.html.

Neither output nor input needs to be measured. Chicken processors contribute to a joint effort that is centred on the operation of the production line. If one worker fails to attend, the productivity of all the others can be affected. Academic staff are required to be at work only when their work necessarily involves the work of others. Research work, which much of the time is individual, is not controlled. Teaching is. The coal miners provide a further interesting example, for, given the two-shift system, the output from each workplace was individualistic, but the work of a man assigned to a particular workplace could be affected by the way in which the other man, his marra, had worked the place. The system of work and pay essentially treated each pair as a single worker, allowing issues to do with their interdependencies to be resolved between the pair themselves.

Technology is therefore an important determinant of whether or not a firm specifies hours of work for its employees, and how precisely it tries to control them. In particular, there are two main features of the production technology that one might point to. One is the extent to which the productivity of one worker is dependent on that of another. The second is the extent to which a loss in production impacts on profits. To see the second point, compare the chicken workers and the academics. If a lecturer does not turn up to give a lecture, the other agents involved in the production of learning – namely the students – will not be as productive in the allotted hour as they might otherwise have been. The consequent loss of total output may not be great, though, since the students can use the time in other learning activities, and the scheduled lecture can be delivered at a later date without any great disruption. In other words, the main costs here are those associated with delay. In the chicken factory, some costs are the same. If one of the chicken hanging stations is not filled, then fewer chickens will start their journey down the production line. They will live to be killed another day. However, if a chicken is killed, and not frozen within a reasonable amount of time, it becomes pet food or waste, and its value on the market is considerably reduced.

Technology and absenteeism

Technological issues determine the costs associated with uncertain labour supply, and are also implicated in employers' efforts to protect themselves from the impact of those uncertainties on profits. The study of the market for absence thus becomes a more general study of the structure of contracts, including their provisions for hours of work, monitoring, pay and its structure.

These examples point to a single cause of fixed hours. The productivity of a worker may not be entirely a result of their own effort, as suggested by Barzel. Flexible hours are usually offered to office workers, a part of whose work involves working as part of a team. Core hours can be seen as an expression of the fact that effective team working requires the simultaneous presence of all the members of the team. Flexible hours are intended to be devoted to those tasks that are better performed by a solitary worker. The chicken workers worked as a team as well, but the main driver of the very precise specification and careful enforcement of their work hours was their relationship with the capital equipment. Not all workers needed to be present at the start of the day, since the first chicken to be hung would not arrive at the freezers until ninety minutes later. Not all needed to be present at the end. The required work hours depended on each worker's place in a production process that took time to complete.

The idea that individual productivity may vary with the presence, or the productivity, of another worker or of a machine is called *complementarity* by economists, and it plays a major role in the arguments in this book. This idea is at the centre of Deardorff and Stafford's (1976) seminal treatment of the consequences of complementarity between workers and between workers and capital equipment. The Deardorff–Stafford model is not stochastic, but it does pinpoint the source of fixed hours in complementarity between inputs. Complementarity plays a key role in Coles and Treble's (1996) model of the market for absence and the same authors' (1993) proposed solution to the puzzle of why employers are prepared to pay sick pay when this clearly encourages absenteeism among their workers.

Complementarity has been strikingly modelled by Kremer (1993), whose O-ring model of production is specifically crafted to accommodate random supply of inputs, which, as well as the 'mistakes' interpretation that Kremer seems to favour, can easily be reinterpreted to allow for other kinds of unreliability. Indeed, Coles and Treble (1996) present a model of equilibrium absenteeism based on a variant of Kremer's model.

An O-ring is a compressible ring with a circular cross-section that is placed in a groove cut in one face of a joint (in a pipe, say). When the joint is tightened, the O-ring is compressed and forms a seal. When the US space shuttle orbiter *Challenger* was sent on its final, fatal voyage on an unusually chilly Florida morning in 1986, some of its O-rings had hardened and lost their compressibility because of the temperature. The failure of this one small part caused the failure of the entire complex machine. Kremer points to a number of examples of production issues in which large failures have apparently small causes. He proposes a model of production with more structure than the standard input(s) and output(s) forms. Here the inputs interact in a manner that can be interpreted as modelling teamwork, or a production line. Suppose initially that there is no capital input. The production process consists of n tasks. In its simplest form, each task is performed by a single worker. The ith worker's quality, q_i, is defined as the percentage of the maximum value that the product retains if the worker performs the task. The definition allows for various ways in which workers can produce less than perfect output: they may produce output that is uniformly of low quality q_i, or produce output that is perfect some percentage of the time and less than perfect the rest, but with an expected value of q_i. B is the output per worker if all tasks are performed perfectly. Total output is thus nB adjusted to take account of worker quality. The ith worker reduces product value by a factor q_i, so that total output can be calculated as

$$nB \prod_{i=1}^{n} q_i \quad 0 \leq q_i \leq 1 \text{ for all } i$$

The key point of difference between this production function and more conventional ones is that quantity cannot be substituted for quality within the production chain. One reason why Adam Smith's pin factory operatives were able to improve productivity so greatly was because specialisation increases q_i for each operative (Smith, 1776: Book 1, chap. 1):

A common smith, who, though accustomed to handle the hammer, has never been used to make nails, if upon some particular occasion he is obliged to attempt it, will scarce, I am assured, be able to make above two or three hundred nails in a day, and those too very bad ones. A smith who has been accustomed to make nails, but whose sole or principal business has not been that of a nailer, can seldom with his utmost diligence make more than eight hundred or a thousand nails in a day.

I have seen several boys under twenty years of age who had never exercised any other trade but that of making nails, and who, when they exerted themselves, could make, each of them, upwards of two thousand three hundred nails in a day.

The multiplicative nature of Kremer's production function implies that a reduction in worker i's quality, q_i reduces the marginal product of every other worker. This is how it represents the complementarity of inputs. Furthermore, a theory of hours fixing can easily be generated by it. If the time at which a worker's task is performed is an aspect of the 'quality' of the work done, then output will be less if it is done at some other time. This happens in personal service industries, when the provider will often need to be present at the same time as the customer; in education, when teachers can teach more effectively if they are present at the same time as their class; and in production line systems, when a 'missing link' can cause supply problems for other workers downstream. Under these circumstances, employers will gain by making attendance at particular hours a feature of the contract.

We have distinguished three theories as to why firms specify how much their workers work or when labour is supplied. The total quantity may be restricted in pursuit of monopoly profits. Daily hours may be restricted because of diurnal variation in a single worker's productivity. Hours will be specified if complementarity effects are present either between members of a work team or between a worker and the capital they work with.

Without hours restrictions, absenteeism cannot exist, but not all firms are alike in their willingness to impose or enforce these restrictions. Such variation between firms generates a 'supply of absence'. The idea of a supply of absence may seem strange to the reader, but in fact it is well engrained in modern human resources management practice and in many developed countries in the law surrounding benefits of various kinds. This was not always so. The idea of paying workers for time when they are not working is linked with the idea of paying workers for time (rather than piece rates); with the idea that the provision of some fringe benefits may lower labour costs; and, in Europe, with the development of the welfare state.

Allen was the first writer to suggest seriously that firms may be willing to tolerate higher absence in exchange for a lower wage rate. His work uses Rosen's 'hedonic pricing' model, in which competition between profit-maximising firms leads to multiple equilibria. For example, in a competitive industry zero profits for any given firm may be consistent with a wide range of different prices so long as the firm's costs differ in a compensatory way. Three papers by Allen in the early 1980s used Rosen's (1974) hedonic pricing framework to estimate the size of the trade-off (Allen, 1981b, 1983) between higher absence and lower wage rates, and a conventional labour supply model (Allen, 1981a), to estimate an absence demand relationship. Allen's work is seminal in the economic literature of absenteeism, and is the original source of many of the ideas in this book.

The hedonic pricing model asserts that firms differ in their circumstances, even though they may share the goal of profit maximisation. Competition should drive economic profits to zero, but this does not imply similar behaviour with respect to all aspects of their operations. A firm with high absence costs may be able to reduce these by paying a higher wage. Such a firm faces a trade-off: offer a high wage in return for good attendance by its workers, or accept that workers are not very reliable and offer a lower wage. The terms of this trade-off are unlikely to be the same for every firm. Figure 2.5 shows a set of isoprofit lines, one for each of three firms. In drawing these lines in this way, we are assuming that all other aspects of the firms' operations are identical, or at least do not affect the wage–absence trade-off in any meaningful way.

Similarly, workers differ in their tastes. Some workers will value highly the freedom that a relatively lax attendance control regime can bring, while others will value this less. Workers are thus confronted with a similar trade-off, which can be represented with a set of indifference curves.

The market relationship between wages and absence rates is then determined by the resolution of these forces of absence supply and absence demand. In general, this will be a downward-sloping relationship (high wages will be associated with low absence rates) running through the points of tangency of isoprofit and indifference curves, in such a way that each worker values their wage–absence mix at the margin in the same way as the firm it is matched to, and each firm employs workers whose wage demands and absence behaviour give it the maximum attainable profit.

This elegant model thus has three elements: firms' decisions as to what to offer to workers; workers' decisions whether to accept a firm's offer or not; and the resolution through the marketplace of these

Absence rate

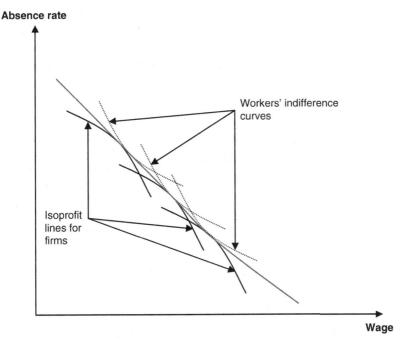

Figure 2.5 The market relationship between absence rates and wages in the hedonic pricing model

decisions. The present chapter delves deeper into the first of these elements, and we deal with the other two in the chapters that follow.

The standard theory of labour demand supposes that firms hire labour as a factor of production – that is, the only rationale for input demand generally and labour demand specifically is that firms believe there to be a demand for whatever it is the firm intends to produce. There are many potential uncertainties in this: the market for output may not have the characteristics that the firm expects; workers, once hired, may prove to be more or less productive than expected, for a variety of reasons including their attendance, the quality of their relationships with other workers, their skill in operating the firm's capital equipment and the reliability of that equipment. Firms' reactions to these uncertainties are an essential part of the study of the market for absence, and so this chapter aims to study them.

The theory was developed in the 1930s by Hicks (1932) and Allen (1938). The first key point distinguishing the firm's demand for an input from a household's demand for some consumer good is that input demands can be shown always to decrease with the price of the input, whereas the demand for a consumption good may be upward-sloping. In either case, a price change generates two distinct effects: substitution and income effects for consumption goods, substitution and scale effects for inputs. In the case of consumption, it is possible for the income effect to be positive and to exceed in absolute the substitution effect; in the case of input demand, the net effect must always be negative, since increasing the scale of output is never an optimal response to increased costs.

The fact that it is possible to be more precise about a firm's demands for inputs than is conventionally possible in the analysis of household demands for consumer goods enables the formulation of the four propositions known as Marshall's laws.[6] These summarise the way in which the elasticity of labour demand depends on characteristics of the output market, and the technology. Marshall's four laws are often referred to as laws of labour demand, but in truth they apply equally to any input to a productive process. They state that the elasticity of demand for an input is greater

(1) the more easily other factors can be substituted for labour (i.e. if the price of an input rises, and that input can easily be replaced by another, the demand for the input will fall more than if the input is not easily substitutable);

(2) the larger the share of the input's costs in total costs (i.e. the importance of being unimportant; if the price of an input rises, the greater the share of that input's costs in total cost, the greater the increase in total cost will be, and the greater the impact on demand);

(3) the smaller the elasticity of supply of other factors (i.e. if the price of an input rises, and replacing it for another leads to a large increase in the cost of the substitute input, the demand for the input will fall by less than if the increase in the cost of the substitute is small); and

(4) the greater the price elasticity of demand for the product (i.e. if the price of an input rises, output costs rise, and price will rise too; the

---

[6] They are named for the great Cambridge economist Alfred Marshall, whose career spanned the end of the nineteenth century and the beginning of the twentieth. Since Marshall formulated them they have gone through several refinements, because Marshall did not quite get his laws right.

larger the impact of the price rise on demand, the less the new quantity demanded will be, and the greater the impact on demand for the input will be).

Although this theory is useful for many applications, it is of limited use for the analysis of absenteeism, since the standard derivation of Marshall's laws[7] assumes that the supply of inputs, the demand for output and the production process are all deterministic. The generalisation of the model to conditions of uncertainty has yet to be completed, though considerable progress has been made. Two early efforts to achieve a generalisation simply assumed that the conditions of the standard theory apply, but that one or more key variables are random rather than deterministic. Sandmo (1971) considers the case in which output demand for a non-durable is uncertain. The assumption of non-durability avoids having to consider the issue of inventory. In this case, one must suppose that the decisions as to what inputs to employ and what output to produce are taken before production takes place. Otherwise, the problem reverts to a series of decisions made with certainty. Comparing situations in which uncertainty increases while preserving the mean of the price distribution, Sandmo shows that output will be smaller the greater the degree of uncertainty.

The second paper to consider a standard approach, this time with a random input, is by Rothschild and Werden (1979). This self-effacing paper[8] takes the standard approach, but replaces deterministic input supply with a random one: 'This notion is meant to capture such phenomena as absenteeism, sloth, and exuberance (for labour) and down time owing to maintenance and repair (for machines).' They show that this leads to increasing returns to scale, but then argue that this is not very important, since the increasing returns are non-negligible only for very small-scale operations. The paper is interesting, though, because it indicates some of the difficulties in modelling absence using conventional techniques of labour demand analysis.

Rothschild and Werden use what they describe as a 'very general' model of production. They assume that the production function is concave and homogeneous of degree one and that output is produced using at most l inputs: $Q = F(x_1, \ldots, x_l)$. They introduce random input supplies by making a distinction between the quantity of each

---

[7] Cahuc and Zylberberg (2001) give a detailed exposition of this in their chapter 4.
[8] It argues for its own lack of importance.

input that is used and the productive services that that quantity delivers. The former can be determined exactly by the firm, the latter cannot. In particular, they assume that hiring n units of input i yields S_{in} units of productive services, where $S_{in} = \sum_{j=1}^{n} Y_{ij}$, and Y_{ij} is the random output of the jth unit of input i hired.

This simple set-up yields an efficiency measure, which compares the expected value of the random output $F(S_{1n}, \ldots, S_{ln})$ to the output that would be produced were certain inputs to be hired in amounts that would yield the mean productive services. This efficiency measure has an upper bound of one and is increasing in n. The latter fact implies increasing returns to scale, the former that these are limited. Some numerical simulations are intended to demonstrate that increases in efficiency become negligible for very low n. Rothschild and Werden end their paper with the observation that '[i]t is of course impossible to prove by illustrative calculations that a phenomenon which could conceivably be important is always unimportant. However, we believe that our calculations indicate that increasing returns to scale owing to random delivery of factor services are likely to be unimportant.'

Viewed from the early twenty-first century, Sandmo's and Rothschild and Werden's attempts to tackle aspects of the problem of production under uncertainty seem worthy rather than successful. They take well-established methods of analysis and modify them in sensible (even ingenious) ways. Unfortunately, neither attempt has stood the test of time, because, despite Rothschild and Werden's claim that their model is 'very general', neither their model nor Sandmo's is general enough. The main reason for this is that both models assume that entrepreneurs have no control over the stochastic processes confronting them.

The question of how to model input demands when the supply of inputs is uncertain is a very complex one, and it has been at the forefront of research in economic theory for the last three decades. The reason it is so problematic is that the complexity of the choices that firms have to make burgeons, even when only one input is in uncertain supply. The analytical issues burgeon as well.

Consider, for instance, a restaurant that buys in meat. The conventional theory says that the proprietor will determine which supplier to choose on the basis of price. The contract between the restaurant and the butcher is therefore very simple. It says something like 'The butcher will deliver daily to the restaurateur x pounds of this and y pounds of that [the definitions of "this" and "that" will include a quality specification]. The restaurateur will pay the butcher $p_x x + p_y y$.' Since there is no uncertainty, what actually happens will be exactly what the contract says. This theory abstracts from questions of quality, either of the meat itself or of the reliability of delivery. When these issues are to be taken into account, the available options increase, too. The restaurateur might not buy at the lowest mean price, preferring perhaps more reliable delivery of a more reliable product. The mix of meats might change. If chicken is more reliable in supply than beef, the demand for it may be enhanced. Furthermore, the restaurateur may be able to influence the distribution of the uncertainty that they face by a number of devices – diversifying their purchasing among a number of suppliers, by vertical integration, by buying insurance of some kind or by introducing flexible menus in which the day's offerings to customers can be varied to take the best advantage of whatever the supplier delivers. More profoundly, the introduction of uncertainty in supply creates issues of adverse selection and moral hazard. Suppliers may not be what they seem and their behaviour may be dependent on the fact that they have a contract. The restaurateur is then confronted with a further set of decisions, which can be conveniently summarised by the question 'What contract should I offer to suppliers?'. In the presence of uncertainty, a contract can specify something different in one contingency from what is specified in another. The enormous literature on contracts that has developed in the last three decades considers answers to this question.

Although there is no currently available neat package of solutions to these issues, the economics profession is making clear progress towards one. Zame (2007) presents the first model in which contracts, firms and technologies are all endogenous. They are the outcome of a competitive process in which every part of the equilibrium is dependent on every other part, so that (for instance) the introduction of a new technology for the dispersal of gallstones using ultrasound can change prices in such a way as to encourage restaurateurs to order more chicken, and to introduce a penalty for delivery after noon. This kind of general equilibrium approach lies largely in the future, and the discussion in this book is necessarily at a rather less exalted level.

The market for absence would not exist if firms allowed workers to come and go as they pleased, contributing to the firm's production when they pleased and taking wages in return for their measured contribution. In many respects, the British coal industry in Victorian times was like this. There is a much-quoted anecdote of a coal miner asked by a royal commission why it was that he turned up to work just four days a week. His reply was that he could not make enough money to feed his family in three. In this example, there was a constraint on hours, but it did not take the form usually envisaged in simple models of hours supply. Here hours are specified as part of a contract, and the worker is expected to deliver the specified number of hours in much the same way as the employer is expected to deliver pay at the end of the week.

In deep-level coal mining, the costs involved in getting the workers to the coalface were great, and were worth incurring in the long run only if the employer could be sure to get a sufficient amount of product to cover them. Thus shift lengths were generally fixed, but the system nonetheless allowed workers freedom to choose whether to work a given shift or not. Other than a loss of wages, which were calculated on a piece-rate basis, there were no penalties for absence from coal mines until mechanisation created a greater degree of teamwork.

The standard way of representing technology in an economic model is with a production function, which is a mathematical representation of how output is related to inputs. In order to avoid issues of waste, 'output' in a production function is always defined as the maximum output that can be made with each specified combination of inputs. Thus, if the production function is just the product of measured input levels of three inputs, x, y and z, then the most that can be produced with $x = 200$, $y = 400$ and $z = 350$ is 28 million units of the output. The study of labour demand has been dominated by the use of comparatively few production functions, chosen largely for their ability to represent in a tractable and compact form the main ideas of diminishing marginal product, economies of scale and substitution. The Cobb–Douglas technology, of which students in mathematics for economists courses get heartily sick, was the first functional form to be used in empirical work. It is no longer widely used, because it imposes constraints on the main parameters of interest that are generally regarded as excessively restrictive. For instance, the standard measure of the ease with which one input may be substituted for another, (the elasticity of substitution), always takes the value one in a Cobb–Douglas technology.

The search for tractable and flexible forms of production functions continues. Hamermesh (1993: 28–33, 38–42) gives a succinct account of the main developments in this field. None of these standard production functions are of much use in the study of systems with uncertain inputs; but Kremer's O-ring production function is, as Kremer (1993) shows.

Kremer incorporates capital into the model by supposing that it is not differentiated by quality, and enters multiplicatively with exponent α, to give the expected production of the n workers as $E(Q) = k^{\alpha}nB \prod_{i=1}^{n} q_i$. The expectation is necessary, because the qs may be random variables in his model of the assignment of workers to firms.

Kremer defines competitive equilibrium in his model as an assignment of workers to firms, a set of quality-specific wage rates, $w(q)$, and a rental price of capital, r, such that firms maximise profits and the market clears for capital and for workers of all skill levels. Workers are assumed not to face any labour–leisure choice and to supply labour inelastically, so that their only decision in this model is which firm they will work for. There is a continuum of workers, whose skill is distributed according to a known, exogenous distribution. Kremer shows that the (unique) competitive equilibrium in this model has workers with similar skill levels clustering in firms – i.e. there is positive assortative matching. Capital is paid its marginal product αy, and workers are paid according to the schedule $w(q) = (1 - \alpha)q^n Bk^{\alpha}$. In this model, firms can be thought of as choosing a skill level and a wage rate along this schedule. High-skill firms pay high wages, low-skill firms pay low wages, but both types of firms make zero economic profit.

In an independent piece of work, Coles and Treble (1996) introduce a form of O-ring technology in which Kremer's concept of 'quality' is replaced by a probability of attendance $(1-p)$. They also derive a similar kind of labour demand schedule. In their model of an 'assembly-line' production process, the success of a production team is determined day by day by the number of workers attending. There is a critical size of team, k. If fewer workers than this turn up on any given day, output will be zero. If k or more workers turn up, production is α. Workers can be substituted one for another, so that the firm can control the probability that the team size is too small by employing excess workers.[9] The Coles–Treble production function is thus

$$E(y) = \alpha P(S_n \geq k) \tag{2.1}$$

where S_n is a random variable measuring the number of workers turning up if n workers are employed. The relationship between employment, which generally will be larger than k, pay and absence is derived in theorem 1 of Coles and Treble's paper.[10]

Labour demand can be calculated for this technology, as a function of p, the probability of absence. The firm offers a package consisting of income, y, and an absence rate, p, that is assumed to be perfectly enforceable. Utility, U, depends only on these two variables, and outside opportunities for workers are worth U_0. The package that the firm offers must therefore satisfy $U(p, y) = U_0$. The firm's problem is to choose a package $\{y, p\}$ and an employment level n, so as to maximise profits subject to the workers' participation constraint:

$$\max_{n,p,y} \alpha P(S_n \geq k) - ny$$
$$\text{subject to } U(p,y) = U_0 \tag{2.2}$$

This problem is tricky, since n is an integer, but because the participation constraint is independent of n it can be solved in two steps: by determining first the optimal hiring level n^*, and then optimal absence, p^*, and pay, y^*, conditional on optimal n^*. The dual problem therefore has n in the constraints only, and can be written as

$$\max_{p,y} U(p,y) \tag{2.3}$$

$$\text{subject to} \quad \alpha P[S_n \geq k] - ny = \Pi_0 \tag{2.4}$$

In other words, we think of maximising the worker's utility subject to a constraint on the firm's profit, rather than the other way round.

What will determine the firm's choice of employment, n^*? Clearly, it will not want to add a worker whose contribution to profit is less than pay, but it will want to add a worker whose contribution to profit

---

[9] Barmby and Stephan (2000) give some empirical evidence on this point.
[10] Readers uninterested in technical detail may skip to the discussion of Figure 2.7 on p. 40.

is greater than pay. Denoting the contribution to profit of the nth hired worker by Δ_n, this gives two further constraints:

$$\Delta_n \geq y; \quad \Delta_{n+1} < y \tag{2.5}$$

The problem represented by equations (2.3) to (2.5) can be tackled by analysing the implications of the constraints (2.4) to (2.5) for the optimal choice of n. This amounts to no more than rewriting the three constraints as a set of constraints, one for each value of n.

To do this, note that (2.4) can be rewritten as $ny = \alpha P[S_n \geq k] - \Pi_0$, and, using (2.5), we have

$$n\Delta_n \geq ny = \alpha P[S_n \geq k] - \Pi_0 > n\Delta_{n+1} \tag{2.6}$$

or

$$n\Delta_n - \alpha P[S_n \geq k] + \Pi_0 \geq 0 > n\Delta_{n+1} - \alpha P[S_n \geq k] + \Pi_0 \tag{2.7}$$

Now take a closer look at Δ_n, the expected contribution to profit of an nth worker. If, of the $n - 1$ workers who are already employed, fewer than $k - 1$ turn up for work, the extra output added by the nth worker will be zero. Similarly, if, of the $n - 1$ workers who are already employed, more than $k - 1$ turn up for work, the extra output added by the nth worker will be zero. The nth worker will have a positive effect on output only if exactly $k - 1$ of his or her fellow workers attend. Such a worker will, of course, have a positive effect on output only if the worker him-/herself attends. If both these conditions are fulfilled, and assuming independence between workers, the nth worker's contribution will be α. It follows that the expected contribution is given by

$$\Delta_n = \alpha(1 - p)P[S_{n-1} = k - 1] \tag{2.8}$$

since the probability of the nth worker's attending is $(1-p)$, and the probability of exactly $k-1$ other workers turning up is, by definition, $P[S_{n-1} = k - 1]$. Substitute (2.8) into (2.7) to obtain

$$\begin{aligned} n\alpha(1 - p)P[S_{n-1} = k - 1] &- \alpha P[S_n \geq k] + \Pi_0 \\ &\geq 0 \\ &> n\alpha(1 - p)P[S_n = k - 1] - \alpha P[S_n \geq k] + \Pi_0 \end{aligned} \tag{2.9}$$

In this expression, α, k and Π_0 are all fixed, so the only variables are n and p. Write the expression on the left-hand side of the first inequality as

$$\phi(n,p) \equiv n\alpha(1-p)P[S_{n-1} = k - 1] - \alpha P[S_n \geq k] + \Pi_0 \qquad (2.10)$$

and it is simple to show that the constraint system (2.4) to (2.5) can be written as

$$\phi(n,p) \geq 0 > \phi(n+1,p) \text{ for each } n \geq k \qquad (2.11)$$

In the light of this result, we now seek to interpret the condition $\phi(n, p) = 0$.

Looking at the definition (2.10), and using the equality in (2.6), we obtain

$$\phi(n,p) = 0 \Rightarrow \Delta_n = y$$

For any employment level, n, the solution to the equation is the absence rate, p_n, that equates pay to the expected marginal product of the nth worker. These conditions state simply that marginal cost should equal marginal benefit.

The solutions take the following form. For each $n \geq k$ there exists a unique $p_n < 1$. This absence rate increases with n, and approaches one as n becomes arbitrarily large.[11] The sequence of absence rates p_k, $p_{k+1}, p_{k+2}, \ldots$ therefore partitions all possible absence rates into sets $[p_n, p_{n+1})_k^\infty$.[12] This means that, for any given level of absence $p \in [0, 1)$, the optimal value of n can now be expressed as $n(p) = m$ if and only if $p \in [p_m, p_{m+1})$. Thus, for any p between p_k and p_{k+1}, the optimal employment level is just k; between p_{k+1} and p_{k+2}, it rises to $k + 1$; and so on. Therefore, for a given technology, more unreliable workers are optimally employed in greater numbers.

Having determined how employment levels vary with the probability of absence, the analysis of the firm's decisions regarding pay and absence can be completed. This is the content of Coles and Treble's (1996) theorem I. There are three results in the theorem. First, the isoprofit relationship between pay, y, and the probability of absence, p, is continuous. Second, the slope of the relationship is not. In fact, for $p \in (p_m, p_{m+1})$, $\frac{dy}{dp}$ is strictly less than its value at p_{m+1}, which is equal to $-\frac{y}{1-p_{m+1}}$. Finally, the proof of theorem I shows that $\lim\limits_{p \to 1} y(p) = 0$.

The theorem is illustrated in Figure 2.7. On the horizontal axis is the probability of absence, p. On the vertical, y is the income of

[11] Coles and Treble (1996: lemma A2).
[12] Coles and Treble (1996: lemma A3). See Figure 2.6.

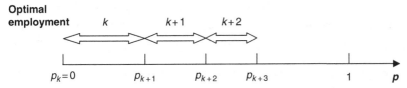

Figure 2.6 Optimal employment and worker reliability in the Coles–Treble model

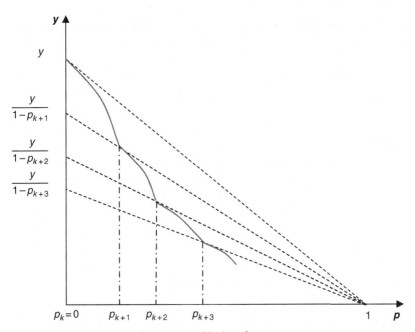

Figure 2.7 Isoprofit line for an assembly-line firm

workers. The bold line is the firm's isoprofit line, $y(p)$. When the probability of absence is zero, the earnings of workers are high. As p increases, they decrease continuously. However, the decrease is not smooth, because, when p attains one of the critical values in the set $\{p_n\}$, it becomes worthwhile for the firm to exercise its option to increase employment. If the probability of absence is zero, there is no reason for the firm to employ any more than k workers, but as p increases it eventually becomes worthwhile to employ an extra worker by way of a buffer against the eventuality that not enough workers may turn up. Once this is done the rate of loss of productivity due to a marginal increase in p becomes lower. The pattern is repeated. As p continues to increase, the firm will eventually find it worthwhile to employ a second buffer worker, and then a third.

So far, we have surveyed the theoretical analysis of labour demand, with especial emphasis on its usefulness as a vehicle for thinking about absenteeism. Conventional methods of analysis, which rely on the idea of labour measured in efficiency units, are not very useful, because they have difficulty explaining why firms offer job packages of wages and hours. There are three possible explanations, one based on the idea that a package enables the extraction of a monopoly profit and two based on characteristics of the production process. The idea that teamwork of some kind is the key production characteristic that leads to a convincing model of the supply of absence is supported by the Coles–Treble model, which predicts several aspects of observed firm behaviour when confronted with a workforce with a positive propensity to go absent. In particular, the use of buffer stocks of workers, and the prediction that remuneration should be less in firms with higher absence rates, are both characteristics that other proposed models are unable to explain. The model also implies that different production technologies have different implications for absence costs, so that these may be relevant in the choice of technology.

These two results of the model also have practical implications for the way in which firms deal with absence, suggesting two ways in which firms might manage their way around the problem rather than putting resources into managing it directly. Offering higher wages in return for a tougher absence policy is one. The other is arranging substitute labour, either in the form of permanent excess employment or in the form of supply arrangements.

The argument above makes clear why and whether firms should care about their rate of absenteeism, and also has policy implications for firms. However, the argument relies heavily on the assumption of a particular production function, in which workers cannot work except as a team. The costs that firms incur from the unreliability of worker attendance are dependent on the probability of absence, p, and the nature of their technology, which is summarised with the single parameter k, representing the minimum team size for successful operation of the equipment. As part of their optimal strategy, firms can control costs by varying the number of workers that they hire, but the outcome for pay, y, and the equilibrium absence rate, p, is then determined by workers selecting a pay–absence package from a menu designed by the firm that suits their own circumstances.

Not all technologies produce the same result. Consider the case when the marginal product of labour is constant. Here the absence of a single worker reduces the output of a team in inverse proportion to its size. The team's expected output is $\alpha(1 - p)$, and the optimal contract satisfies

$$\frac{U_p}{U_y} = \alpha \text{ and } y = \alpha(1 - p)$$

The second condition ensures zero profits. The first condition states that, at the optimum, the marginal rate of substitution (MRS) between absence and earnings should be equal to the worker's marginal revenue product. In other words, the worker's subjective evaluation of a small decrease in their rate of absence should equal the firm's gain. This outcome is clearly efficient, but it does not require firms to hire a buffer stock of workers in an attempt to control the probability of having insufficient workers turn up. This is because, under the linear technology, the marginal cost of a worker is equal to their marginal revenue. The marginal profit yielded by each worker is identically zero. That this is not the case with the assembly-line technology follows from the fact that the marginal worker can reduce the output of the rest of the team to zero. The marginal profit yielded by such a worker is equal to the revenue of the entire team.

The explanation of absence supply proposed here is that firms differ in the costs that absence imposes on them. These differences arise because firms' production functions are not all identical. In particular, they differ in the complementarity characteristics that they display. Indeed, strictly speaking, the model described here does not refer to firms at all, but to jobs, since different jobs within the same firm or organisation can easily have different complementarity structures. Consider the office staff at a chicken-processing plant. Their output does not need to be kept moving along a production line in the same urgent way. While a stream of invoices or correspondence may lose some value from delay, they do not decay in the same way that a slaughtered chicken does. As a consequence, the attitude of the firm to these workers' absence behaviour is likely to be different. Indeed, according to the argument above, all other things being equal,[13] it *should* be different, if the firm is to maximise profit.

The supply of sick pay

So far, the discussion has supposed that job offers to workers can be adequately described by a wage rate and an 'acceptable' absence rate. This is insufficient for a complete understanding of the issues involved in absence supply, because of the complications introduced by the fact that many firms provide sick pay (or paid sick leave).[14] We defer an integrated treatment of the issues surrounding sick pay to Chapter 4, but it is appropriate in this chapter devoted to the supply of absence to ask why employers provide it.

To many continental European readers, this may appear to be a strange question, since in their own country sick pay is not provided by employers but by the state or perhaps since in their country employers provide sick pay because government regulations require labour contracts to include sick pay provision. It is nonetheless a question worth asking, for two reasons. The first is that asking this question opens up a debate about the role of government in the provision of sick pay. In particular, is there any reason why we would expect market failure, and, if there is, what appropriate steps may be taken to correct it? The second is that, while in many countries governments do intervene in the market for sick pay, it remains a fact that, when employers are able, many of them provide sick pay in excess of what is required by regulation. Of the developed economies, the United States and United Kingdom are probably the least regulated in this respect. Figures for sick pay coverage are hard to come by for the United Kingdom, but we have only ever encountered one firm in which the only sick pay coverage was at the minimum statutory sick pay rates. One firm that we have studied in detail actually uses the possible reduction of sick pay entitlements to the statutory minimum as a threat, its normal replacement rate for short-term absence being 100 per cent. The United Kingdom's statutory minimum rates are not

---

[13] This argument ignores issues of equity within the workforce, which may be costly if ignored. These issues are raised in more detail in Chapter 8.

[14] In this chapter we make no distinction between sick pay and paid sick leave, referring to both simply as 'sick pay'.

generous, but even in France, where sick pay is tightly regulated by the state, with quite generous replacement rates, many employers and unions have voluntarily negotiated higher levels of replacement than are legally required (Lanfranchi and Treble, 2010).

The remainder of the present chapter is devoted to a discussion of two issues that arise from the model of absence supply described here. The argument of the last few paragraphs refers to p, the probability of absence, which is assumed to be an enforceable characteristic of the contract offered by the firm. This is not an assumption one would like to insist on, though. There is plenty of evidence to suggest that attendance probabilities are determined partially by workers 'playing the system'.[15] Indeed, human resource managers seem to spend many resources recording, monitoring and attempting to control the attendance of their workers,[16] while there is much discussion and implementation of incentive schemes of a wide variety of types and degrees of sophistication. Simple schemes include those in which good attenders become eligible for some kind of prize, such as an attendance bonus or lottery ticket. The firm studied by Barmby, Orme and Treble (1991) runs a much more sophisticated scheme, specifically introduced to tackle a perceived moral hazard problem. In essence, the insurance against loss of income provided by the firm is subject to an experience-rated excess: it uses information about each worker's absence in the recent past to determine their current eligibility for sick pay. The scheme is not cheap to run, since it involves the employment of at least one dedicated administrative worker in each of its plants, whose main task is to manage the collection of data and the assignment of sick pay grades.

There are two routes that a firm can take to avoid moral hazard of this sort. It can buffer itself from its impact, or it can try to control it. One aspect of buffering that we have discussed above is to employ excess workers. Another is to choose technologies that are robust to absenteeism. For example, a fully automated process that requires no

---

[15] See Butler, Gardner and Gardner (1998), or, perhaps even more convincingly, the advice to workers on how to fake sickness given by Bishop (2006).

[16] In Britain, an 'absence management toolkit' developed by the Chartered Institute of Personnel Development (CIPD), the Health and Safety Executive and the Arbitration and Conciliation Advisory Service is available online. See www.cipd.co.uk/subjects/hrpract/absence/absmantool?vanity=http://www.cipd.co.uk/absencemanagementtool

human input would be immune from the impact of absence. Two major types of control include attempts to change the distribution of the shocks hitting the households that workers inhabit and the changing of incentives. For instance, hiring (and firing) criteria may be designed to select low- (or high-) absence individuals, or the firm may be able to protect households from shocks, perhaps by the provision of childcare facilities or reliable transportation. Incentives can be built into contracts by the schemes such as those described in the last paragraph, or by disciplinary arrangements – which brings us full circle back to firing. Consideration of selection, childcare and other issues we defer to a later chapter. The remainder of the present chapter concerns the provision of incentives.

It is a curious fact, noted above, that many firms apparently choose to create incentives for absence by paying workers when they are off sick. Given the difficulties experienced in monitoring sickness, one would think that this would simply be a way of creating more incentives for moral hazard, but there are at least two reasons why firms might do it. The first is the standard argument from the principal–agent model,[17] to the effect that a risk-neutral employer can pay lower wages if employees can be protected from risk. The second is more unfamiliar, and is explained in full in Chapter 4: by 'supplying' absence and paying workers when they claim to be sick, firms create a tool, other than the wage, that they can use to control workers' behaviour.

The simplest form of principal–agent model envisages a decision-maker (the principal) who wishes to delegate some task to another decision-maker (the agent). The principal has to offer a sufficiently good contract to enable the agent to take it. This would be simple enough were it not for the complication that the performance of the task cannot be observed directly by the principal. This means that, without appropriate incentives, the agent may cheat. The contract design therefore has to take into account potential cheating by employees.

Imperfect information is now thought of as a key factor in the structure of labour contracts. The labour market that can usefully be thought of as a spot market is rare, and the explicit or implicit

---

[17] An exhaustive account of the principal–agent problem has been provided by Laffont and Martimort (2001).

long-term arrangements that are made between employer and employee have to take account of several complicating factors. Chief among these are monitoring costs and measurement costs. The costs of measurement are a key factor in determining whether workers are paid by the piece or by time. If it is expensive to pay a piece rate, perhaps because output itself is not easily measurable, or because it is hard to attribute a measurable output to an individual, then paying by the hour can be an attractive prospect.[18]

Principal–agent problems can have efficient solutions in the absence of monitoring costs. If the principal were able to observe exactly what effort the agent puts into the performance of their allotted task, the contract could simply specify an effort level and a schedule of rewards for different effort levels. This is why piece rates are sometimes said to be *self-monitoring*, by which is meant that they provide suitable incentives for optimal effort levels, though they do require some monitoring in the sense that employers would be unlikely to accept self-reported output measures. A good example of these kinds of problems is described in Treble and Vicary's (1993) account of coal mining in late Victorian County Durham. The elaborate and expensive arrangements at the head of coal pits for measuring the quantity and quality of individual output of coal also served to check (on behalf of the workers) that the measuring was done accurately.

Why is it, therefore, that firms offer contracts that contain sick pay entitlements among their provisions? This question seems to have been broached first by Coles and Treble (1993), who propose an explanation based on the chief insight of the principal–agent model–namely that it is sometimes possible to construct systems of payments that are made to the agent conditionally on some observable outcome that is correlated with the unobservable characteristic. In the case of sick pay, absence is certainly observable, and it is correlated with sickness if no moral hazard is present. Coles and Treble (1993) first consider an industry with free entry, in which all firms are profit maximisers with identical linear technologies, output markets are competitive, and so is the market for the sole input, labour. The price of output is normalised to one. The technology is $Q = n$, where Q represents the quantity of output, and n the number of workers who

---

[18] These issues are discussed by Lazear (2000), and are the focus of a number of papers by Shearer, such as Shearer (1996) and (2004).

Table 2.1 *Pay-offs in Coles and Treble's (1993) model*

State		Behaviour	Pay-off	Probability
Sick		Absent	$U_s(s)$	p_s
Not sick	Additional utility not available	Attends	$U(w)$	$1 - p_s - p_t$
	Additional utility available	$\begin{cases} \text{Absent} \\ \text{Attends} \end{cases}$	$\left.\begin{array}{l} U(s)+U_t \\ U(w) \end{array}\right\}$	p_t

attend. Contracts of work, which are written before any production takes place, specify a wage, w, and a sick pay rate, s. The wage is payable if the worker attends, the sick pay rate is payable if they do not. The model distinguishes between 'genuine' absenteeism and moral hazard by assuming two kinds of shocks: the worker is too sick to work, with probability p_s. This yields utility $U_s(s)$. With independent probability p_t, absence gives the worker additional utility U_t, which the worker does not receive if they attend work. The pay-offs are summarised in Table 2.1.

The firm can choose whether it is better off with its workers attending when they are sick or not, and can engineer either outcome by appropriate choices in its contract structure. If it wants to control absence, it can do so by ensuring that the workers are better off attending when the valuable alternative crops up. It can do this by ensuring that the contract satisfies the incentive compatibility constraint:

$$U(w) \geq U(s) + U_t \tag{2.12}$$

This constraint says that the wage has to be sufficiently high to encourage workers to attend when they have the opportunity to obtain the extra utility U_t, and, in particular, implies that $w > s$.

A standard assumption in principal–agent models is that the principal is risk-neutral and the agent is risk-averse – or, at least, that the principal's degree of risk aversion is less than the agent's. The firm minimises income risk subject to (2.12), which will therefore always hold with equality. The 'low-absentee' contract is easily computed as $\{w, s\}$, satisfying (2.12) with equality and

$$(1 - p_s)w + p_s s = 1 - p_s \tag{2.13}$$

The second condition is derived from the competitive structure of the industry. Because entry is free, expected profits must be zero.

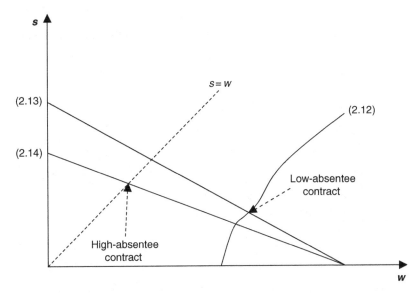

Figure 2.8 Two possible equilibrium contracts

The left-hand side is expected costs if workers attend when they can obtain U_t; the right, expected revenue.

The 'high-absentee' contract must also satisfy a free entry condition, but the probabilities are different, because workers are absent both when they are sick and when U_t is available. This contract does not have to satisfy any incentive compatibility constraint, since it permits workers to take absences whenever they benefit from doing so. It therefore must satisfy the single condition

$$(1 - p_s - p_t)\, w + (p_s + p_t)\, s = 1 - p_s - p_t \qquad (2.14)$$

which implies that $w = s = 1 - p_s - p_t$ (see Figure 2.8).

The model is set up in such a way that firms do not care which of these two contracts they offer. In either case, expected profits are zero and firms are risk-neutral, so that any differences in risk are irrelevant. However, workers care, and which contract they prefer depends on the size of the utility, U_t. As this approaches zero, workers prefer the low-absentee contract, since, for U_t close to zero, $w_l \approx 1 - p_s > 1 - p_s - p_t = w_h$. Therefore, $\lim_{U_t \to 0} U(w_l) > U(w_h) > (1 - p_t)U(w_h)$. The left-hand side of this inequality is the limiting utility of a worker under the low-absence contract as $U_t \to 0$, while the right-hand side is the limiting utility under

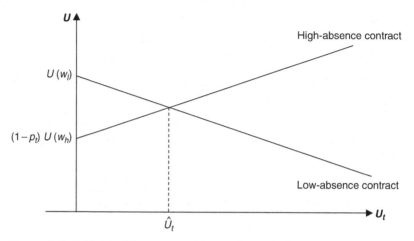

Figure 2.9 Optimal sick pay provision with perfectly competitive linear-technology firms

the high-absence contract. For low values of U_t, workers prefer the low-absence contract. Clearly, utility under the high-absentee contract increases, and utility under the low-absentee contract decreases, as U_t increases. There is therefore a critical utility level, $\hat{U}_t$, such that if U_t is less than $\hat{U}_t$ workers prefer the low-absence contract. For values of U_t greater than $\hat{U}_t$, they will prefer the high-absence contract (see Figure 2.9).

This simple model thus predicts that sick pay will be paid if workers value it highly enough. Receiving sick pay lowers the wage. The model so far says nothing about what kinds of firms will pay sick pay. Since all firms are identical, they all behave in the same way, but the model does argue that the supply of sick pay is driven by the existence of a demand for insurance against loss of income due to sickness. This can be provided profitably, even though it is paid to workers who the firms know are certainly going to cheat them by taking absence when they are not sick.

In this model, though, sick pay will be paid only if workers value the opportunity to exploit it highly enough, but Coles and Treble (1993) also show that heterogeneity among firms can cause sick pay to be paid by some firms but not by others. The argument is that the introduction into the economy described above of a firm with the assembly-line technology defined by equation (2.1) can generate an equilibrium in which the linear technology firms pay sick pay and the assembly-line firm does not. The argument is quite subtle. The equilibrium can arise if

U_t lies in the neighbourhood of $\hat{U}_t$, such that $U_t > \hat{U}_t$. Then the linear-technology firms offer the high-absentee contract, insuring workers fully against sickness and paying also for the moral hazard of workers who sometimes have things they prefer to do (under the offered contract) than go to work. If the assembly-line firm offers the same contract as the linear-technology firms, its absentee rate is $p_s + p_t$. If it wanted to offer a low-absentee contract, it would choose wages and sick pay so as to minimise the cost of the contract:[19]

$$\min_{w_l, w_s} (1 - p_s)w_l + p_s s \qquad (2.15)$$

The contract has to be incentive-compatible, so that (2.12) still applies:

$$U(w_l) \geq U(s) + U_t = U(s) + \hat{U}_t + \varepsilon \qquad (2.16)$$

In this expression, $\varepsilon > 0$ is the excess of the external utility U_t over its critical value $\hat{U}_t$. In addition, there is a participation constraint, since workers need to be attracted to the contract. This constraint is

$$(1 - p_s)\, U(w_l) + p_s U(s) \geq (1 - p_t)\, U(w_h) + p_t \left(\hat{U}_t + \varepsilon\right) \qquad (2.17)$$

The equality in (2.17) must always hold, since if it did not w_l and w_s could always be reduced without violating (2.16). Given that (2.17) binds, (2.16) must as well, for otherwise the first-order conditions would imply full insurance. Constraint (2.16) can thus be rewritten as

$$U(w_l) = U(s) + \hat{U}_t + \varepsilon \qquad (2.18)$$

Substituting into (2.17) (with the equality holding) gives

$$(1 - p_s - p_t)\, U(w_l) + (p_s + p_t)\, U(s) = (1 - p_t)\, U(w_h) \qquad (2.19)$$

which describes all the feasible pairs $\{w, s\}$ given that the probability of absence is $p_s + p_t$. This expression summarises the two constraints, both of which must hold with equality.[20] All feasible contracts must satisfy (2.19) and $w \geq s$, which is shown in Figure 2.10.

---

[19] Note that, since we are conditioning on low absenteeism, production and hence revenues are independent of the form of the contract. Thus it is sufficient to minimise costs.

[20] Coles and Treble (1993) describe it as an 'indifference curve'. This is not really accurate; a more accurate description would be 'the zero-profit isoprofit line'.

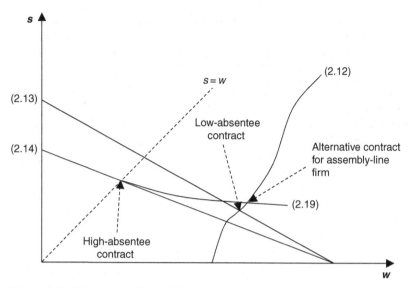

Figure 2.10 Three possible equilibrium contracts

Figure 2.10 reproduces Figure 2.8, with this constraint labelled as (2.19). The alternative contract must satisfy this as well as the incentive compatibility constraint (2.12). This contract is thus indicated in the figure as the intersection of these two constraints. The incentive compatibility constraint (2.12) varies with ε, while (2.19) is independent of it. In fact, increases in ε generate rightward shifts in the incentive compatibility constraint. Furthermore, if $\varepsilon = 0$ the low-absentee contract and the alternative contract are coincident. Proposition I of Coles and Treble (1993)[21] shows that the assembly-line firm's profits are decreasing in p at the market contract. Thus, if $\varepsilon = 0$, the assembly-line firm strictly prefers the low-absentee contract, since by doing so it reduces its probability of absence from $p_s + p_t$ to p_s. As ε increases, the assembly-line firm's expected costs increase, but only by a small amount. The firm will therefore continue to offer its alternative contract unless it encounters a point at which the additional expected costs of doing so are no longer smaller than the value of the productivity gain from reduced absenteeism. This is proposition II in the published paper.

---

[21] The proof is technical and similar to the argument on pages 49–50.

The proposition says that, even in a perfectly competitive market, a firm with high costs of absence may find it profitable to offer no sick pay, even if other firms (which have different technology) do not. If workers (who are homogeneous in this model) value absence sufficiently highly, then both kinds of firm will offer full sick pay, so the main insight is that variations between firms in the provision of sick pay can arise for technological reasons, although if the available workforce is sufficiently idle, or has a sufficiently lively social life or is particularly prone to sick children, even firms with high absence costs can find it too expensive to try to control their workforce's absence behaviour.

Coles and Treble have been criticised by Chatterji and Tilley (2002), who argue that their model provides no real rationale for the payment of sick pay, and that it ignores the fact that firms may want to discourage the attendance of workers who are sick. They pick up one of the themes of the literature on absence since its inception[22] – namely that absence rates may be driven too low if sick pay is not sufficiently generous – but they do not address the central point of Coles and Treble's work, which has to do with variations in sick pay provision across firms.

Chatterji and Tilley (2002) construct a variant of the standard principal–agent model, with three constraints rather than the two specified in the basic model:

(1) participation – the worker prefers this contract to the best alternative;
(2) incentive compatibility I – the worker is better off turning up to work when healthy; and
(3) incentive compatibility II – the worker is better off staying at home when sick.

The argument follows the standard exposition of the principal–agent model, in terms of first establishing the nature of the optimal contract when there is full information, then seeing how the introduction of an informational asymmetry affects the structure of this contract. In the full-information case, the firm chooses a wage rate, w, and a sick pay rate, s, in such a way as to maximise its expected profit. Expected profit depends on the productivity of the worker, and on

[22] In particular, Buzzard (1954) is persuasive on this point.

labour costs. In particular, suppose that a healthy worker produces output x and a sick one produces nothing (because, in the optimal contract, sick workers do not attend), and that the probability of the worker being healthy is s. Expected profit is

$$\Pi = p(x - w) - (1 - p)s \qquad (2.20)$$

In the full-information case, only the participation constraint is necessary. It ensures that the worker is at least as well off having signed the contract as not. Suppose the worker's well-being depends on income, i, the effort they expend, ε, and their health status, σ. If the worker is well, $\sigma = \sigma_L$. If not, $\sigma = \sigma_H$. If the worker attends, work income is w and effort e. If not, income is $i = w_s$ and effort $e = 0$. The worker is supposed to evaluate these states according to an additive utility function:

$$U(i, \sigma, \varepsilon) =$$
$$\begin{cases} U(w, \sigma_L, e) = u(w) - v(e, \sigma_L) & \text{if worker is well and attends} \\ U(s, \sigma_L, 0) = u(s) - v(0, \sigma_L) & \text{if worker is well and is absent} \\ U(s, \sigma_H, 0) = u(s) - v(0, \sigma_H) & \text{if worker is sick and is absent} \\ U(w, \sigma_H, e) = u(w) - v(e, \sigma_H) & \text{if worker is sick and attends} \end{cases}$$

Finally, suppose that alternative income, b, is independent of health and that effort is $\varepsilon = e$.

The participation constraint says that the worker must be at least as well off having signed the contract as not. Expected utility under the contract is given by

$$U_C \equiv pU(w, \sigma_L, e) + (1 - p)\, U(s, \sigma_H, 0)$$
$$= p[u(w) - v(e, \sigma_L)] + (1 - p)[u(s) - v(0, \sigma_H)]$$

Otherwise, expected utility is given by:

$$U_N \equiv pU(b, \sigma_L, 0) + (1 - p)\, U(b, \sigma_H, 0)$$
$$= p[u(b) - v(0, \sigma_L)] + (1 - p)[u(b) - v(0, \sigma_H)]$$

If the worker is to participate in the contract, it is necessary that $U_C \geq U_N$, or, adopting the separable form,

$$p[u(w) - v(e, \sigma_L) + v(0, \sigma_L)] + (1 - p)[u(s)] \geq u(b) \qquad (2.21)$$

The contracting problem can thus be formulated as:

choose w and s to maximise expression (2.20), subject to the participation constraint (2.21) and $w, s \geq 0$.

First, observe that the participation constraint must always bind, since the principal is always better off with w and s as low as possible. w and s cannot both be zero, since if they are (2.21) becomes $u(0) + p[- v(e, \sigma_L) + v(0, \sigma_L)] \geq u(b)$. If this is to be true, it must also be true that $v(e, \sigma_L) < v(0, \sigma_L)$ – that is, the worker must have positive marginal utility of effort (when they are healthy). This seems an unreasonable condition, and we assume that it is not true. Thus, adopting the assumption $v(e, \sigma_L) > v(0, \sigma_L)$, we can conclude that $w = s = 0$ is not a solution to the problem.

The problem is analysed in the standard way, by setting up the Lagrangean function and deriving the Kuhn–Tucker conditions, which are necessary and sufficient for a solution to the problem.

The Lagrangean problem is

$$\max_{w,s,\lambda} p(x - w) - (1 - p)s \\ + \lambda\{p[u(w) - v(e, \sigma_L) + v(0, \sigma_L)] + (1 - p)u(s) - u(b)\} \tag{2.22}$$

from which we can write the first-order Kuhn–Tucker conditions:

$$u'(w) \leq \frac{1}{\lambda} \text{ (equality if } w > 0) \tag{2.23}$$

$$u'(s) \leq \frac{1}{\lambda} \text{ (equality if } s > 0) \tag{2.24}$$

$$p[u(w) - v(e, \sigma_L) + v(0, \sigma_L)] + (1 - p)[u(s)] = u(b) \tag{2.25}$$

Suppose $w > 0$, $s = 0$, then from (2.23) and (2.24) $u'(w) \geq u'(0)$, so this could not hold unless u were convex. Similarly, $w = 0$, $s > 0$, implies that $u'(s) \geq u'(0)$. In principal–agent models, it is usual to suppose strict concavity in terms of an agent's utility, and we maintain this assumption here.

We have now eliminated all possibilities except for $w > 0$, $s > 0$. If this is true, (2.23) and (2.24) imply that $u'(w) = u'(s)$, which, with strict concavity of u, implies that $w = s$. As we know from our previous treatment of the principal–agent problem, full observability implies full insurance of a risk-averse party, when the other party is risk-neutral. We can assess the sensitivity of the optimal wage, $\tilde{w}$, and sick pay, $\tilde{s}$, to other parameters of the problem by using equation (2.25):

$$u(\tilde{w}) = u(\tilde{s}) = u(b) + p[v(e, \sigma_L) - v(0, \sigma_L)] \tag{2.26}$$

Thus the optimal payment is higher for more highly valued outside opportunities; the greater the probability, p, of being healthy, the more the worker dislikes effort when healthy and the greater the required effort is.

This contract (in which the worker is fully insured) is not feasible unless monitoring is cheap, or there is some other device, such as reputation, to keep workers honest. To see why, simply note that a healthy worker is better off not attending work because pay is independent of attendance and effort has to be supplied if they attend, but not if they do not. There is ample evidence that this is in fact what happens from experience with paid sick leave schemes. These are often criticised on the grounds that the sick leave allowance is treated as additional holiday – that is, healthy workers who suffer no financial penalty from absence will pretend to be sick if they have the opportunity.

In this case we need to add the second constraint listed above to the problem. This ensures that healthy workers have no incentive to report sick. Thus we require

$$u(w) - v(e, \sigma_L) \geq u(s) - v(0, \sigma_L) \tag{2.27}$$

Chatterji and Tilley (2002) claim that this is the problem analysed by Coles and Treble (1993): maximise (2.20) subject to the participation constraint (2.21) and the incentive compatibility constraint (2.27). The result is what they call the 'low-absence' contract, which does bear a superficial resemblance to the low-absentee contract described in the discussion of Coles and Treble (1993) above.

The Lagrangean problem is

$$\max_{w,s,\lambda,\mu_1} p(x - w) - (1 - p)s$$
$$+ \lambda\{p[u(w) - v(e, \sigma_L) + v(0, \sigma_L)] + (1 - p)u(s) - u(b)\} \tag{2.28}$$
$$+ \mu_1\{u(w) - v(e, \sigma_L) - u(s) + v(0, \sigma_L)\}$$

from which we can write the first-order Kuhn–Tucker conditions:

$$u'(w) < \frac{p}{\lambda p + \mu_1} \quad \text{(if } w = 0) \tag{2.29}$$

$$u'(s) < \frac{1 - p}{\lambda(1 - p) - \mu_1} \quad \text{(if } w_s = 0) \tag{2.30}$$

$$u'(w) = \frac{p}{\lambda p + \mu_1} < \frac{1}{\lambda} \text{ (if } w > 0) \tag{2.31}$$

$$u'(s) = \frac{1-p}{\lambda(1-p) - \mu_1} > \frac{1}{\lambda} \text{ (if } s > 0) \tag{2.32}$$

$$p[u(w) - v(e, \sigma_L) + v(0, \sigma_L)] + (1-p)[u(s)] = u(b) \tag{2.33}$$

$$u(w) - v(e, \sigma_L) - u(s) + v(0, \sigma_L) = 0 \tag{2.34}$$

which can be manipulated to characterise the solution.

Once again, (2.33) binds, as does (2.34) (this is the argument made above). These two conditions imply that $u(\tilde{s}) = u(b)$ and $u(\tilde{w}) = u(b) + v(e, \sigma_L) - v(0, \sigma_L)$. Thus, by monotonicity of u, and the assumption $v(e, \sigma_L) > v(0, \sigma_L)$, $\tilde{w} > b = \tilde{s}$. Sick pay is set at the value of the outside opportunity, and the wage is greater than sick pay.

Finally, Chatterji and Tilley (2002) add a third constraint to the model that guarantees that workers will not want to attend when they are sick:

$$u(w) - v(e, \sigma_H) \leq u(s) - v(0, \sigma_H) \tag{2.35}$$

Rewriting this and (2.34) gives

$$u(w) - u(s) = v(e, \sigma_L) - v(0, \sigma_L)$$

$$u(w) - u(s) \leq v(e, \sigma_H) - v(0, \sigma_H)$$

so that, if the discomfort felt by an ill person at turning up to work (relative to staying at home) is the same as the discomfort felt by a well person, the extra constraint adds nothing. If sick people suffer more discomfort from turning up to work than well people do, $v(e, \sigma_L) - v(0, \sigma_L) < v(e, \sigma_H) - v(0, \sigma_H)$. This means that the added incentive compatibility constraint never binds, since it is never as restrictive as the first. The added constraint makes a difference only if $v(e, \sigma_L) - v(0, \sigma_L) > v(e, \sigma_H) - v(0, \sigma_H)$. In this case, it is the second constraint only that binds:

$$p[u(w) - v(e, \sigma_L) + v(0, \sigma_L)] + (1-p)[u(s)] = u(b) \tag{2.36}$$

$$u(w) - v(e, \sigma_H) - u(s) + v(0, \sigma_H) = 0 \tag{2.37}$$

Under these circumstances, which might be interpreted as a worker with a troubled conscience in the event of going absent without being sick, sick pay must be set above b. This follows because (2.37) implies that $u(w) - u(s) = v(e, \sigma_H) - v(0, \sigma_H) < v(e, \sigma_L) - v(0, \sigma_L)$. Combining this with (2.36) yields $\tilde{s} > b$. If the worker feels bad about taking absences anyway, he or she does not have to be exposed to as great a degree of risk as otherwise.

Comparison of Chatterji and Tilley's model with Coles and Treble's is revealing only in the sense that it underlines the complexity of the issues at stake. In truth, they are strictly incomparable, since the models are so different. The principal–agent framework as used by Chatterji and Tilley assumes that there exists an outside opportunity for the agent that is fixed exogenously and that competition in the output market is irrelevant to the contract design, whereas Coles and Treble assume that there are markets for labour and for output both of which clear when firms make their contract design decisions. While it is true that the design of Coles and Treble's low-absentee contract is similar to that of Chatterji and Tilley's two-constraint model, the design emerges from quite different considerations. In both cases, it is a consequence of firms' (or the firm's, in Chatterji and Tilley's case) inability to monitor the true state of workers' (the worker's) utility, but the alternative design (full insurance) in Chatterji and Tilley's model can be efficient only if their firm is well informed. In Coles and Treble's model, the full-insurance contract can be optimal even with asymmetric information if the workers' alternative utility is sufficiently high. This outcome arises because there are two sources of utility variation to which Coles and Treble's workers are subject. The first is sickness (or whatever eventuality it is that the sick pay is intended to insure against), the second is other shocks to workers' utilities, such as 'It's a good day to go fishing'. In the Coles–Treble set-up, as U_t approaches zero, the low-absentee contract dominates, because sickness is verifiable in their model whereas the second source of utility variation is not.

While Chatterji and Tilley argue that sick workers attending may be just as worth worrying about as healthy workers not attending, their model does not include any good reason a firm should worry about excess attendance. There are several, especially the following. (1) Workers whose incentives get them back to work prematurely may be less productive than if they are able to make a full recovery before returning to work. (2) Workers with infectious or contagious diseases may spread diseases among their fellow workers. Skåtun (2003) addresses some of these problems, but his paper also raises others that are troubling. This paper is in the principal–agent mould, and features three wage rates, rather than two. The extra wage rate is paid to sick workers who turn up to work. Turning up to work while sick enables an employer to monitor the worker's state of health better, so that the appropriate wage rate can always be paid to attending workers. Skåtun concludes that the wage paid to sick workers who attend must be greater than the wage paid to well workers, while the sick pay paid to absent workers lies between these two.[23] The theoretical possibility that one may want to pay sick workers differently from healthy workers is of some interest, although we know of no examples of firms that do this. The main point of interest raised by Skåtun (2003), though, is the technical one that, because ill agents at work are more likely to infect others, the probability of illness is an increasing function of the probability that an ill agent turns up to work. However, the firm knows this, and so can internalise this infection externality. From the perspective of workers, the probability of being healthy is therefore fixed, so that the provision of appropriate incentives in the presence of contagion can be analysed using the same methods as appropriate for the case without contagion.[24]

Although these papers raise interesting questions, neither of them is really satisfactory as a theoretical approach to the supply of absence. This apparently dismissive remark is based on one important observation: while it is seductive to use received theoretical structures (in this case the standard principal–agent model), it is rarely the case that an off-the-shelf solution will suit any particular problem without modification. The difficulty in the present case is that, if the only random shock affecting the attendance behaviour of a worker is whether they are sick or not, then that worker's attendance or absence will reveal exactly to the employer when they are sick and when they are not. To make a credible model of absenteeism it is necessary to have at least *two* random shocks disturbing the workers' tastes: the sickness shock, and something else that will generate an occasional desire on the part of the worker to be absent when they are not sick. In the absence of the

---

[23] Chatterji and Tilley (2003) contend that this ordering is wrong, and that one of the incentive compatibility constraints is in fact redundant. This last claim implies that only two wage rates are necessary to provide the desired incentives.

[24] Some empirical evidence on contagion effects is given by Barmby and Larguem (2009).

second shock, which we might call a *utility shock*, the fact that the worker has accepted the contract and is not absent from work is sufficient to enable the employer to infer correctly that the worker is truly sick, so that sickness cannot be unobservable.

Finally, it is probably worth emphasising the novelty of the idea of a supply of absence, in the context of the extant literature. This literature, and the advice that is regularly given to HR practitioners, is based uniformly on the idea that absenteeism is a problem that arises because of workers. There is some truth in this, but there seems little point in complaining about the human frailties of workers. This chapter proposes that in order to understand observed rates of absenteeism, it is necessary to understand not only the behaviour of workers, but also the responses of firms and their managers to it. We have used conventional ideas of profit maximisation to argue that these responses are likely to be complex. Wage-fixing and acceptable absence will be associated with technology, which can itself be managed. Managing absence is not simply a matter of trying to modify or exploit human psychology. Technological choices can be important drivers of how costly absence will be to a firm. This claim applies not only to absence without the moral hazard induced by sick pay, but also to moral hazard itself. What a firm can do or wants to do about it is connected to the technology it uses.

Summary

This chapter observes that absenteeism can exist only if workers are required by their contracts to be present. Not all work contracts insist on this. We argue that the ones that do relate to jobs in which the absence of one worker incurs costs for the firm that are greater than the marginal product of the absent worker. The technical or shorthand phrase for this is that complementarities are important. These may be complementarities between workers, or complementarities between workers and the capital equipment that they work with. A firm's willingness to supply absence depends on the degree of complementarity that its production processes display.

A second aspect of absence supply is the apparent willingness of firms to provide sick pay to their workers. The reason for this is not obvious, partly because the payment of sick pay can create moral hazard problems. Once again, we argue that firms' provision of sick pay varies according to the costs implied by the technology they adopt, just as their tolerance of absence does.

We conclude that explanations of observed patterns of absenteeism and sick pay provision will involve consideration not only of the tastes of workers and their proneness to sickness, but also on the technologies adopted by their employers.

Finally, it is worth stressing that the models described here all involve workers whose utility is random, either because they are prone to sickness, or for some other reason. In fact, if an appeal is to be made in a theory to the non-observability of sickness by an employer, it is necessary that there be at least two sources of random shocks to workers' utilities: sickness and a utility shock to create the moral hazard.

3 | *The demand for absence*

We show in this chapter how the demand for absence may be modelled either as a response to a fixed-hours contract, or as a consequence of shocks disturbing household production, or worker tastes. We consider how the models may be modified to include sick pay – either individual or group-based. Finally, we pursue two issues that arise: shocks to workers' ability to attend work (such as unreliable buses) and the impact on two-employee households of sick pay.

The allocation of time

For the most part, the literature on labour supply has created a bleak world for its decision-makers to inhabit. You probably would not wish to spend long in the company of the decision-makers themselves. Their home life, if it exists at all, is limited, their decisions (until quite recently) were independent of their nearest and dearest, and their consumption unidimensional. The literature has developed in this way for very good reasons, but the approach looks increasingly inadequate as a basis for understanding real-life decision-makers. The availability of increasingly detailed, complex data sets and of statistical methods of analysis has led to an interplay between theoretical developments and empirical practice, which is yielding new insights into the way in which households operate. At the same time, an increasingly rich theoretical description of house-hold life is being created against which individual workers' relationships with the labour market can be analysed.

The early literature on labour supply, such as that reviewed by Killingsworth (1983), was based on consideration of a simple model in which individuals allocated time between work and non-work activities. Their decisions were made in the light of the wage that they might receive and non-wage income. In many accounts of worker absenteeism, the stress is on the behaviour of workers. They are purely supply-side explanations, which take the work environment within which workers make their decisions as given, and ask how workers respond to it.

In order to explain the demand for absenteeism, something more complex is required. As we have already observed, in order to be absent, a worker needs to have been required to attend. In turn, this requires that they have agreed to a contract requiring attendance. If we can suppose that there is no coercion, workers would not sign such a contract unless there were some gain to them in doing so. There are two possible ways in which such a gain might arise. One is that the set of available contracts is incomplete, and does not include one that matches the number of hours that the worker would seek to supply at the offered wage. The second is that there are shocks to workers' labour supply functions, such that sometimes the offered wage will be sufficient to secure labour supply, but sometimes it will not. This second possibility also requires that the contract be acceptable to the worker and the employer.

The simplest theory of labour supply is a model of the allocation of time. People allocate the hours of the day to various uses according to the value they believe they will yield. These values are not usually purely financial, so the model is presented in terms of utility. A simple version stresses the concentration on labour supply by dividing time into work and non-work time, and supposes that only one job is held. Non-work time is often unhelpfully referred to by economists as 'leisure'.

In this simple model, people value time spent not working and income. These tastes (or preferences) are summarised in a utility function

$$U = U(T - h, y) \tag{3.1}$$

where T represents total time available, h represents time spent on work and y represents income. Non-work time, $T-h$, and income, y, are both goods in the sense that utility rises if either of them rises independently of the other – that is, $U_1 \equiv \partial U / \partial (T - h) > 0; U_2 \equiv \partial U / \partial y > 0$.

Work time and income are not independent of each other for many workers. To keep things as simple as possible in these initial stages of the argument, we assume that work contracts specify a wage: a fixed rate of payment per hour of work. This assumption begs many questions about piece rates, sick pay, overtime, fringe benefits, taxation, etc. We tackle many of these questions in the course of what follows, but for the time being suppose that the wage, w, yields an income of wh to a worker who works h hours. Workers may, of course, receive income from sources other than work; call this non-work income V. Total income is then given by the sum of income from work and non-work income, or

$$y = V + wh, \; h \in [0, T] \tag{3.2}$$

The decision facing a person with tastes represented by U can then be described as choosing a number of hours of work that will make U as large as possible, given the constraint on hours of work and income in (3.2):

$$\max_{h \in [0,T]} U(T - h, y) \text{ subject to } y = V + wh \tag{3.3}$$

The first-order conditions for interior solutions to this problem are

$$\frac{U_1}{U_2} = w$$
$$y = V + wh \tag{3.4}$$

which is to say that, at the optimal choice of hours, the marginal rate of substitution between non-work hours and income is equal to the wage rate, and the constraint is satisfied. If there is no positive solution to (3.4) then optimal hours $h^* = 0$.

The solution is illustrated in Figure 3.1, in which income is measured on the vertical axis and non-work time on the horizontal. Thus any point on the diagram represents a particular combination of income and non-work hours. The curved line represents an indifference curve, which is a contour of the utility function. Consider any income–hours combination on the indifference curve. The indifference curve separates those combinations that are preferred to the chosen one (which are above and to the right of it) from those that are not preferred. The worker is indifferent between any two combinations on the line. The straight line represents the constraint (3.2), for a given wage and unearned income. It separates those income–hours combinations that are attainable by the worker from those that are not. The wage rate is insufficiently high to enable the worker to achieve combinations above and to the right of the straight line. Any combinations below the line, or to the left, are feasible. Of course, if the wage or unearned income change, the constraint will change as well. The

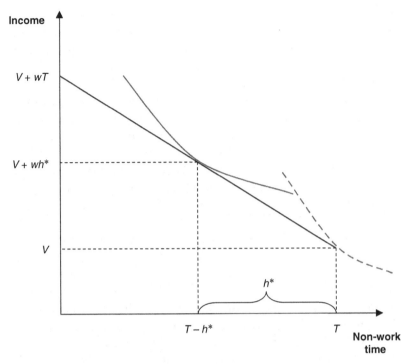

Figure 3.1 The simplest model of labour supply

income–hours configuration indicated by the dotted lines represents the best attainable combination given the wage rate, w. The easiest way to see why this must be so is to note that any combination that is preferred by the worker is above the constraint line, and is therefore unattainable. All attainable income–hours configurations are below the indifference curve, and therefore not preferred. The optimal labour supply can be read off the figure as the distance h^*.

It is sometimes useful to think of this problem in a slightly different way. Becker's 'theory of the allocation of time' (1965) introduced the idea of 'full income' – the maximal income that would be generated by someone whose only interest in life was gaining income. In a very simple model, which ignored the necessities of eating, sleeping and recreation, this might be thought of as the income that would be earned if all available time were devoted to work. Under these rather dreary circumstances, full income would be $y = V + wT$. In the model of Figure 3.1, the worker can be thought of as allocating full income to different uses of time – work and non-work. Of course, this reinterpretation makes no difference to the result. It is just more natural sometimes to think of the worker spending some of their full income on non-work and taking the rest as money than to think of them spending some of their time on work, some on non-work and then calculating the money income.

The condition expressed in equations (3.4) appears in the diagram in the following form. The right-hand side, w, is the negative of the slope of the constraint, which falls from a height of $V + wT$ to a height of V over the horizontal distance T. Each extra hour of time devoted to non-work is worth w in lost income. Alternatively, w is the full-income price of an hour of non-work. This slope thus represents the 'objective' valuation of an hour of the worker's time by the market. The slope of the indifference curve represents the worker's own subjective relative valuations of income and non-work time. The marginal rate of substitution (as the slope is called) tells us how much extra income the worker would need in order to give up a marginal amount of non-work time. At the optimal point, these two quantities are equal. Condition (3.4) expresses the idea that the optimum occurs where the subjective and objective valuations are identical. If this were not the case, the worker would either feel that their hours were too long or too short (given the wage that they command).

It is important to note as well that the optimal choice of hours depends on who is making the decision. People who potentially supply labour differ in their tastes. In the model outlined here, tastes are captured by the utility function, or its geometric counterpart, the indifference map. Looking at Figure 3.1, consider someone with steeper indifference curves than the one illustrated. A steeper indifference curve means that the marginal rate of substitution for any given income–hours combination is greater. With the wage rate fixed, this implies that the optimal non-work hours will be higher (labour supply lower) and income lower. Steeper indifference curves produce a choice further to the right on the constraint line. For some people, the optimum choice will be to supply no work at all, and receive an income of V. The dotted indifference curve in Figure 3.1 illustrates this case.

Fixed hours

This basic model of labour supply does not lead immediately to a model of absenteeism. The missing vital element is that the only characteristic of a job in the model is the wage that it pays, and, as we pointed out in Chapter 1, absenteeism is impossible unless a worker is required to turn up to work. To create a meaningful theory of absence demand, it is necessary to have job packages that specify hours. Otherwise, there is nothing for the worker to be absent from.

The theory can be adapted to include contractual hours. In problem (3.3), the worker freely chose some number of hours between 0 and T. Choosing zero hours amounts to non-participation. If the job also specifies a number of hours that the worker is required to attend, this choice is constrained to non-participation, or accepting the contractual hours specified in the job description. Call these H, and (3.3) becomes

$$\max_{h \in [0, H]} U(T - h, y) \text{ subject to } y = V + wh \qquad (3.5)$$

where the braces indicate that the choice of hours can be made only over the *pair* $\{0, H\}$. The worker can choose either non-participation or the contract with H hours of work. Income is V in the case of non-participation, or $V + wH$ if the contract is chosen. The situation is illustrated in Figure 3.2.

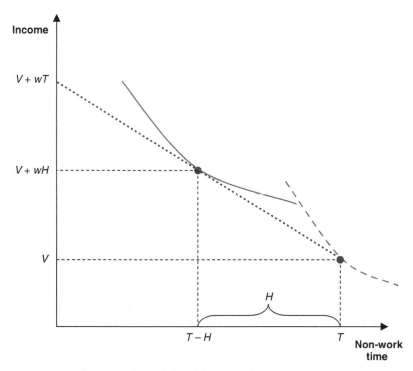

Figure 3.2 Labour supply with fixed hours

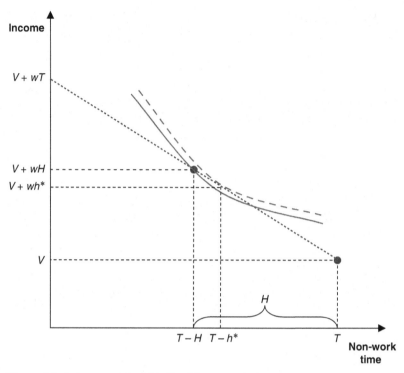

Figure 3.3 Labour supply with fixed hours and absenteeism

The figure shows a worker whose tastes lead them to choose the offered contract, but other people's tastes will be different. For this person, just as before, condition (3.4) applies. The marginal rate of substitution is equal to the wage rate. As in Figure 3.1, the dotted indifference curve shows a person who would choose not to take the job.

The apparent simplicity of the choice here masks a greater complexity in this model than in the basic labour supply model. In particular, it is possible to imagine a person with indifference curves that are steeper at the offered contract, for whom the optimal choice is still to take the job, but for whom condition (3.4) does not apply. Figure 3.3 shows such a person. Notice, first, that the option not to work at an income of V lies below the indifference curve that runs through the option to work H hours for an income of $V + wH$. Thus working is preferred to not working. Second, the subjective relative valuations of non-work time and income, measured by the slope of the indifference curve, imply that non-work is valued more highly by the individual concerned than the market valuation, w.[1] Such a worker, given the current wage rate and a free choice of hours, would choose to work fewer hours than H. The optimal labour supply is shown as h^* in the figure.

Note that the lower hours worked are preferred even though, according to the argument so far, the worker would lose income for every hour that actual hours, h^*, fell short of contractual hours, H. Formally, the solution to this problem satisfies the same first-order conditions as problem (3.3), unless $U(V,T) > U(V + wT, T-H)$, in which case $h^* = 0$.

A random utility model

The model outlined here is essentially that of Dunn and Youngblood (1986) and Dunn (1990).[2] It posits that the demand for absenteeism arises because firms see some benefit in offering a wage–hours package, and workers are able, because of imperfect monitoring and control on the part of the employer, to undermine the terms of their contracts. This seems a rather limited view of absenteeism demand, suggesting that all absenteeism should be viewed as subversive by firms. As was pointed out in Chapter 2, though, firms willingly set in place policies permitting absenteeism, because they recognise that not all absenteeism is subversive. Instead, it arises from circumstances such as illness, children's illness and a long list of other disruptions of everyday life – late buses, broken-down cars and domestic crises of various kinds. Given these sources of uncertainty in domestic life, it would be an unwise employer who tried to enforce 'zero tolerance'.

Furthermore, the idea of absenteeism as exclusively a mechanism by which workers can redress a discrepancy between their desired hours and those on offer from an employer cannot easily answer the question of monitoring. If Dunn and Youngblood's proposal were the *sole* source of absence behaviour, employers could easily detect those workers whose desired hours fell short of contractual hours. They would be those who took absences.

---

[1] The wage rate is still indicated by the slope of the line joining the two options, but intermediate points on this line, which is shown dotted, are not feasible choices.

[2] Vistnes (1997) also uses this idea, but does not attempt to test it.

An alternative has been proposed by Barmby, Sessions and Treble (1994) in which workers' utilities are not fixed. Instead, they vary stochastically from time to time. The key parameter in studies of labour supply is the marginal rate of substitution of income for non-work time. In the model developed by Barmby, Sessions and Treble, a utility function is used for which the marginal rate of substitution varies randomly according to some probability distribution.

The idea here is that labour supply is not entirely controllable by workers. People get ill, some of them have responsibility for others who might get ill, domestic capital is not perfectly reliable, and nor are transport systems, whether private or public. The random utility approach to modelling absence deals with this by claiming that it can be captured by a single parameter: the rate at which workers are prepared to exchange non-work time for income. If a child is sick, time spent caring for it becomes more valuable to its parent. Sickness generally makes it hard for people to engage in work, so the disutility of time spent at work increases when a worker is sick. If the plumber is coming to fix the sink, and needs access, then the worker's subjective valuation of time spent providing that access increases. It is harder perhaps to justify random utility as a way of modelling variations in transportation costs, so we deal with these in a different way below.

The empirical work reported in Dunn and Youngblood's paper is aimed at measuring the difference between the marginal rate of substitution of workers and the marginal wage rate. They find that '[h]ours lost due to non-medical absence is found to increase with increases in the difference between a worker's marginal rate of substitution and his marginal wage rate. Increases in this difference are also found to increase the frequency of illness absences.'

Their technique leaves a large part of the total variation of absence unexplained. In order to make this work it is necessary to measure the marginal rate of substitution at the contractual hours of work, rather than at actual hours. Marginal wage rates are routinely recorded by employers, but marginal rates of substitution are not. Dunn and Youngblood use a survey instrument that asks people to evaluate a set of job benefits twice – once in terms of money, once in terms of time. The marginal rate of substitution is then taken to be the ratio of these two evaluations. However, it does not estimate the marginal rate of substitution at the contractual hours. Instead, it estimates the marginal rate of substitution at the workers' actual choices.

Of course, there is no reason why the Dunn and Youngblood model and the random utility model should be regarded as mutually exclusive. The random utility model starts with the idea that the marginal rate of substitution is not constant. Suppose that what Dunn and Youngblood measure with their survey is a mean marginal rate of substitution for each respondent. Those respondents with a high measured marginal rate of substitution would then be more likely to be absent than those with a low measured marginal rate of substitution at the same marginal wage. This 'hybrid' model is almost certainly able to explain more of the variation in absence rates than a deterministic model, and it also resolves the question of monitoring, since inferring bad behaviour on the part of a worker for whom it is accepted that behaviour will be unreliable is a lot more difficult than inferring bad behaviour in a world of certainty.

How does the random utility model work? People cannot be in two places at once. Being at work is binary: either one is or one is not.[3] McFadden (1981) in his survey of discrete choice models makes the following general observation (205):

Suppose a probabilistic choice system is consistent with a random utility model. Are there alternative theories of individual behaviour which generate the same probabilistic choice model, but which for reasons of generality are to be preferred to the classical model of individual utility maximization? One more general alternative is immediate. We might view the individual himself as drawing a utility function from a random distribution each time a decision is made. Then the individual is a classical utility maximizer given his state of mind, but his state of mind varies randomly from one choice situation to the next.

This is the approach taken in our model, although what we do is probably rather different from what McFadden had in mind.

Suppose, then, that a worker has a utility function of the form $U = U(a,b \mid \theta)$. Here a represents the worker's attendance choice, taking the value zero if the worker attends and one if they are absent. The second argument, b, is the current realisation of a random shock, σ, and θ is a vector of parameters representing other aspects of the worker or their choice situation that are relevant to the choice. Fix a particular value for σ, and the situation is as illustrated in Figure 3.4, which is a version

---

[3] This is true so long as the work contract specifies what is meant by 'attendance'.

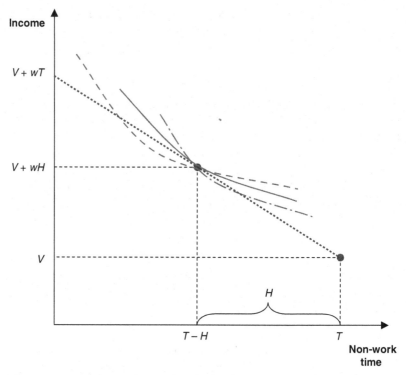

Figure 3.4 A random utility model of absenteeism

of the standard income–leisure choice diagram reproduced in many labour economics texts.

Now suppose that σ controls the marginal rate of substitution between non-work time and income in such a way that an increase in σ increases both the relative value of non-work time and the marginal rate of substitution. The solid indifference curve in Figure 3.4 represents the worker's tastes when σ happens to generate a marginal rate of substitution just equal to the slope of the budget line implied by the fixed-hours contract shown. Increases in σ steepen the slopes of the indifference curves derived from the utility function U, yielding something like the dot-and-dash indifference curve in the figure. Given the same wage rate and non-wage income, optimal hours h^* fall. Similarly, a smaller value of σ will increase optimal hours of labour supply, as show by the dotted indifference curve.

With a utility structure such as this, absenteeism can be explained as follows. The worker understands that their personal circumstances imply a particular distribution, $\Phi(.)$, of σ. A firm offers a contract that specifies a wage and a number of hours of work. It may also specify an absence policy. Workers can then assess whether or not their own $\Phi(.)$ makes it worthwhile for them to sign the contract. They know what their own propensity for sickness is, they know what their childcare responsibilities are and they are familiar with any other aspects of their lives that may be relevant to the reliability of their labour supply. They can therefore figure out the implications of a particular contract structure for their own circumstances.

Absence distributions and mean absence rates can be calculated from the model. Under reasonably general conditions[4] a reservation level of σ, $\tilde{\sigma}(\theta)$, exists such that $U(0, \tilde{\sigma}|\theta) = U(1, \tilde{\sigma}|\theta)$. The agent's optimal decision is then to attend if the actual realised value of σ is less than the reservation level, and to stay away if it is greater. It follows that the probability of attendance is just $\Phi(\tilde{\sigma}(\theta))$, and the probability of absence is $1 - \Phi(\tilde{\sigma}(\theta))$. For this agent, then, the distribution of absences during any sample of days of size n is binomial with mean $n[1 - \Phi(\tilde{\sigma}(\theta))]$, while the mean absence rate will be just $1 - \Phi(\tilde{\sigma}(\theta))$.

Here is an example using a Cobb–Douglas utility function:

$$U(y, T - h) = (T - h)^{\sigma} y^{(1-\sigma)} \tag{3.6}$$

Suppose that a daily decision is made as to whether to attend or not. Just as in the fixed-hours model, a worker will attend if $U(V,T) \leq U(V + wH, T-H)$ and stay absent if $U(V,T) > U(V + wH, T-H)$. The reservation value of σ solves the equation $U(V,T) = U(V + wH, T - H)$ or $\left(\frac{T}{T-H}\right)^{\sigma} = \left(\frac{V+wH}{V}\right)^{(1-\sigma)}$. This equation has a unique solution, since, when $\sigma = 0$, the left-hand side is one, and the right-hand side is greater than one and, when $\sigma = 1$, the left-hand side is greater than one, and the right-hand side is equal to one. Both sides are continuous and monotonic, and therefore there is a unique crossing point, given by

$$\tilde{\sigma} = \frac{\ln\left(\frac{V}{V+wH}\right)}{\ln\frac{T-H}{T} + \ln\left(\frac{V}{V+wH}\right)} \tag{3.7}$$

---

[4] The optimality of reservation level rules has been widely discussed in the literature on job search; see, for example, McCall (1970) and Rothschild (1974).

The reservation value is independent of the distribution of σ, although the implied binomial distribution of the absence count is, of course, not.[5]

The key variable in determining the absence rate here is $\tilde{\sigma}(\theta)$. Since $\Phi(.)$ is a distribution function it is increasing in its argument, higher reservation levels imply lower absence rates. It is worthwhile asking what characteristics of the problem would raise or lower the value of $\tilde{\sigma}(\theta)$. A glance at Figure 3.4 suggests that there are only two types of factors: characteristics of the budget constraint, which is determined by non-labour income and the terms of the job contract, and the characteristics of the utility function. Since this model is based firmly on the standard model of labour supply, and the predictions of that model are ambiguous, it will also be the case that the predictions of this model are ambiguous.

(1) Just as the labour supply curve may be backward-bending in the standard model, so may the relationship between wage and mean hours supply be backward-bending in the random utility model. This implies that, holding contractual hours fixed, the relationship between absence and the wage rate is likely to be ambiguously signed as well.

(2) So far as the utility function is concerned, the key issue is how changes in the elements of θ (the vector of worker characteristics) affect the distribution of the marginal rate of substitution. The birth of a child is likely to increase variance, thus increasing absenteeism, but the impact on the mean is uncertain. Some may think that it is gendered – that the value of time at work relative to time at home is increased for men, and decreased for women – but this is, ultimately, an empirical matter.

Introducing sick pay

In Chapter 2 we argued that there are circumstances under which firms will find it profitable to offer sick pay to workers, since this leads to an efficient sorting of workers between firms. What will the impact of this be on the absence demand of workers? First, consider the standard labour supply model (3.3). Although there is no rationale

---

[5] A recent working paper by Lindbeck and Persson (2006) uses a similar stochastic model in an investigation of absence and income insurance.

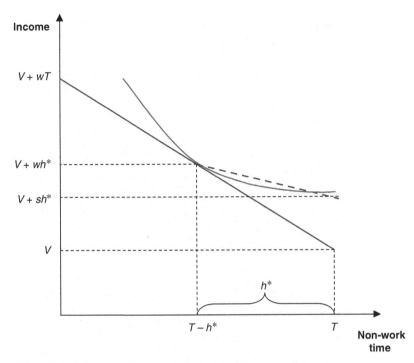

Figure 3.5 Sick pay in the simplest model of labour supply

for sick pay or absenteeism if this is how the world is, it is worthwhile asking what the impact of sick pay would be, because something similar to this model seems to be the basis of many managerial attitudes to absence.

Figure 3.5 reproduces Figure 3.1 with the addition of a sick pay constraint, indicated with a straight dotted line. This emanates from the chosen hours of the worker, and is flatter than the original budget constraint, indicating that sick pay is lower than the wage rate.[6] Optimal hours supply with sick pay is unambiguously lower than without, since there is no income effect involved in the comparison of the original budget constraint and the budget constraint representing the

---

[6] This is not necessarily the case. An aspect of the chaotic benefit system in Britain in the early 1980s was that sick pay was not taxable. Those who were entitled to sick pay at 100 per cent replacement – civil servants and university teachers, among others – thus received greater post-tax sick pay than their normal earnings. This anomaly has now been removed.

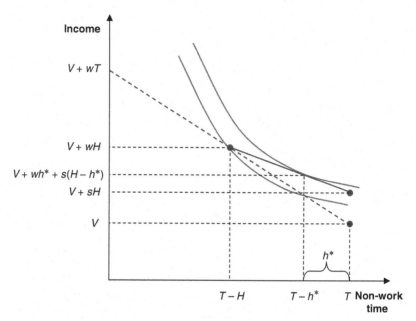

Figure 3.6 Sick pay in the fixed-hours model

sick pay scheme. In fact, with sick pay at 100 per cent replacement, this model predicts 100 per cent absence – an implication routinely rejected by data.[7]

The model with fixed hours has rather different implications, which are illustrated in Figure 3.6. This is identical to Figure 3.1 with the addition of the constraint that applies when sick pay is payable. Because this constraint does not cross the original budget constraint at the optimum, income effects will apply, so that a backward-bending labour supply (forward-bending absence demand) is possible.[8]

Third, consider the introduction of sick pay into the model with random utility. This model predicts a distribution of absence rates, which changes in the budget constraint will alter. In particular, it will

[7] For example, among the workforce studied by Barmby, Orme and Treble (1991), workers with replacement rates of 100 per cent had an absence rate of 2.87 per cent. However, the models presented here are incomplete, since few employers tolerate paying sick pay to someone with an absence rate of 100 per cent for very long. In other words, these simple models omit aspects of contracts, such as disciplinary proceedings, that threaten the continuation of the contract.

[8] Vistnes (1997: 309) claims otherwise, but it is not clear from her discussion exactly what model she is referring to.

lower the optimal reservation morbidity level, $\tilde{\sigma}$, thus increasing the probability of absence, and changing the parameter of the binomial distribution of absence accordingly. In particular, mean absence will rise. To see this, note that

$$\tilde{\sigma}_s = \frac{\ln\left(\frac{V+sH}{V+wH}\right)}{\ln\frac{T-H}{T} + \ln\left(\frac{V+sH}{V+wH}\right)} \tag{3.8}$$

It is easy to show that this is smaller than $\tilde{\sigma}$ calculated from equation (3.7), so the probability of absence rises, and mean absence with it.

More generally, it is true that $\tilde{\sigma}_s$ is decreasing in the replacement rate s; it is decreasing in V and H, and increasing in w and T. The probability of an absence increases with non-labour income and contractual hours, and decreases with an increase in the wage rate or the total available time.

It is probably impossible to provide a complete analysis of the way in which the absence behaviour of an individual worker may respond to different schemes of remuneration and particularly sick pay, for two reasons. First, the range of available incentive structures is enormous (in particular, we have said little about dynamic schemes); and, second, their impact in general will depend on the relationship of the individual to the work group and to the household. The rest of the chapter is taken up with a discussion of these issues.

The design of sick pay schemes is usually more complex than a simple insurance scheme with a fixed replacement rate. In Chapter 4 we discuss the variety of these schemes, and the reasons for their adoption. Here we consider their impact on the demand for absence. It is very common for sick pay schemes to be *experience-rated*, by which is meant that replacement rates depend in some way on past behaviour. For example, paid sick leave schemes often involve replacement at 100 per cent for a fixed number of days per year, with the rate dropping to zero when the number of accumulated days in the year exceeds this number. Many state-regulated sick pay schemes specify that the first few days of each absence spell should attract no replacement, with a higher rate beginning after these days of waiting have expired.

How do experience-rated schemes affect the behaviour of workers? They are clearly designed in an attempt to control attendance, but the impact of even a simple design can be complex and hard to predict, for two reasons. First, these designs tend to generate perverse incentives, by which is meant they can encourage undesirable behaviour. As an example, consider the generic sick leave scheme, in which a fixed number of days of paid absence are granted. These days are usually counted from the beginning of the year, creating an end-year effect. A worker whose paid sick leave has not been exhausted at the end of year has little reason other than conscience not to take it, so that the moral hazard is enhanced at the end of the sick leave year. It is for this reason that sick leave has acquired a poor reputation (at least in Britain).

The second difficulty created by experience-rated schemes is that, since they are dynamic, they affect both workers' decisions to begin a spell of absence and their decisions to return to work. We would expect many absence spells to end on exactly the day that a sick leave allowance expires.

These issues are hard to discuss in general. However, it is possible to write down a model that uses the specific structure of any scheme and derives the pattern of absence demand generated by it, and it is this that we now explain. Our discussion is restricted to a subset of experience-rated schemes. These may be called *redemptive* schemes, because they have the property that, whatever state of grace or disgrace the decision-maker may currently be in, it is always possible to exit it, and return to it given an appropriate pattern of behaviour. While non-redemptive schemes exist,[9] we have not yet devoted any time or effort to analysing them.

The example worked out in full below comes from a snack-food-packaging plant in the English town of Ashby-de-la-Zouch. We concentrate on it because we have completed an analysis of its effects, in an attempt to develop a general method of analysis. The method is described in detail by Treble (2009b), and is readily adaptable to produce what one might call 'incentive profiles' for any dynamic scheme.

Here, workers who take more than one spell of absence in a rolling five-week period are banned from eligibility for overtime for a period of four weeks following the end of the most recent spell. This is a

---

[9] Hassink and Koning (2009) describe a scheme in which workers with good attendance are given a lottery ticket. Those workers whose tickets win become ineligible for future lottery tickets, and are therefore in effect permanently thrown out of the scheme. This means that the scheme is non-redemptive.

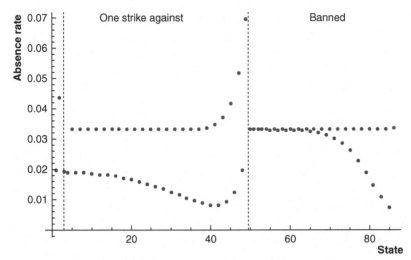

Note: Upper rows refer to workers who are in an ongoing spell of absence; lower rows to workers who are currently attending.

Figure 3.7 Incentives in an experience-rated scheme

redemptive scheme[10] in which optimal behaviour depends on the number of spells of absence that a worker has accumulated during the previous five weeks, and the dates on which they ended. These can be represented by a set of eighty-six states, each one indexed to indicate the number of absence spells they have experienced in the last five weeks (none, one or more than one); the time elapsed since the end of the last absence spell; and whether or not the worker is absent at the moment.

Each state is characterised by a distinct set of constraints, and transitions between states depend on the current decision whether or not to be absent. It follows that the decision to be absent will be influenced by both the current set of constraints and the constraints that will face the decision-maker in the future. In essence, the model that we have devised to study these kinds of systems takes the random utility framework, and extends it to this more general set-up in which the future is important.

The plot in Figure 3.7 shows a simulated pattern of incentives. The eighty-six states are plotted on the horizontal axis. In the first

---

[10] Ed Lazear has observed in conversation with one of the authors that, since workers always have the option to quit, this claim is not quite true.

and second states, the worker has no absences in the previous five weeks. In states 3 to 49 they have one completed absence spell at some time in the past five weeks. State 3 and even-numbered states refer to workers who are currently attending. Odd-numbered states (but not state 3) refer to workers who are not. Within each of these groups the end date of the worker's last completed absence spell is further in the past the greater the number of the state. Similarly, for states 50 to 86, workers are banned from overtime working. State 50 and odd-numbered states refer to workers who are currently attending. Even-numbered states (but not state 50) refer to workers who are not.

Perhaps the easiest way to see how the plot relates to the rules of the scheme is to imagine how a worker's state changes as time passes. Workers who are never absent remain permanently in state 1. On starting an absence spell, someone in state 1 will switch to state 2, and then to state 3 when they return to work. Assuming no further absences, they will move through even-numbered states 4 to 48. A worker in state 48 who continues to attend will then return to state 1, since their last spell will have expired. However, if another spell is started by a worker occupying one of the states 4 to 48, they will move to the odd-numbered state three higher than their current one. So a worker who is in state 10 and is absent will move into state 13. If a worker in one of the odd-numbered states 5 to 47 attends they complete a second spell and will move to the first banned state (state 50). Otherwise, the second spell will remain uncompleted, and they will continue to move through the odd-numbered states 5 to 49. From state 49, an attending worker will move to state 2, because the absence spell prior to their current one will have ended more than five weeks previously. Similar remarks apply to the banned states. The only additional point that needs emphasis is that a worker at the end of a ban will move from state 85 (or 86) to state 21, at which the spell that triggered their ban has five days to run. This is because bans last for four weeks, while the currency of a spell is five weeks.

In the first and second states, the worker has no absences in the previous five weeks. The two states differ according to whether the worker is already absent or not. State 1 is the clear state (present yesterday). State 2 is the clear state (absent yesterday). It is apparent from the plot that the incentives for attendance are quite different for these two states, since the state 2 absence rate is more than twice the state 1 rates. It is important to note that this is *not* because of any autocorrelation in the stochastic process underlying the model, or temporal dependence in tastes. In this simulation we used identically and independently distributed random variables in the underlying stochastic process. The reason for the higher probability of absence among workers in state 2 is that, if they attend, they will switch states to one strike against.

States 3 to 49 are states in which the worker has one strike against, incurred at various times in the past. Once again, the incentives for workers who are currently attending are quite different from those for workers who are currently absent. For the former group, absence rates are comparatively low, and they have a distinctive pattern: initially falling as the end of their most recent absence spell recedes into the past, but rising from state 40 onwards. Those workers who are in an ongoing spell of absence have weaker incentives to attend than those who are not. This is because, on their return to work, they will incur a ban. In fact, as the date of their most recent absence spell recedes into the past, their incentives get increasingly weaker, reaching a high of 7 per cent in state 49. This is because an absence spell started in spell 49 is quite likely not to finish until after the existing strike against expires. By extending their absence spell until the current strike has expired, workers can avoid a ban and continue to work overtime with a new, fresher strike against them. The same remarks apply, with rather less force, to those workers who have a strike against, and who are not in an ongoing absence spell. Starting an absence spell is potentially less expensive for them, because a spell started now can extend into the future to the point where the current strike has expired. These workers are less likely to be absent, the further into the past their last absence spell is. This is a consequence of the discounting in the model. Starting a second spell of absence will attract a ban as soon as the spell ends, but workers who do not start a second spell will return to the more valuable 'free' state sooner, the further their first spell is in the past. This is why the profile of absence rates falls through states 3 to 40.

States 50 to 86 are banned states. The incentives to attend are, once again, stronger for workers who are not in an ongoing spell of absence. Towards the end of a ban, such workers are keen not to start a new spell, because doing so would trigger a further ban of almost maximum length.

There are several lessons to be learned from this analysis. What appears to be a simple set of rules intended to deter people from taking excessive absence has effects that are far more complicated than its designers probably intended. It is unlikely that all the unintended consequences are captured in our analysis, but they include: the impacts of the scheme on the timing of the return to work as well as on starting a spell; the impact of the scheme on workers at the start of a ban;[11] the increasing effectiveness of a strike against as it ages; and the countervailing 'deadline effects' described above, which tend to increase absence as a ban approaches its end, or as a spell nears expiry.

Group-based sick pay

Many attempts to control absence try to do it on a group basis. Ultimately, though, these have to operate on individual decisions, with the result that the kind of analysis that we have discussed here remains valid, except to the extent that utility functions depend in some way on the actions, or welfare, of others. Skåtun and Skåtun (2004) develop a model in which attending workers cover for absent workers. In the model, attendance levels become strategic complements, so that it is worthwhile for firms to encourage this kind of behaviour (see Rotemberg, 1994) by increasing wages and improving working conditions. They also show that rigorously enforced firing rules can benefit workers.

Group-based schemes are often designed to give a group bonus or impose a group penalty. One such scheme is described in Hansard[12] as follows: 'In 1986, Vauxhall had sickness absenteeism of 8.8 per cent. Today (December 1993) it is down to 4.5 per cent. That was after the company introduced a negotiated incentive scheme which saved employees £4 a week in contributions to the company's sick pay scheme if average levels of sick pay [*sic*] could be kept below 5 per cent.' Low group absence led to a group bonus of £4 per worker per week. What Hansard does not report is the kind of unintended consequences recounted by Evans and Walters (2002), who tell a story of Iveco Ford trucks. This firm introduced a group scheme similar to the Vauxhall Motors one described above, under which sick pay was more generous for everyone if overall absence fell below some threshold. This apparently reduced overall absence rates, but had the

---

[11] This is analysed in detail by Brown (1999).
[12] Hansard is the official record of the proceedings of the British parliament. See www.publications.parliament.uk/pa/cm199394/cmhansrd/1993-12-15/ Debate-7.html, column 1140.

unanticipated side effect of inducing a cycle of rising and falling absence rates. When the aggregate absence rate was below the threshold, sick pay entitlement rose, and absence rose; when it was above, sick pay entitlement fell, and absence fell. Evans and Walters suggest that switching to an individual, rather than a group, scheme may be a solution to this 'problem'.

Between the one extreme of holding each employee responsible for their own absenteeism and the other of holding all employees responsible for aggregate absence lie myriad possibilities. It is hard to judge exactly how many firms introduce these schemes, how long they survive or how successful they are. There are many reports in the management literature of how a particular scheme was introduced, and attributing subsequent changes in the absence rate to the scheme. It is hard to take these reports very seriously, since they rarely control for any other changes that may have been taking place at the same time as the introduction of the scheme that is being considered. In particular, they do not account for the fact that simply letting workers know that their behaviour is being monitored changes observed rates of absence (see, for instance, Gardiner, 1992).

As far as we are aware, there is no discussion in the academic literature of the theory of group schemes, and many popular schemes seem to lack very good incentive properties. One basic criterion for judging the incentives provided by a scheme is to ask what Nash equilibrium behaviour is under the scheme. Jacobson (1989) describes a scheme introduced by New York State School Board in 1986/7, which has some promise. A pari-mutuel pool was created, from which teachers would draw one share for each day absent less than seven. If teachers are interested only in cash, and all absences are discretionary, this clearly works, since each teacher's bonus would be the proportion of the pool given by the number of shares earned by that teacher divided by the total number of shares earned. This proportion falls with each absence, so that the bonus-maximising behaviour is to take no absence whatever the behaviour of one's colleagues. Whether or not this is utility-maximising behaviour depends on many things, including the marginal rate of substitution between income and non-work time, but, clearly, this scheme's structure has some potential to shift behaviour in the direction of reduced absence.

Compare this with the Vauxhall scheme described above. In this scheme, each individual worker's behaviour has no impact on their sick pay contribution, unless only one additional attendance is required to push the absence rate below the 5 per cent threshold. If workers ever knew that this was the situation, there is no particularly good reason why they should volunteer to be the one to tip the balance. There is little reason to suppose that this scheme would be successful in reducing absence rates.

The idea of a pari-mutuel pool brings gambling to mind, and, while the element of gambling involved in the New York teachers' scheme is small, the idea of creating incentives with a lottery surfaces every now and then. The average bonus earned among the New York teachers was small at about 0.25 per cent. Lotteries seem attractive, because they give a group reward, but only one member of the group actually needs to be rewarded. They therefore appear to be cheap. Assuming incentives to be unaffected, setting up a single-prize lottery for the New York teachers would have allowed one of them to get a bonus of more than three years' salary. Of course, risk-averse teachers would rather have the scheme as it was implemented.

The attribution to B. F. Skinner by O'Hara, Johnson and Beehr (1985) of the notion of using a lottery for absence control is almost certainly misplaced.[13] Thirty years before Skinner's remark appeared, Consolidated-Vultee was building B-24 Liberator bombers and PBY Catalina flying boats at two plants in San Diego and spending $300,000 a year on prizes in a lottery designed to reduce absenteeism. *Time* magazine,[14] pointing out that the scheme met with only grudging approval from the regional War Labor Board on the grounds that '[l]oyalty cannot be bought', is also distinctly dubious about its impact:

Every Consolidated worker who had not missed a day's work in the month preceding the drawing or had not been tardy (later relaxed to allow one ten-minute tardiness per week) was eligible. At the first drawing (March 15) Consolidated's president, Harry Woodhead, announced that after one month of the plan there had been a drop in absenteeism, enabling the company to push out six and a half more bombers that month. But successive drawings brought no announcements of lessened absenteeism or production increases. Consolidated is mum on just how much improved

---

[13] Skinner (1973) actually proposes (for reasons that are unclear to us) that there may be merit in all remuneration being stochastic.

[14] 16 August 1943.

attendance it has got for its $70,000 so far. But it is no secret that Consolidated is still plagued by absenteeism; and recently it has soft-pedaled its lottery to concentrate on social service, to help employes [*sic*] work out domestic problems which keep them from their jobs.

The *Time* article goes on to recount tales from other plants:

In one Chicago plant, a lottery slashed absenteeism and tardiness two-thirds. In several others, lotteries were dropped when they produced no improvement in attendance. Another plant found no improvement, but kept the lottery anyway. Said one official: 'Maybe we're chumps. While things haven't gotten any better, they could easily get worse if we dropped the lottery, now that it's accepted and expected by employees.' Lotteries have substantial limitations. They have no effect on many basic absenteeism causes – lack of anyone to care for children, sickness, bad transportation, stormy weather or simply need of rest. And chronic absentees balance the long chance of winning a prize against the sure shot of a day of loafing, and take the day. People who always worked regularly still do.

Wherever or whenever the idea originated, it seems unlikely to go away. Having enjoyed something of a vogue among organizational behaviourists in the 1970s (along with numerous other applications of Skinner's ideas), academic interest in lotteries as a method of controlling absenteeism seems to have been supplanted by the occasional journalist[15] or management consultant[16] getting excited about the idea. A recent attempt to introduce a lottery to control absence by a Dutch employer has been analysed by Hassink and Koning (2009). Their work is discussed in Chapter 7.

Other kinds of shock

In this section, we deal with the observation that variations in household 'tastes' may not be the only source of randomness. In particular, the costs of getting to work may vary in an unpredictable way.

Much lateness, and some absence, arises from the fact that many workers have to get to work somehow. When a worker makes a participation decision, the costs of getting to and getting from work will be a factor that is taken into account. These costs can be entered

---

[15] For example, Umiker (1988).
[16] For example, Gregory P. Smith; see www.careerknowhow.com/absenteeism. htm.

into the standard model in the following rather basic way: let transport costs for an attending worker be τ, and then we have

$$y = V - \tau + wh, \ h \in (0, T] \qquad (3.9)$$

Higher transport costs in this kind of formulation cause changes in behaviour that are exactly the same as a reduction in non-labour income of the same size. Although one might intuitively think of higher transport costs reducing labour supply, this is not necessarily what the standard model predicts, since 'income' effects in models of this kind may be positive or negative.

The equivalent decision to that described in equation (3.3) is

$$\max_{h \in [0,T]} U(T - h, y) \text{ subject to } y = V - \tau + wh \qquad (3.10)$$

The first-order conditions for this problem are then

$$\frac{U_1}{U_2} = w$$
$$y = V - \tau + wh \qquad (3.11)$$

which is to say that, at the optimal choice of hours, the marginal rate of substitution between non-work hours and income is equal to the wage rate, and the constraint is satisfied. Random shocks to transport costs τ will generate random shocks to desired hours with no predictable sign. This model does not seem to make a lot of sense, and a similar application of the same idea to the fixed-hours model does little better. In order to generate a set-up that is able to say anything about these issues, a more sophisticated model, such as that offered by Barzel (1973), is needed. Like the fixed-hours model, Barzel's model can easily be adapted to include the idea that hours are *set* – by which we mean that the contract specifies not only that the worker should work a given number of hours, but also that the hours they work are specified. A contract that says 'eight hours a day' is a fixed-hours contract. If those hours are also specified to be, say, '9:00 to 5:00', it is a set-hours contract as well. The two types of contract can be mixed. Flexitime frequently specifies fixed hours, but not all of them are set. A flexitime contract might read 'eight hours a day, to include 10:30 to 3:30'.

Let us see what happens in Barzel's model, under these different kinds of contract. Figure 3.8 reproduces Figure 2.4. Curve VDP,

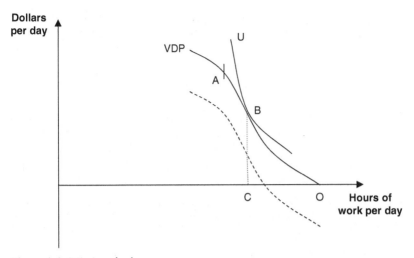

Figure 3.8 Missing the bus

value of daily product, need not be affected by a late start with a fixed-hours contract with no set hours. All that will happen is that the worker starts at 9:15 instead of at 9:00, and completes the fixed number of hours a quarter of an hour later than the usual time. Long delays could generate changes in VDP, since the interaction of work rhythms with biological rhythms may be disturbed. A person used to starting work at 9:00 a.m. and finishing at 5:00 p.m. might find it hard to be exactly as productive starting at 1:00 p.m. and finishing at 9:00 p.m.

Now consider a set-hours contract. Here, turning up at 9:15 rather than at 9:00 means that the first fifteen minutes of the day yield no product. VDP can be thought of as shifting vertically downwards by some amount.[17] A shorter day will lead to lower average wages, although, once again, it is not possible to make any clear prediction about desired hours of work. We can conclude, then, that uncertainty in the arrival time of transport will unequivocally not increase

---

[17] This might be equal to the value of the first quarter of an hour's production, but the size of the shift might be more complicated. For instance, if the worker is part of a team, the reduction in VDP might be greater than proportional to the time lost; alternatively, the daily pattern of output might change as a consequence of a delay in the start time. In the latter case, the shape of the curve would change in more complicated ways than a simple shift.

productivity per day, with the result that it leads to lower average wages, as well as lower average productivity.

Sick pay in two-employee households

Finally, we broach a question that we do not think has been raised previously: how does household structure affect the impact of absence control schemes and sick pay? How and to what extent might individual absence decisions be affected by the household responsibilities of individual workers? It seems likely that the almost universal excess of female absence rates over male ones (see Chapter 6) is due to the differing household roles that are adopted by these groups.

We think of the household here as a productive enterprise, usually small in scale (see Becker, 1993). In fact, we restrict our view to households in which two partners contribute both to household production and to financing the household by supplying labour to the market. Perhaps the main distinguishing feature of household production is that a large part of the labour input is provided by the principals – that is, the household members themselves.

The dominance of self-help in the management of household production implies that the constraints on attendance in the household are considerable. A buffer stock of workers who can cover for absent household members is, for many households, hard to arrange, unless there are obliging parents or friends living nearby. One consequence of this is that household members will tend to specialise in the provision of reliable labour supply. Of two parents, for instance, we might expect one to specialise in reliable labour supply to the household, and the other in reliable labour supply to the market. If they do not do this, they will not be using their labour market opportunities efficiently. We develop a very simple model, in which cover has to be provided in the household with probability p. This may be because there are young (or sick) children or an ailing parent present requiring frequent attention, or because of problems with the physical capital of the household. Represent this by a binary variable:

$$C_t = \begin{cases} 1 \text{ with probability } p \\ 0 \text{ with probability } 1 - p \end{cases}$$

Suppose that the household consists of two decision-makers, F and M, both of whom have labour market opportunities. These pay wages and sick pay of $\{w^m, s^m\}$ to M and $\{w^f, s^f\}$ to F. Sick pay is paid when a worker is absent from work. We denote day t absent from work (present in the household) as $a_t^f \in \{0,1\}$ and $a_t^m \in \{0,1\}$ for F and M, respectively. Since at least one of F and M must be present in the household when cover is required, it must be true that $a_t^f + a_t^m > 0$, which is equivalent to $\left(1 - a_t^f\right)\left(1 - a_t^m\right) = 0$ for all t such that $C_t = 1$. Suppose the household wants to maximise its income over period $t = 1, \ldots, T$, with T perhaps being infinite. The problem is then

$$\max_{\{a_t^f, a_t^m\}_1^T} \sum_{t=1}^T \left(1 - a_t^f\right)w^f + a_t^f s^f + \left(1 - a_t^m\right)w^m + a_t^m s^m$$

subject to

$$\left(1 - a_t^f\right)\left(1 - a_t^m\right) = 0 \text{ for } t \text{ such that } C_t = 1$$

(3.12)

This problem is easy to solve, since there is no intertemporal dependence. When there is no constraint, both partners work, but when $C_t = 1$ the constraints imply that either $a_t^f = 1$ or $a_t^m = 1$, or both. If the latter is true, the maximand is

$$\left(1 - a_t^f\right)w^f + a_t^f s^f + s^m$$

which has its maximum at $a_t^f = 0$. If the former is true, the maximand is

$$\left(1 - a_t^m\right)w^m + a_t^m s^m + s^f$$

which has its maximum at $a_t^m = 0$. The solution is thus that $a_t^f = 1$ or $a_t^m = 1$, but not both. This very simple model of household responsibility and absence demand therefore predicts that, when household responsibilities require attendance at home, they will be covered by M if $w^f - s^f > w^m - s^m$ and by F otherwise. In other words, it is the partner who loses less when they are absent who will specialise in household cover.

Now suppose that $s^m = \rho^m w^m$ and $s^f = \rho^f w^f$ for all t, with the ρs representing the replacement rates in an insurance scheme. Then the cover will be provided by whichever partner has the lower value of $w(1-\rho)$, which may be the partner with the higher replacement rate rather than the partner with the lower wage.

In a sick leave scheme (in which the replacement rate eventually falls to zero), the optimal provider of cover may change. Suppose that F has a sick leave allowance of d^f days, and that M has d^m days. Sick leave allowances typically apply over a calendar year. Consider, then, a couple whose employers both specify the same calendar year, but for whom $\{w^m, d^m\} \neq \{w^f, d^f\}$. Then, at the start of the year, it will be the partner with the lower wage who will cover. Suppose this is M. M will continue to cover until the total number of sick days claimed is d^m. At this time $w^m - s^m = w^m$ and $w^f - s^f = 0$, so F will take over.

This argument clearly has testable implications for seasonal patterns of absence. So far as we know, none of these have been tested.

Summary

The demand for absence cannot be analysed using the standard labour supply model, since this assumes that workers have a free choice as to their hours of work. There are two ideas in the literature as to how absence arises: a pre-contractual view, which supposes that workers sign contracts that do not match their desired hours; and a post-contractual view, which supposes that, once workers have signed a contract, their desired hours are subject to random variation.

The random utility model is useful in the evaluation of sick pay arrangements, and also permits analysis of the effects of household structure on attendance behaviour.

4 | *The markets for absence and for sick pay*

Having discussed the two sides of the market for absence in the last two chapters, we now put the two together to produce a theory of how the market operates. We have also discussed the rationale as to why firms might find it worthwhile to provide sick pay, and later in this chapter we argue that there seems to be no pressing reason an efficient market for sick pay (or, to be more precise, insurance against loss of income due to sickness) should not be organised, with firms providing experience-rated sick pay to their own workers.

Sorting in the market for absence

We would have liked this chapter to follow on from the previous two to form a seamless whole, in which firms make decisions about hiring and remuneration systems, and households make decisions about labour supply and absence. Chapter 2 argued that the supply of absence arises because it is cheaper for firms to agree to some level of absence than for them not to. The demand arises because of a multitude of influences on workers and their households, which cause variations in the workers' valuation of time or in their costs of attendance. Since a full equilibrium approach to modelling this market is impossible in the current state of knowledge, we follow the approach of Coles and Treble (1996), in which the demand side of the market is modelled simply as a set of households with heterogeneous utilities, and the supply side as a set of firms with heterogeneous technologies. This framework leads to insights into the nature of observed absence rates that we believe to be novel, largely because of the role that firm heterogeneity plays. The past literature has ignored this aspect of things, partly because it is written from the point of view of managers who are concerned with their own firms only, partly because tractable ways of capturing the idea of complementarity have not been developed.

In this chapter we continue to adopt the approach taken in Chapter 2, and concentrate on the two polar cases of production using an assembly-line production method, or a constant marginal product production function. In the latter case, the optimal contract sets pay and absence rates in such a way as to equate the worker's expected marginal product to their shadow value of attendance. For the assembly-line technology, things were much more complicated, since the worker's expected marginal product depends on the attendance probabilities of other workers, and on the number of workers the firm chooses to employ.

It is easy to show that, if firms with both kinds of technology coexist in an economy with homogeneous workers, there will be variation in the rate of absence between the two types of firm, compensated by variation in pay. This is an important result, because it shows that, *even if all workers are identical,* variation in optimal absence rates can be generated by firm differences alone. Therefore, any complete explanation of observed absence rates must take account of firm differences. In this world, some workers will display low absenteeism, because that is what their employer wants and is prepared to pay for. It has nothing to do with the workers themselves. They do not care whether they work for a high- or a low-absence employer, since the wage differential is exactly right to compensate the marginal worker for the difference in utility generated by the different absence levels required by the two jobs.

To see why the result is true, suppose that both types of firm make zero profits and that it is optimal for assembly-line firms to set $n = k$. Both types of firm must offer a contract that satisfies the workers' participation constraint, $U(p,y) = U_0$. The linear-technology firm chooses y_c and p_c so that $\frac{U_{pc}}{U_{yc}} = \frac{y_c}{1-p_c}$, while the assembly-line firm chooses y_a and p_a so that $\frac{U_{pa}}{U_{ya}} = k\frac{y_a}{1-p_a}$. Now, for any given p, and in particular for p_c, the slope of the assembly-line firm's isoprofit line must be less than the slope of the linear-technology firm's, therefore $\frac{U_{pc}}{U_{yc}} \leq \frac{U_{pa}}{U_{ya}}$ or $\frac{y_c}{1-p_c} \leq k\frac{y_a}{1-p_a}$, and with concave indifference curves $p_c > p_a$ and $y_c < y_a$. That the result remains true for $n > k$ is shown in theorem 2 of Coles and Treble (1996).

The result is illustrated in Figure 4.1 for $n = k + 1$. Here the dots and dashes indicate the linear-technology firm's isoprofit line, and the splined line is the assembly-line firm's. The heavy convex curve is a worker's indifference curve. Since workers are homogeneous in this argument, drawing the relevant indifference curve for one is sufficient to stand for all. The indifference curve must touch both firms'

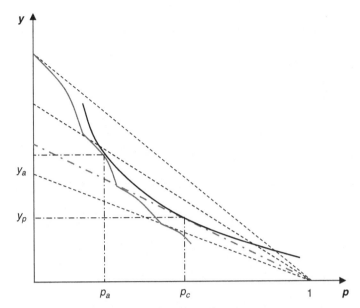

Figure 4.1 Theorem 2, Coles and Treble (1996)

isoprofit lines, for if it did not one firm would not be able to hire any workers, and the assumption that both firms coexist would be violated. Since the indifference curve touches both isoprofit lines, there will be a separation of the workforce between firms.

A similar separation occurs when workers are heterogeneous in tastes. Suppose that there are two types of worker, characterised by a difference in their valuation of time spent in non-work activities: type 1 has $\frac{U_p}{U_y}$ greater than type 2 for any given p, and so values time spent at work less than type 2. Then there are two types of sorting equilibrium: one in which all the type 1 workers work in the constant marginal product firm, while the type 2 workers are divided between the two; the other in which type 1 workers are divided between the two types of firm, while type 2 workers all work in the assembly-line firm. Once again, the wage differential has to be sufficient to make workers whose type works for both kinds of firm indifferent between the two kinds of job. These equilibria are illustrated in Figure 4.2.[1]

---

[1] Of course, the system may fortuitously produce a perfect sorting in which all type 1 workers work for constant marginal product firms, and all type 2 workers work for assembly-line firms.

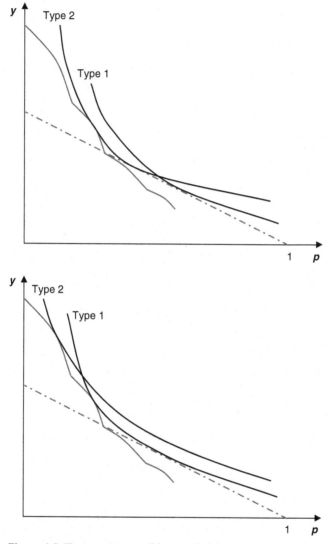

Figure 4.2 Two sorting equilibria with heterogeneous workers and heterogeneous firms

Most of the remainder of the chapter is devoted to a discussion of the
meaning and implications of these sorting outcomes.

Firms seek a reliability in the supply of inputs that they rarely
achieve. Machines break down, suppliers can be late making deliver-
ies, workers do not always turn up to work. These are facts of life that,

since they cannot be changed easily or cheaply, must be recognised and lived with. The previous literature on absenteeism has tended to think of it as a problem connected exclusively with the labour supply. In this book, we think of it not so much as a problem but as a phenomenon to be understood, and the results described above suggest that understanding it is not possible without taking account of firms' interests.

The idea of an optimal sorting of heterogeneous workers into heterogeneous jobs has efficiency implications. In particular, it suggests that an efficient solution of the problem of the assignment of workers with differing degrees of unreliability to jobs is available. This claim may seem odd to an employer who spends a lot of time worrying about keeping production going, and thinks of absence as creating nothing but trouble. Such an employer does not, of course, necessarily take account of the household production process that their absent worker is attending to, and which an absent worker presumably believes to be a more valuable use of their time than fulfilling their market production contract.

Figure 4.2 shows an equilibrium in which workers are also heterogeneous – say workers with different family responsibilities. In this case, a competitive labour market implies equilibrium sorting by firms and workers. Assembly-line firms require a low level of absenteeism and pay a relatively high wage to compensate workers for attending work reliably.

All other things being equal, workers who have a comparative advantage in attending work reliably – say those who do not have to look after children when those children are sick – take employment in assembly-line firms and enjoy the wage premium attached to employment there. Conversely, those who appreciate greater flexibility in work attendance take employment in the linear-technology firms and in equilibrium earn a lower average wage rate.

Although absenteeism may be costly to firms, observed absenteeism rates are not necessarily inefficient when viewed in the context of the economy as a whole; the worker who misses a day at work to look after sick children (or enjoy a sports event) is expressing a trade-off between workplace production and home production, with home productivity perhaps subject to idiosyncratic shocks. Efficient contracting implies that firms and workers agree to an acceptable absenteeism rate and a compensating wage differential. Efficient sorting implies that those workers who can commit themselves to attending work reliably accept employment in assembly-line occupations, and so earn a wage premium reflecting the shadow price of absenteeism.

The outcome of the argument so far is that absenteeism will exist in an economic equilibrium since there is a demand for it, and because firms are better off satisfying that demand than trying to enforce absence rates that are too low. In equilibrium there is an assignment of workers to firms so that workers who can cheaply supply reliable work time to firms will tend to work for firms that find it costly to tolerate an unreliable labour supply. However, there is one gap in the argument, which we will now fill. Jobs in the Coles–Treble framework have two dimensions: pay and an acceptable absence rate. Specifying what absence rate is acceptable is different from enforcing that rate, though.

The structure of sick pay

We now argue that firms can enforce an acceptable rate of absence by offering appropriately structured sick pay. What 'appropriately structured' means in practice is something of an open question, but the design of the sick pay scheme must include some form of experience rating. Paid sick leave schemes, for instance, can do the trick, but there are a wide variety of other ways in which sick pay can be experience-rated.

The fundamental problem here is one of moral hazard. In the context of a long-term contract of employment, only an unreasonable employer would expect perfect attendance. There are certain kinds of shocks to labour supply that employers will regard as justified or acceptable, and others that are not.[2] It is important to understand that moral hazard will arise only if there are other sources of shocks to household labour supply than acceptable ones (see Chapter 2). To see this, suppose that there are no unacceptable sources of shock. Then the only reason for a worker's absence (given that a contract has been signed) is that the worker's household has experienced an acceptable shock. Therefore, no moral hazard can arise, for contracts would be self-monitoring. Unlike conventional principal–agent models, a satisfactory explanation of moral hazard that manifests itself as

---

[2] The question of whether the sources of absence that different employers regard as acceptable may differ is left uninvestigated here. We suppose that views of what are or are not acceptable causes of absence are shared by all employers.

absenteeism must rely on there being at least two kinds of shock. Acceptable shocks create the notion of acceptable equilibrium absenteeism, while other shocks allow the moral hazard under the pretence that they are acceptable.

We have already seen, in Chapter 2, how Coles and Treble (1993) use this idea to create a model of sick pay provision by firms. They contrast a linear technology with an assembly-line technology, and demonstrate an equilibrium in which linear-technology firms provide sick pay while assembly-line firms do not.

A more elaborate treatment of the theory of sick pay provision by firms is provided by Treble (2009a). This paper takes the equilibrium demonstrated by Coles and Treble (1996) and argues that, in this context, it is more efficient for firms to provide this insurance against loss of income due to sickness than private insurance contracts, because firms have an interest in maintaining absence rates at a particular level. An insurance contract between the worker and a third party would not take this interest into account, whereas a contract written between the firm and its workers can internalise the interests of both parties.

The idea of experience rating as a means of avoiding moral hazard is now well established in the literature on optimal insurance. Cooper and Hayes (1987) show that multi-period contracts in which excessive claims can be punished by raised premiums can ensure that insurance companies' customers will truthfully reveal their exposure to risk. Dionne and Lasserre (1987) discuss a market in which insurance companies offer contracts to customers who face differing probabilities of loss. Their market has an equilibrium in which customers truthfully reveal their risk of loss, despite a finite time horizon. Cheating is averted by contracts featuring experience rating, which has to be constructed in such a way as to ensure that a misrepresentation will yield less utility to customers than they would get by telling the truth. Experience rating in Dionne and Lasserre's model works in the following way. Customers announce their risk, and this information is used by insurance companies to determine what premium to offer. Should it appear that a customer has misrepresented their risk, the premium will be raised *ex post*. In order for this to work, the conditions under which a penalty premium will be charged has to be such as to ensure that customers' announcements are truthful.

Malueg's (1988) model is used as the basis for Treble's (2009a) argument about the structuring of the experience rating. His treatment, like Dionne and Lasserre's, is rooted in the approach first proposed by Radner (1981). It is more general than Dionne and Lasserre's in that it allows for learning about absence proneness on both sides of the relationship. The idea of all these papers is that a contract specifies a statistical test of whether or not an insured agent's behaviour is consistent with their declared risk status. If the test statistic suggests that they are actually more risky than they claim to be, they are punished with a high premium. Exactly how this punishment works varies from paper to paper, but all have in common that the test statistic is the difference between the observed mean loss and the expected mean loss. Of course, an honest declarer may be unlucky, and by pure chance claim more than the expected loss. Radner (1981), Dionne and Lasserre (1985, 1987) and Malueg (1988) all show that, in order to elicit truthful revelation, the permitted mean loss will be greater than the expected mean loss and that this difference will fall in accordance with the law of the iterated logarithm, which is a standard result describing how the mean of a random walk evolves as the walk progresses.

The point here is that, as time goes on, the insurer's information about the insured improves. The actual mean loss becomes a better indicator of the true expected mean loss. The margin of error that an insurer should optimally permit should therefore become smaller over time, and the law of the iterated logarithm describes exactly how the margin of error should fall.

Specifically, in all these papers at a time t, the optimal statistical margin of error, α_t, between permitted mean loss and the expected mean loss is given by

$$\alpha_t = \sqrt{\frac{2\lambda\sigma^2 \log\log t}{t}} \tag{4.1}$$

where σ^2 is the variance of losses and $\lambda > 1$ is an arbitrary parameter. The law of the iterated logarithm is a statement about the asymptotic behaviour of a stochastic process, so that small values of t can be ignored. It is easy to check that, for $t \geq 6$, the right-hand side of equation (4.1) decreases monotonically in t.

This expression applies for an insurance company facing a customer with whom there is no other connection than the insurance contract.

Treble (2009a) derives a variant of it for the case in which a firm is insuring a worker, and every time a worker goes absent it suffers a correlated loss.

The scheme of sick pay proposed by Treble differs from the Dionne–Lasserre structure in two ways. First, firms bundle up insurance with a job contract, consisting of a wage offer and a declaration of an acceptable level of absence. Second, it is firms that announce the level of risk they are prepared to accept. Instead of competing with each other across the spectrum of risks, they effectively segregate the market, with each firm appealing only to potential workers with a risk that they regard as acceptable. Under these circumstances, workers who wish to engage in morally hazardous behaviour can do so by joining a firm that is able to accept a higher rate of absence than their true exposure to sickness would justify. The moral hazard thus incurs a wage penalty for the worker, who implicitly bears its cost. The firm is content not to enquire whether there is any moral hazard, since it can be confident that its acceptable level of absence will be adhered to.

Interested readers can find a formal statement and proofs of these propositions in the paper by Treble (2009a). Here, suffice it to say that the main claim of this section is that there exist experience-rated schemes of sick pay that are optimal in the sense that, if they were universally adopted, they would enable the creation of a labour market in which moral hazard in sickness absence is eliminated. In this market, workers and firms are sorted, so that more unreliable workers work at firms that find absence relatively cheap, and reliable workers at firms that find absence relatively costly. Reliable workers earn a premium for their virtue. Workers are discouraged from taking excess absence by experience-rated sick pay schemes, which enforce a firm-specified acceptable rate of absence. The experience rating may take the form of sick leave, with the threshold for absence determined by the acceptable absence rate and a margin that is determined by the law of the iterated logarithm. This implies that it should fall over time. Such a scheme will not only attract workers whose tastes and household circumstances match the technological profile of the firm, but also discourage moral hazard *ex post*. It requires no monitoring of sickness, other than sickness that is self-declared by the worker in the form of an absence.

We have now completed the main theoretical development of the book, which concludes with the proposition that market solutions are available for the provision of absence and sick pay. These market solutions are similar in form to paid sick leave arrangements. They are therefore similar in structure to the arrangements commonly in place in the United States. Chapter 9 deals with this point in more detail.

Firm and worker heterogeneity

In the rest of this chapter, we look at the nature of the equilibrium, and in particular the sources of firm and worker heterogeneity. Workers, being human, vary in their tastes, and in their capacity for and interest in work and non-work activities. They vary in health and, furthermore, they are all engaged in production processes (broadly defined) that carry on outside the workplace. These may include the production of children and of child quality, the care and nurturing of other adults or any kind of 'leisure' activity. Many of these characteristics of workers imply not only that workers are different from each other, but that any individual worker's evaluation of time spent at work will vary from time to time. This is why we have been insistent in Chapter 3 that analysis of worker absence requires a random utility model, because some, at least, of these time variations will be unpredictable.

The incidence of illness is the most obvious of these. Employers and regulators in many developed economies recognise that workers will sometimes be ill, and institutions have developed to cope with this. That a worker's children, parents or other dependants may also be ill, and that this illness may affect the worker's evaluation of time spent at work, is less widely recognised. In the United States, laws protect workers from the threat of firing for absence with a wide range of these causes. Many Scandinavian countries insure workers against loss of income due to children's sickness. Many other countries do not, though, including the United Kingdom and France.[3]

The fact that 'leisure' time may vary in value is institutionally recognised. The coordinated weekend is perhaps the most pervasive example of this, and the most persuasive evidence of its enormous

---

[3] There are exceptions, though, in the form of some industry-specific agreements (Joseph Lanfranchi, personal communication).

value as an economic institution is the fact that even Stalin failed to get rid of it in the Soviet Union in pursuit of increased capital utilisation rates.[4] In Britain and elsewhere, ad hoc public holidays are sometimes declared on occasions of national celebration or commiseration. Special arrangements are often made for amateur sportspeople to accommodate training, and so forth.

Complicating matters is the fact that none of these sources of variation and uncertainty remain constant. As people age, the incidence of sickness tends to increase. The number of household members who may need care changes with household formation and dissolution, births, deaths and other departures.

From the point of view of the firm and its supply of absence, the tastes of individuals will not usually be of much interest. Firms will have regard more for the characteristics of local labour markets when formulating their policies. The indifference curves in Figures 4.1 and 4.2 can be interpreted as relating to an aggregate of tastes within a local labour market; a firm located in a large urban area may, for instance, develop different policies from an otherwise identical rurally based firm.

Whatever the sources of these differences or their changes over time, it is convenient to think of them as a bipartite structure in which some elements are relatively constant and others vary randomly. The model of absenteeism demand discussed in Chapter 3 is built around this idea. There we assumed that workers chose a contract having regard to their average demand for absence, while actual absence was generated by random deviations from this, in particular those deviations that caused workers to value time spent at work less highly.

How should those jobs having a high cost of absence be characterised? The underlying issue is one of worker complementarity in the production process, whereby the absence of one worker adversely affects the marginal productivity of the others. There is no simple way of identifying all such complementarities in a given workplace. However, there are indicators that can successfully be used to proxy the idea of complementarity. For example, in the empirical work described in Chapter 7, the use of just-in-time production techniques is treated in this way. The just-in-time system is a production

---

[4] Zerubavel (1985) gives a careful account of this episode. Nadezhda Krupskaya, Lenin's widow and minister of education in the 1930s under Stalin, apparently thought of it as a means of eliminating the family as a social institution.

technique in which the firm's production process might be considered as one long assembly line, with each component of the production process relying immediately on the production of an intermediate input. If one part of the process fails because of worker absenteeism, the whole production process fails.[5] This is not the case for non-just-in-time technologies, in which inventories of intermediate product can be held against the eventuality of an interruption in the flow of output from prior processes in the production sequence.

To see how and why inventories impact on absence costs, consider the following example. Suppose that there are two sub-processes in the production process, each operated by a single worker. Worker 1 takes input from outside the firm. This is in perfectly elastic supply. Worker 2 takes input either directly from worker 1 or from an inventory of worker 1's output. So long as there is sufficient flow of input from these sources to enable worker 2 to work, their output is one. Otherwise, it is $s < 1$. If the workers are each absent with independent probabilities, p, their joint output is

$$q = \begin{cases} 1 \text{ with probability } (1-p)^2 \\ s \text{ with probability } (1-p)p \\ 0 \text{ with probability } p \end{cases}$$

Clearly, the greater the elasticity of supply of semi-finished goods, the greater output will be. In particular, if the elasticity of supply is perfect (which might be achieved with an infinite stock of semi-processed product),

$$q = \begin{cases} 1 & \text{with probability } 1-p \\ 0 & \text{with probability } p \end{cases} , \text{ with } E(q) = 1-p$$

If stocks are always zero (perfect just-in-time functioning), worker 2 is wholly dependent on worker 1 attending, and output is zero if worker 2 does not turn up.

---

[5] Aoki (1988) explicitly relates just-in-time techniques to absenteeism: 'The "zero inventory" requirement to dispense with buffer inventory necessitates the effective control of local shocks, such as the malfunction of machines, absenteeism of workers, and quality defects, in order to minimize their effect on the smooth operation of horizontal coordination.'

$$q = \begin{cases} 1 & \text{with probability } (1-p)^2 \\ 0 & \text{with probability } 1-(1-p)^2 \end{cases}, \text{ with } E(q) = (1-p)^2$$

This is formally identical to the assembly-line technology defined on page 37. Note that, since $(1-p)^2 < (1-p)$ for $p < 1$, just-in-time technology lowers the expected output of the workforce at a given absence rate.

The demonstration in this chapter that an equilibrium configuration of institutions is available is, we believe, of interest in itself. It does not, of course, imply that this, or anything like it, is mirrored in the way that real-world economies work, but it does provide a standard of comparison or benchmark against which actual arrangements might be measured. It also enables structure to be given to debates over absence, its costs and what can or should be done about it by firms or governments. These issues are taken up in later chapters.

Summary

The market for absence generates variations in absence rates that depend on the characteristics of workers and of firms alike. If workers are risk-averse, firms can reduce costs by offering sick pay. Furthermore, if sick pay is structured in such a way as to avoid moral hazard and adverse selection, a market for absence can produce efficient outcomes.

5 | *A brief introduction to identification*

What is identification?

Among economists, the conventional way of finding out what demand or supply functions look like is statistical: one gathers appropriate data and then asks what the relationship between them is. Early attempts to estimate demand functions, particularly by Moore (1914), led to a number of puzzles, chief among which was that some demand curves were apparently upward-sloping, in particular the demand for pig iron. This strange finding was ultimately explained in Working's (1927) elegant article, which marks the first statement[1] of what has come to be known in economics as the 'identification problem'. This is the question of when data drawn from observation of the world is able to identify a theoretical construct. It stands at the heart of applied economics, for economists are very fond of constructing theories, but perhaps less fond of testing or calibrating them with care. Working's explanation of why Moore's 'demand curve' for pig iron had the 'wrong' slope is still instructive, and has led to great improvements in the quality and usefulness of economic measurements.

Working's insight seems simple, but it has profound consequences. It is that economic theory says that observed prices and quantities are generated not by a demand curve alone, but by the intersection of a demand and a supply curve. Thus, in order to trace out a demand curve, one needs not just data on the price and quantity demanded, but also to be sure that variations in these are generated by shifts in supply (see case B in Figure 5.1). If they are not, then what is measured will not be the demand curve. Indeed, if the observations are taken of a system in which the demand curve alone shifts from observation to observation, it will be the supply curve that is measured, or, as Working put it, '[I]s it not evident that Professor Moore's "law of

---

[1] Working (1927) credits a 1915 review of Moore's book by P. G. Wright with making a similar observation.

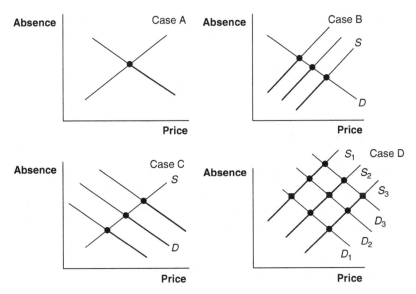

Figure 5.1 Identification

demand" for pig iron is in reality a "law of supply" instead?' (see case C in Figure 5.1). The answer to this question turns out to be 'No' – it is not evident at all. Working argues that, in a situation in which both demand and supply are shifting about (which will be the usual case), the interpretation of what one finds is crucially dependent on whether the shifts are coordinated or not.

Consider case D in Figure 5.1, and suppose that the three possible demand curves, and the three possible supply curves, are chosen at random, but independently. Fitting a line to the scatter of points generated will produce an estimated schedule that is neither supply nor demand.

The identification problem lies at the boundary between theory and observation. It logically precedes inference by asking what can be learned from observed data.[2] In order to be able to interpret a particular set of observations as having been generated by a particular theoretical construct, it is necessary to be sure that they were generated by that structure, and only by that structure. A downward-sloping relationship between sales volume and price is not sufficient

---

[2] For a recent discussion of identification and the continuing work in this research area, see Manski (2007).

to identify a demand curve; for this one needs to know also that the supply curve alone is changing across observations, or that any shifts in the demand curve are uncorrelated with shifts in supply.

These remarks apply equally to other kinds of equilibria. For instance, some of the work discussed in Chapter 6 is based on the idea that observations are generated by points of tangency between a constraint and an objective function. Here one needs exactly the same kinds of conditions for identification of the objective function: either the constraint alone shifts, or, if there are shifts of the constraint, they must be uncorrelated with the shifts in the objective. Similarly, for identification of the constraint: either the objective function alone shifts, or, if there are shifts of the objective function, they must be uncorrelated with the shifts in the constraint.

Identifying demand and supply for absence

Fundamentally, the identification problem arises because of the co-determination of variables in systems (in our case a market system), which we describe as

$$Q_d = \alpha_d + \beta_d p + \varepsilon_d$$
$$Q_s = \alpha_s + \beta_s p + \varepsilon_s \qquad\qquad (5.1)$$

The first equation describes the quantity (of absence) demanded, Q_d, by workers as a function of the 'price' of absence, p, and a random error, ε_d. The second equation describes the supply of absence by firms. The systematic parts of the two equations give case A in Figure 5.1. In equilibrium $Q_d = Q_s = Q$, so that what is observed by an empirical analyst is quantity traded Q and price p, and both variables are determined within the system. These are called *endogenous variables*.

One way of seeing the problem of identification is to consider the relationship between two different ways of representing the system. The first is the *structural form* (SF):

$$BY = \Gamma X + \varepsilon \qquad\qquad (5.2)$$

Here Y is a vector of endogenous variables, X exogenous and B and ε conformable matrices of parameters. Expressing the system (5.1) in this way gives

$$\begin{bmatrix} 1 & -\beta_d \\ 1 & -\beta_s \end{bmatrix} \begin{pmatrix} Q \\ p \end{pmatrix} = \begin{pmatrix} \alpha_d \\ \alpha_s \end{pmatrix} + \begin{pmatrix} \varepsilon_d \\ \varepsilon_s \end{pmatrix} \tag{5.3}$$

If we were to consider estimation at this stage, we would want the dependent variable(s) on the left-hand side of the equation and any explanatory variables, if there are any, on the right-hand side. We can do this straightforwardly by manipulating (5.2) as

$$Y = B^{-1}\Gamma X + B^{-1}\varepsilon$$

or, defining $\Pi \equiv B^{-1}\,\Gamma$ and $v \equiv B^{-1}\,\varepsilon$,

$$Y = \Pi X + v \tag{5.4}$$

This is known as the *reduced form* (RF), which for system (5.1) is

$$\begin{pmatrix} Q \\ p \end{pmatrix} = \frac{1}{\beta_d - \beta_s} \begin{bmatrix} -\beta_s & \beta_d \\ -1 & 1 \end{bmatrix} \begin{pmatrix} \alpha_d \\ \alpha_s \end{pmatrix} + \frac{1}{\beta_d - \beta_s} \begin{bmatrix} -\beta_s & \beta_d \\ -1 & 1 \end{bmatrix} \begin{pmatrix} \varepsilon_d \\ \varepsilon_s \end{pmatrix} \tag{5.5}$$

Here the two elements of Π in the RF (π_1, π_2) are related to the parameters of the SF (α_1, β_1, α_2, β_2) by

$$\begin{aligned} \pi_1 &= (\beta_d\alpha_s - \beta_s\alpha_d)/(\beta_d - \beta_s) \\ \pi_2 &= (\alpha_s - \alpha_d)/(\beta_d - \beta_s) \end{aligned} \tag{5.6}$$

These two reduced-form parameters can be estimated from the data, but knowledge of these values will not identify the structural parameters. The essential point is that, without extra information, it is not possible to recover the structural parameters from knowledge of the reduced-form parameters. It is still possible to perform estimation in the sense of regressing Q on p, but this tells you nothing about the slope either of the demand schedule or of the supply schedule since neither β_d nor β_s can be computed from (5.6).

The way forward involves finding extra information that relates to the situation. The obvious question is: what form might this extra information take? The first possible source is the use of what is commonly termed instrumental variable (IV) estimation. Imagine you have knowledge of a variable, v, that has the following properties:

$$Cov(v, \varepsilon_d) = 0$$
$$Cov(v, p) \neq 0 \tag{5.7}$$

This means that v is correlated with and therefore carries some information about the price, p, but is not correlated with the error, ε_d. In a sense, one is giving up some of the information in p to buy identification. To see how the slope of the demand function is identified, note that the first line of (5.7) implies that

$$
\begin{aligned}
0 &= Cov(v, Q - \alpha_d - \beta_d p) \\
&= E[v(Q - \alpha_d - \beta_d p)] - E(v)E(Q - \alpha_d - \beta_d p) \\
&= E(vQ) - \alpha_d E(v) - \beta_d E(vp) - E(v)E(Q) + \\
&\quad \alpha_d E(v) - \beta_d E(v)E(p) \\
&= Cov(v, Q) - \beta_d Cov(v, p) \\
\Rightarrow \beta_d &= \frac{Cov(v, Q)}{Cov(v, p)}
\end{aligned} \tag{5.8}
$$

The slope of the demand function is the ratio of the covariances of v with Q and p.

In Chapter 7, we give an extended example of how IV estimation can be used to establish the slope of the demand schedule for absence in a particular firm for which we have data. The purpose of this is to try and establish an elasticity of absence with respect to its price – a quantity that is important for firm policy.

The other main route to identification is to exploit information regarding variables that may affect one of either the demand or supply schedule, but not the other. These are known as *exclusion restrictions*. To see how they work, consider case C in Figure 5.1 again. Here the demand curve is shifting and the supply curve is not, so the observations generated by the system enable estimation of the supply curve. Such a system can be represented with a pair of equations:

$$Q_s = \alpha_s + \beta_s p$$
$$Q_d = \alpha_d + \beta_d p + \gamma_d Z \tag{5.9}$$

where Q_s, Q_d and p denote the quantities supplied and demanded,[3] and price, respectively. The variable Z (which may be a vector of variables, in which case γ is a vector too) represents whatever it is that causes the demand curve to shift. If this were a model of the supply of fur hats, this might be seasons. The changes in Z cause shifts in the demand curve, which identify the supply curve.

Now consider case D. Here, if shifts in the supply curve are correlated with shifts in the demand curve so that if the supply is S_i the demand is D_i, neither is identified by the observed data. If the makers of fur hats are able to predict that the demand for them varies seasonally, and they also tailor their supply to this seasonal variation, we would not be able to identify either supply or demand. We might write such a system as

$$Q_s = \alpha_s + \beta_s p + \gamma_s Z$$
$$Q_d = \alpha_d + \beta_d p + \gamma_d Z \tag{5.10}$$

In this system, the variable(s) Z that shift supply also shift demand.

The difference between the two sets of equations is that the case C equations don't include the $\gamma_s Z$ term that accounts for shifts in the supply curve. This gives us the basis for the statistical methods of identification. In a two-equation system, one of the equations must include variables that are excluded from the other. These are the exclusion restrictions mentioned above.[4]

The idea here is that, if we want to estimate a supply curve, there must be variation in the demand curve from a source that does not cause variation in the supply curve. Similarly, if we want to estimate a demand curve, there must be variation in the supply curve from a source that does not cause variation in the demand curve.

To identify β_d we need something that affects supply and not demand, as in the following system:

---

[3] The distinction between these two quantities exists in theory only. All that we observe, of course, is the volume of trade. Indeed, the identification problem might be posed as: does the observed volume of trade represent the quantity supplied or the quantity demanded?

[4] Similar requirements apply to systems with more than two equations, but this book does not include discussion of any higher-order systems of this kind.

$$Q_d = \alpha_d + \beta_d p$$
$$Q_s = \alpha_s + \beta_s p + \gamma_s Z \qquad\qquad (5.11)$$

Here the SF looks like

$$\begin{bmatrix} 1 & -\beta_d \\ 1 & -\beta_s \end{bmatrix} \begin{pmatrix} Q \\ p \end{pmatrix} = \begin{pmatrix} \alpha_d & 0 \\ \alpha_s & \gamma_s \end{pmatrix} \begin{pmatrix} 1 \\ Z \end{pmatrix} + \begin{pmatrix} \varepsilon_d \\ \varepsilon_s \end{pmatrix} \qquad (5.12)$$

which is similar to (5.3) except that $\begin{pmatrix} \alpha_d \\ \alpha_s \end{pmatrix}$ has been replaced by $\begin{pmatrix} \alpha_d \\ \alpha_s + \gamma_s Z \end{pmatrix}$. The RF corresponding to (5.12) is

$$\begin{pmatrix} Q \\ p \end{pmatrix} = \frac{1}{\beta_d - \beta_s} \begin{bmatrix} -\beta_s & \beta_d \\ -1 & 1 \end{bmatrix} \begin{pmatrix} \alpha_d & 0 \\ \alpha_s & \gamma_s \end{pmatrix} \begin{pmatrix} 1 \\ Z \end{pmatrix} +$$
$$\frac{1}{\beta_d - \beta_s} \begin{bmatrix} -\beta_s & \beta_d \\ -1 & 1 \end{bmatrix} \begin{pmatrix} \varepsilon_d \\ \varepsilon_s \end{pmatrix}$$

or

$$\begin{pmatrix} Q \\ p \end{pmatrix} = \begin{pmatrix} \pi_{11} & \pi_{12} \\ \pi_{21} & \pi_{22} \end{pmatrix} \begin{pmatrix} 1 \\ Z \end{pmatrix} + \frac{1}{\beta_d - \beta_s} \begin{bmatrix} -\beta_s & \beta_d \\ -1 & 1 \end{bmatrix} \begin{pmatrix} \varepsilon_d \\ \varepsilon_s \end{pmatrix} \qquad (5.13)$$

where $\Pi \equiv \begin{pmatrix} \pi_{11} & \pi_{12} \\ \pi_{21} & \pi_{22} \end{pmatrix} \equiv \begin{pmatrix} \dfrac{\beta_d \alpha_s - \beta_s \alpha_d}{\beta_d - \beta_s} & \dfrac{\beta_d \gamma_s}{\beta_d - \beta_s} \\ \dfrac{\alpha_s - \alpha_d}{\beta_d - \beta_s} & \dfrac{\gamma_s}{\beta_d - \beta_s} \end{pmatrix}$.

Note that the elements of the first column of the matrix of RF parameters, Π, are the same as in (5.6), but the slope of the demand schedule, β_d, can be computed by taking the ratio of elements in the second column. Therefore, we have illustrated two methods of recovering the slope of the demand for absence, instrumental variables and exclusion restrictions. Although the methods look dissimilar, (5.8) and (5.13) are effectively the same. As Manski (2007) points out, the IV result relies on the covariance restrictions in (5.7), while the exclusion restrictions will imply similar restrictions on covariances.

Economists and econometricians have spilled large amounts of ink in discussions of identification, yet in many other sciences the issue is barely considered. Economics draws most of its data from records kept by governments, firms and individuals, and sometimes from social surveys. All these sources report behaviour within an ongoing system, in which change is taking place almost continuously.

Identification in practice

There are several ways of identifying relationships in practice, but they all amount to ensuring the fixity of the relationship that one is trying to estimate, and that some change is taking place that implies that the system generates a number of points along the 'fixed' relationship. The econometric methods described above do this by statistical means, but there are other ways of achieving the same objective. One classic technique, widely used in the natural sciences but not yet generally established in economics, is the use of laboratory experiments. The advantage of a laboratory is that conditions under which phenomena can be observed can be controlled more easily than in nature. For instance, demonstrations of Boyle's law can hold pressure constant and observe the effect on volume of an increase or decrease in temperature in a gas. Alternatively, they can hold volume constant and observe the effect of an increase of pressure on temperature; and so on.

Empirical work in economics has recently distinguished laboratory experiments, field experiments and 'natural' experiments. In the same way that laboratory experiments in the natural sciences seek to control an environment in such a way as to yield information about a specific phenomenon, so do these experiments seek to control decision-makers' environments and ask them to make decisions that will be informative about some aspect of decision-making. The difference between the three types of experimental approach lies in the way in which the experiment is administered.

Laboratory experiments in economics take place in a laboratory, usually equipped with networked computers to present the experiment to subjects and record their responses. Experiments usually take the form of a sequence of choices. Sometimes these are individual choices, intended to reveal something about individuals and ways in which they vary; other laboratory experiments seek to understand how choices of individuals are affected by the choices of others. Holt and Laury's (2002, 2005) experiments designed to measure the risk aversion of individuals are good examples of experiments focused on the individual, as are the fashionable attempts to find out what parts of brains are activated when people make decisions (see McCabe, 2003). Cox and Oaxaca (1999) use laboratory experiments to demonstrate that the performance of a variety of commonly used estimators of supply and demand systems is sensitive to the institutional price-setting arrangements in place. It matters not just that there is a supply curve and a demand curve, but also whether prices are posted by sellers or determined by some kind of auction process.

Field experiments require the cooperation of some outside organisation. Thus, to estimate the labour supply elasticity for workers at factory X, one might persuade the management at X to shift the demand curve artificially (by offering a different contract to all or some of its workers) and then observe the result. Fehr and Goette (2007) provide an example of such a field experiment involving bicycle messengers in Zurich. Many of the same issues that arise in the design of experiments in natural science arise in this context too. It is therefore useful to have a control group of subjects who do not experience the experimental shift in the demand, so that changes that might occur during the experiment to both groups can be controlled for.

Natural experiments are not designed by investigators. They arise during the normal working of the economy. A good example is the work of Treble (2003), in which a group of coal miners was observed working in a fixed set of workplaces. The geological conditions differed at each workplace, and also changed as the coal was extracted. In order to allow for the productivity differences that this created, a different piece rate was paid on each workplace, but, because the geological conditions changed over time, these piece rates had to be revised. While the changes in conditions tended to be gradual, the structure of piece rates was changed only occasionally. Comparing workers' output for comparatively brief periods of time before and after a revision of the piece rates thus enabled the response to changed rates at the same workplaces to be measured and analysed.

All three types of experimental method – laboratory, field and natural – rely on the idea that either supply or demand (or a constraint or an objective) can be disturbed in such a way as to reveal the shape of demand or supply (the objective or the constraint). The identification problem is thus solved by these shifts, as suggested by Working (1927).

A carefully designed experiment will often be able to make use of what has become known as a *difference-in-differences estimator*. Suppose that observations of a control group and of a treatment group are available. Differences in behaviour will then be due either to the treatment or (if things have been set up well) to influences that affect both groups equally. By comparing the differences in behaviour between the two groups, and in particular by computing the difference in these differences, any influences on both groups will be netted out, leaving only the impact of the treatment. In the case of the work by Treble (2003), for example, the same workers were observed at the same workplaces both before and after the piece rate structure had been varied. Any variations in productivity between workers that might be due to their personal characteristics (strength, the number of mouths to feed, etc.) or to the characteristics of their assigned workplaces (the thickness of the seam, the incidence of rock among the coal, the travel distance underground, etc.), could be differenced out, leaving any residual variation in productivity attributable to the change in rates.[5]

To finish off this brief discussion of identification, we look by way of examples at a few of the studies in the literature, and assess what they tell us about absence and its correlates. In particular, we look at what papers by Pedalino and Gamboa (1974), Thoursie (2004) and Buzzard and Shaw (1952) identify. A large number of papers in the management literature on absence consist of accounts of the introduction of particular schemes and reporting their impact on absence. It is our contention that, because they have ignored the identification problem, none of these papers have much to offer in the way of useful results.

Pedalino and Gamboa (1974) conducted a field experiment in which members of several work groups were given a poker card for each day they attended work on time. At the end of each week the worker in each work group with the best poker hand won $20, equivalent to about half a day's pay. This experiment clearly adjusts the expected price of absence, so that gathering data about attendance before and after the introduction of the experiment should yield a data set that shifts the supply of absence, and identifies the demand curve. Unfortunately, it does not, because changes in absence are attributed to the change in the price alone, while there are other things going on in this experiment that are ignored. In particular, these workers knew that they were being watched, and it is quite possible that they believed that other penalties were likely to be imposed on them. In this case the measured change in the absence rate is not due to the

---

[5] For another instructive example of a difference-in-differences estimator, see Chemin and Wasmer (2009).

measured change in the price, but to some change greater than the price change alone.[6] The idea that something else is going on in this experiment than simply the changes in rewards due to the poker game is reinforced by the reaction of workers to a hitch in the experiment. In a second phase of the experiment, the authors reduced the frequency of the poker game to once a fortnight, but for some reason were unable to run one of the games. This meant that workers were without their extra incentive for attendance for three weeks. The response was for absence to rise not only above the rate established by the first phase of the experiment (2.3 per cent) but also well above the pre-experimental level (3.01 per cent), to 3.9 per cent. There is not enough information given in the paper to evaluate why this might have happened, but it suggests that, whatever the disruption was that caused the failure to administer the experiment, it, too, disrupted attendance independently of the experiment.

Thoursie (2004) examines the impact on absence of two televised sporting events widely followed by Swedes, and especially by Swedish men. Here, though, the assumption that the change in the cost of absence is small is justified by the nature of the Swedish system, which for most people implied that taking extra time off to watch Olympic cross-country skiing did not affect their pay at all. This means that his study simply recovers a vertical segment of the supply curve, and is probably a true representation of the size of the shift in demand for absence when these events were being televised.

Finally, Buzzard and Shaw (1952) examine a data set that records the response of workers to a supply curve shift. The shift does enable the estimation of an elasticity of demand, through a comparison of two groups that were differentially affected by the introduction of a sick pay scheme when previously there had been none. The two groups differed according to whether or not they received incentive pay

---

[6] There are numerous similar scheme introductions described in the literature, many of which are less carefully structured than the Pedalino–Gamboa experiment. For a typical example, consider Turner (1982), who describes the introduction of a bonus for workers who took no sick pay. The scheme not only involved computation and examination by managers of sick leave, in order to determine eligibility for the bonus, but it was introduced along with measures to improve employee fitness, which would have shifted the demand curve as well as supply. Despite being described as meeting 'with tremendous success', the scheme has apparently not survived.

in the form of piece rates. 'Incentive pay' workers had a two-part remuneration scheme, with a fixed, time-based element, and a piece rate element that depended on each worker's individual production. They were entitled under the sick pay scheme to replacement of their basic pay only, and not to any earnings that they may have lost from the piece rate component. The other group of workers were on time-based pay only. Both groups were entitled to 100 per cent replacement of their time-based pay, so that workers who were not on incentive pay were entitled to 100 per cent replacement, while those who were not had a replacement rate that depended on how large their individual output was.

The calculation of a demand elasticity for absence can be done if we are justified in supposing that the supply and demand curves are the same for the two groups prior to the change.[7] Buzzard and Shaw (1952: 293) raise the question of whether or not the demand curves are the same (293): 'We do find a distinct and striking difference between workers who receive incentive pay and those who do not. It is possible that part of this difference might arise from selection, the less fit workers gravitating to jobs requiring less speed. However, not only the sick rate but the proportional increase in days lost after the introduction of the scheme is lower for the incentive worker, and this suggests that the smaller absence rate of the latter is in part due to the fact that he receives less money when absent sick than when at work.' There is no suggestion in the paper that the two groups of workers were treated differently so far as the monitoring of absence or disciplinary procedures were concerned. Indeed, the idea that establishment difference may be partially due to the difference between incentive and non-incentive workers is explicitly ruled out (289).

How would this calculation be done? Buzzard and Shaw's data included records of absence before and after the introduction of the sick pay scheme. It also included details of pay. So, with price and quantity information both before and after the introduction of the scheme, the slope of the demand curve could have been calculated for each group, and compared both before and after for each group and, after the intervention, between groups.

What prevents us from actually doing this calculation is that, rather frustratingly, 'no attempt was made to calculate the relative

[7] We do this calculation as best we can on page 171.

differences in payments received at work or when sick in these two groups' (290). Why Buzzard and Shaw did not do this calculation we shall never know.

Summary

In order to understand fully the workings of any market, it is necessary not to confuse demand and supply movements, by ensuring that measured relationships are identified properly. There are several ways of doing this, which include instrumental variables techniques and a variety of experimental or quasi-experimental methods.

6 | *The market for absence: empirical evidence*

For a topic of such interest to employers, employees and people who live in households with employees, good-quality information about absenteeism is remarkably hard to find. While there are scattered surveys of firms and of households and individuals, an ideal data set must include information on both. We discuss some studies that have exploited such data at the end of this chapter, but, to begin with, we present what we think of as a statement of the problem that this book addresses: can patterns be detected in absenteeism? If so, what are they? Are they robust across economies? Why are they the way they are?

Fixed hours

In Chapter 2 we pointed out that there would be no absence, were it not for the fact that employers insist on particular hours (or a fixed number of hours) being worked. The last twenty-five years have seen several attempts to establish whether, in fact, workers sign up for more hours than they wish to work. These range from the crude and not very convincing technique of asking them, to attempts to establish, using micro-data sets and econometric techniques, whether marginal rates of substitution are equal to the wage, as theory suggests it should be if workers are unconstrained.

Lundberg (1985) points out that, if the menu of hours choices available to workers at whatever wage rate they may command is sufficiently rich for them to choose their hours as part of their choice of employer, it must be the case that there is a correlation between offered hours and offered wages. If lower hours imply a lower hourly wage, then the choice of low hours carries with it a penalty of a low wage, and a high wage can be earned only by accepting high hours. She concludes, using quite a small data set drawn from the Denver Income Maintenance Experiment, that there is indeed a correlation, although the wage cost of lower hours is not large.

More direct is the approach taken by Dunn (1990), who tries to interpret the responses to questions about how much extra income, or how many fewer hours, a worker would need in order to persuade them to give up a specified benefit:

Each worker is asked (1) how much, if any, money per week he would be willing to pay to have each of a set of specified benefits on his job if they were not provided by the employer; and (2) alternatively, how much time he would be willing to work longer each week with no pay in order to have each of the same benefits. The equivalence between the money and the time evaluations gives the worker's MRS. Without going into theoretical detail, one can see intuitively that if a worker says that he would pay $5 per week for a certain retirement pension, or alternatively that he would work one hour per week longer with no pay to have the pension, then the internal value of his time (or MRS) is about $5 per hour.

Using this information, Dunn studies three separate markets. In a market in which an overtime premium was in effect but fixed employment costs were high, the MRS of workers was found to be greater than their wage rate, indicating that contractual work hours were greater than desired hours. This market was also characterised by absenteeism. In a market in which an overtime premium was in effect and fixed employment costs were low, the MRS of workers was found to be less than their marginal wage rate, indicating that contractual work hours were fewer than desired hours. This market was also characterised by multiple job holding. In the case in which neither the overtime premium nor high fixed employment costs were present, the MRS of workers was found to be essentially equal to their marginal wage rate, as would be predicted by the standard competitive model.

Since these early, rather inconclusive attempts to discover whether workers are generally constrained in their choices of hours, much work has been done, but the question remains controversial. Blundell, Brewer and Francesconi (2008) argue that much of this work is flawed, because 'changes in labour supply preferences or other individual variables may not be exogenous to hours levels or changes'. The authors use the exogenous shocks to the labour to identify hours adjustments in the employment of single mothers in Britain. Their conclusion suggests that, while there is little hours adjustment within jobs, movements of workers between jobs creates enough flexibility in the labour market to prevent outright rejection of the canonical model in which workers choose their own hours. As far as absenteeism is concerned, this suggests that mismatched hours may be less of a problem than the post-contractual random variations in tastes proposed by Barmby, Sessions and Treble (1994), but the fact of the matter is that this literature is not sufficiently well developed to enable a clear-cut rejection of either possibility.

Major characteristics of absence

Perhaps the most promising development in the study of absenteeism and its relationship with industrial and demographic variables has been the recent construction of internationally comparable data on absence. One the first published attempts at this is by the present authors and Marco Ercolani (Barmby, Ercolani and Treble, 2002), which uses data for a number of countries drawn from their national labour force surveys. These ask a number of questions of their respondents and are used in a number of countries, including member states of the European Union and the Organisation for Economic Co-operation and Development. The data used in the study were drawn from the Luxembourg Employment Study (LES). Unfortunately, at that time the LES did not have more than one sweep of the surveys for each country.[1] The intertemporal picture given by these data is therefore seriously limited. Worse than that, they do not constitute a cross-section, since the sweeps for the various countries are not all for the same year. Furthermore, even if an international panel could be assembled, there are difficulties in comparing the survey results across countries. Although the surveys feature a common core of questions that are asked of respondents in all countries, the sampling and survey methods used differ considerably from country to country.

As a vehicle for the serious analysis of international and intertemporal patterns of absenteeism, therefore, these data have clear limitations, but viewed for each year, in each country taken separately, they

---

[1] We have been told by a source in the United Kingdom's Office for National Statistics that confidentiality rules are incompatible with attempts to merge the full data from the labour force surveys for different countries, but that ways of surmounting this are currently under discussion between the relevant statistical agencies. Until this issue is resolved, much valuable work on these data will remain undone.

can be of use, and – as we shall see – some suggestive common patterns arise. In particular:

absenteeism rates are nearly always higher for women than for men;[2]
they are nearly always higher for married people than for singles;
they increase non-linearly with age;
they increase with job tenure, even when the age effect is accounted for separately;
inter-industrial patterns of absence show some consistency across countries, with heavy industry experiencing higher rates than services or other manufacturing;
there is an identifiable occupational structure; and
absence rates are lower among managerial and supervisory grades of workers than among blue-collar workers.

The labour force surveys elicit information from respondents about work during a 'reference week', which is the last full week before the interview date. Specifically, they are asked if they do any paid work, or if they are away from a job or business that they would normally attend. Those who do some paid work are then asked what their usual hours and actual hours of work are, and the reason for any difference. Respondents who report being away from an occupation are also asked what their usual hours are, and a reason for their absence. Our estimated absence rates are constructed by treating usual hours as contractual hours, and any difference between usual hours and actual hours as absence. We consider only those absences that are regarded by the labour force surveys as due to sickness.

The absence rate R_t is the ratio of the hours reported absent due to illness in the reference week (A_{it}) to contracted hours (C_{it}):

$$R_t = \frac{\sum_{i=1}^{n} A_{it}}{\sum_{i=1}^{n} C_{it}} \tag{6.1}$$

To construct A_{it}, our measure of absence hours due to illness, we take the difference between usual hours C_{it}^u and actual hours C_{it}^w and multiply it by an indicator of absence due to illness in the reference week,

---

[2] Kremer *et al.* (2005, 2006) report a striking exception to this general rule. They find (using a system of enumerators visiting schools and checking who is in work and who is absent) that the absence rate is higher among male Indian teachers than among females. Ichino and Moretti (2009) consider biological foundations for the difference between female and male absence rates.

$$s_{it} = \begin{cases} 1 \text{ if absence is due to illness} \\ 0 \text{ otherwise} \end{cases}$$

Then A_{it} is defined as

$$A_{it} = (C_{it}^u - C_{it}^w)s_{it} \tag{6.2}$$

There are two problems with this procedure.

(1) It is possible for A_{it} constructed in this way to be negative in some cases. This occurred only in 0.02 per cent of cases in the study carried out by Barmby, Ercolani and Treble (1999). We conclude that the error from this is very small.
(2) This measure may misrepresent absence in cases in which over-time is worked. We can assess the extent of the bias induced by the omission by comparing the 1989 UK rates reported here and those given by Barmby, Ercolani and Treble (1999). When over-time is excluded the overall rate is 3.17 per cent, which decomposes into 2.87 per cent for men and 3.82 per cent for women. Comparable rates when overtime is included are 3.21 per cent overall, 2.91 per cent for men and 3.87 per cent for women. These facts are inconsistent with the idea that absence on over-time hours should be lower, as the rate increases when overtime is included.

The variables C_{it}^u, C_{it}^w and s_{it} are also used to construct the measure of contracted work hours C_{it} as

$$C_{it} = C_{it}^w(1 - s_{it}) + C_{it}^u s_{it} \tag{6.3}$$

This says that contracted hours are measured by actual hours worked if there was no absence due to sickness in the reference week and by usual hours if there was some absence due to sickness.[3]

---

[3] Bliksvær and Helliesen (1997) use a measure of absence based only on observing whether an individual has been absent from work for the *whole* of the reference week. This ignores short absences, which can constitute a large proportion of total absence (Barmby, Orme and Treble, 1991) and almost certainly underestimates the overall rate.

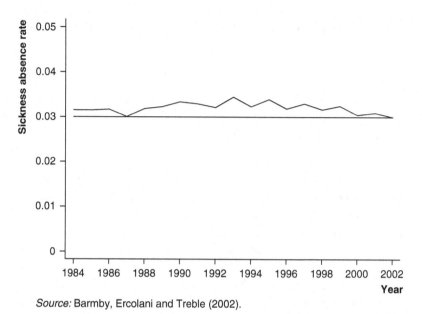

Source: Barmby, Ercolani and Treble (2002).

Figure 6.1 Yearly absence rates in the United Kingdom, 1984–2002

We have been able to examine the time variation of absence most closely for the United Kingdom using the above formula for its Labour Force Survey (LFS), so this is where we start. This reveals relatively little annual variation but substantial seasonal variation, as Figures 6.1 to 6.3 show. Throughout the period of our study, annual average absence rates remained a little above 3 per cent. This steadiness across years disguises the fact that absence tends to be higher in the winter quarters (quarters 1 and 4) than in the summer (quarters 2 and 3). The highest quarterly rates approach 4 per cent, while the lowest are about 2.75 per cent. The way in which the United Kingdom's LFS is conducted implies that calculated monthly rates are not nationally representative, with the result that Figure 6.3 needs to be treated with care. The highest recorded monthly absence rates are more than 50 per cent above the lowest. It is easy to think that this seasonal variation is due to the incidence of illness, but there are almost certainly other factors at work.

Figure 6.4 shows the relationship between absence rates and the logarithm of the hourly wage rate. There is a marked pattern here also,

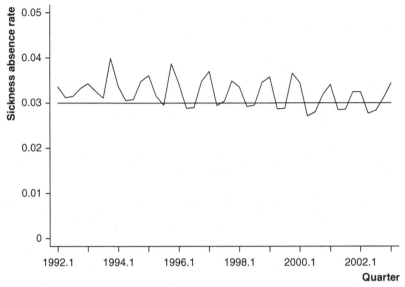

Source: Barmby, Ercolani and Treble (2002).

Figure 6.2 Quarterly absence rates in the United Kingdom, 1992.1–2003.1

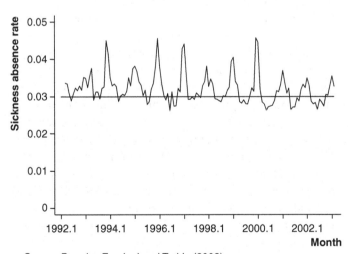

Source: Barmby, Ercolani and Treble (2002).

Figure 6.3 Monthly absence rates in the United Kingdom, 1992.1–2003.1

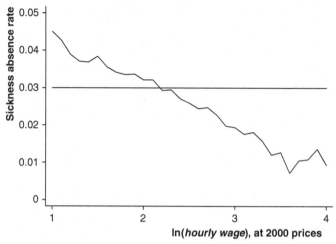

Source: Barmby, Ercolani and Treble (2004).

Figure 6.4 Absence rates by natural log of hourly wage rate, United Kingdom, 1993–2002

with absence rates falling by about 80 per cent between the lowest and the highest wages. Of course, this figure confounds many other influences on absence, since wage rates are correlated with, among other things, gender, age, contractual hours, tenure and occupation, and the figure is drawn without controlling for any of these factors.

The following figures document some of these relationships. Figure 6.5 shows that absence in the United Kingdom is higher for women than men who are below the age at which they become eligible for the state retirement pension, which is sixty for women and sixty-five for men. Absence rates for people above these ages who continue to work show much lower absence rates. This is suggestive of some selection effect, but, again, HR managers are typically constrained in the extent to which they can control the age and gender composition of their workforces. However, they tend to have more control over the terms of employment, wages and contracted hours of work.

Figure 6.6 shows an apparently quite complicated relationship between hours and absence, which might be simply characterised as 'absence rates rise with hours for part-time workers, but fall for full time workers'.

These six figures give us some idea of the variation in the absence rate for the United Kingdom, and how it covaries with other variables.

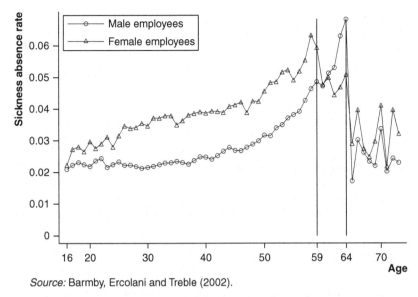

Source: Barmby, Ercolani and Treble (2002).

Figure 6.5 Absence rates by age and gender, United Kingdom, 1993–2002

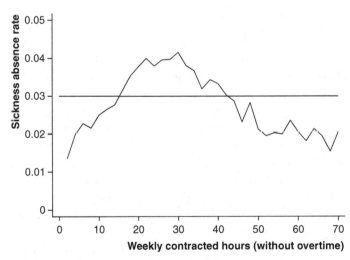

Source: Barmby, Ercolani and Treble (2002).

Figure 6.6 Absence rates by weekly contracted work hours, excluding all overtime

Table 6.1 *Sickness absence rates by country and gender*

Date	Country	Female	Male	Total	Observations
1997	Canada	3.83%	2.58%	3.07%	36,015
1997	Czech Republic	4.75%	3.34%	3.95%	23,656
1997	France	2.76%	2.49%	2.59%	42,835
1992	Luxembourg	1.62%	1.92%	1.83%	5,345
1994	Slovenia	3.48%	3.62%	3.56%	8,494
1993	Spain	2.47%	2.49%	2.48%	39,019
1990	Sweden	8.42%	5.13%	6.31%	24,933
1997	Switzerland	2.69%	1.40%	1.78%	5,301
1989	United Kingdom	3.87%	2.91%	3.21%	48,189

Source: Barmby, Ercolani and Treble (2002).

The question arises as to whether the patterns described here are unique to Britain, or whether there are any cross-national similarities in absence patterns. This question is addressed by Barmby, Ercolani and Treble (2002), who provide the data reproduced here as Table 6.1. It shows the international variation in mean absence rates, computed using the method described above, which is as close to being consistent across national boundaries as it is possible to get. The rates are also shown for males and females separately. As we observed above, the Luxembourg Employment Study data do not all refer to the same year, so comparisons are rather dangerous. Sweden's absence rates, in particular, have shown large fluctuations in recent years.

Perhaps the most striking thing about this table is the fact that, despite the wide variation in national arrangements for sick pay or sick leave, the female absence rate is above the male rate in all these countries except for Luxembourg, Slovenia and Spain. In the last of these the rates are almost identical.

There is also remarkable uniformity in the fact that absence rates for married people are consistently higher than for single people. This is true for all nine countries for which we were able to do the calculations. Once again, the caveat that these observations refer to different years in different countries must be borne in mind when considering the graphical representation of these findings, given in Figure 6.7.

These observations can be taken as indicators of the required scope of candidate theories of absence. They must embrace individual and

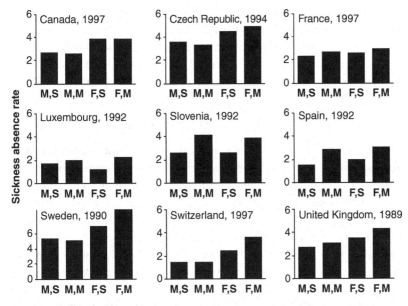

Notes: M,S = male and single; M,M = male and married; F,S = female and single;
F,M = female and married.
Source: Barmby, Ercolani and Treble (2002).

Figure 6.7 Absence rates by gender, marital status and country

household factors, in order to account for the gender and marital status patterns. They must include firm characteristics, so as to account for the industrial patterns, and they must include job characteristics, in order to account for the occupational structure. Finally, the relationship between firm and worker must be important independently of the characteristics of either, otherwise tenure would not be important.

More recently, consistent data have become available for European Union countries from the European Survey on Working Conditions, which began in 2000. So far two analyses of these data have been published. A descriptive paper by Gimeno *et al.* (2004) does little more than calculate the raw percentages of men and women who had any absences during the year. Frick and Malo (2008) use the same data set to some effect, by regressing annual counts of absences on a number of indices of the policy regimes in place in the various countries covered, as well as on the more usual variables measuring individual and job characteristics. They find that both enhanced job security and higher sickness benefits increase absence rates, but that the aggregate effect of these institutional differences is small relative to that of individual variables such as gender, the presence of work-related health problems and the type of the labour contract.

Demand-side and supply-side determinants of absence rates

In this chapter we deal with empirical evidence for the market for absence. Since in this book we are emphasising a market interpretation of absenteeism, we should be very clear exactly what the two sides of the market constitute. There is plenty of evidence to suggest that absenteeism rates respond not only to the behaviour of workers but also to that of firms. Katz (1986), in a review of efficiency wage models, refers to Allen (1984), saying that he 'finds consistently in an analysis of several data sets that positive wage differentials are associated with reduced absenteeism. Although absenteeism is something that can easily be observed by a firm, the reasons for absenteeism are not easily monitored. High wages combined with the threat of job loss for too much absenteeism might be an effective personnel policy.'[4]

Lindeboom and Kerkhofs (2000) analyse a very large and detailed data set recording day by day the individual absence histories of almost 5,000 Dutch teachers working in 426 schools. They are unable to estimate demand schedules for absence because they have insufficient variation in the cost of absence to identify such a relationship. However, they do analyse the incidence and duration of absences and of work spells. One of their main conclusions concerns the importance of understanding the supply side. Their attempt to find any satisfactory explanation of the large variations in absence rates between schools is unsuccessful, except that they reject firmly the idea that it has anything to with the demand side of the absence market. In their data, teachers do not cluster together to produce local gatherings of workers with similar morbidity. It is, rather, that the schools themselves induce 'healthy' or 'sick' workforces:

---

[4] Katz (1986) also refers to the working paper version of the study by Krueger and Summers (1988), which he says includes the claim that '[i]ndustry wage premiums are found to be negatively related to absenteeism (due to weather)'. Sadly, this intriguing part of the working paper has not survived into the published version.

In the analyses, we find strong effects of both observed personal characteristics and school characteristics. From a comparison of a range of models, we conclude that it is important to allow for unobserved school heterogeneity in the most flexible way. Unobserved workplace-specific effects account to a large extent for the observed variation of sickness absenteeism across schools. We also find that the observed clustering in 'healthy' schools and 'sick' schools is a result of unobserved school heterogeneity instead of (self-)selection of teachers (the sorting hypothesis). In an additional analysis, we relate the school-specific fixed effects to a range of observed exogenous school variables. The estimates indicate that the school-specific effects are hardly related to the exogenous variables of the type available in the data. It remains, however, that workplace effects are important in explaining the observed patterns of sickness absence. A better understanding of these workplace conditions is therefore essential for developing successful policies aimed at reducing sickness absenteeism.

Allen argues that absenteeism can be seen as a non-pecuniary characteristic of the compensation package, which some firms can, as we observed earlier in this chapter, allow as a characteristic of their offered job at greater or lower cost. Using Rosen's (1974) hedonic framework, Allen shows how market interactions generate a sorting of workers between firms – that is, workers who place higher value on being able to take absence sort themselves into jobs with employers who can provide this at relatively low cost. The sorting thus generates a market trade-off between absence rates and wages.

What Allen finds in his estimation is a negative relationship between absence rates and wages, which in the light of the theory is interpreted as the locus of tangency points of firms' isoprofit schedules, and workers' indifference curves, as illustrated in Figure 2.5. Such studies do not directly recover the demand and supply schedules that we have been referring to, therefore, but may recover other aspects of the firm's technology, such as the shape of their isoprofit schedules, and the shape of their workers' indifference curves.[5] These in turn can sometimes be used to recover the demand and supply schedules themselves. Exactly when this can and cannot be done is not known.

---

[5] Ekeland, Heckman and Nesheim (2004) discuss identification in hedonic models.

Allen (1981a) puts the issues clearly:

First, do higher wage rates encourage workers to report to work more regularly? Simple labor supply models predict that the effect of wages on absenteeism is ambiguous because of income and substitution effects working in opposite directions. However, if one considers absences as an agreeable employment characteristic and one allows for differences in worker preferences and employer cost functions, then this ambiguity no longer prevails – there should be an inverse relationship between absence and wage rates across plants.

Second, how do fringe benefits influence the attendance of workers? Since retirement income, paid time off work, health insurance coverage, and similar benefits do not vary with hours or days worked per year, over one-third of a worker's total compensation is unaffected bv his attendance record (unless he loses his job on account of absenteeism). Large amounts of non-wage income lead workers to demand more leisure. In addition, some companies pay workers for days missed because of illness or injury, thus subsidizing absenteeism. To establish the magnitude of these effects, retirement and short-term disability benefits are included as independent variables in the model.

Third, does absenteeism fall in response to improved safety? The net reward for working on any given day will be lower in a job where work hazards are present. An objective measure of workplace safety – the illness and injury incidence rate – is used to assess the impact of safety on absenteeism.

To answer these questions, he uses data relating to seventy-two US paper mills. He finds a decreasing relationship between absenteeism and wage rates, with an elasticity somewhere in the range between -1.2 and -2.1. The evidence relating to fringe benefits is unconvincing, while absentee rates tend to be lower in safer workplaces.

Allen (1983) estimates the slopes of workers' indifference curves, and from these estimates calculates the implied gain to employers of a one day per worker-year reduction in absence, as well as the impact of lowered absence on productivity. Once again, the range of these estimates is quite large, but the implied impacts are much smaller than estimates arrived at using the cost-accounting methods that are commonly used by commercial absenteeism analysts.

Using a similar theoretical framework, Allen (1984) establishes a large union–non-union absenteeism differential. The estimate of the size of this differential varies across the three data sets that Allen uses, the smallest being around 30 per cent and the largest around 100 per cent. In the light of his earlier estimates of the relationship between absenteeism and productivity, though, even differentials of this size have impacts on productivity that are less than 1 per cent.

Allen's pioneering work does not seem to have engendered much in the way of further investigation using the hedonic model, despite the quite specific calls in his papers for further investigation. In particular, Allen (1981b) calls for [f]urther study using other data sets ... before one places much confidence in the quantitative results presented here. Employer reported absence and wage data over a longer interval such as a year combined with interviews of individual workers would be ideal. This call has not proved to be a very effective rallying cry, until quite recently.

In the spirit of Allen's work are two papers examining the structure of absenteeism in a market setting using French data that partially fill the need identified by Allen. The first, by Coles *et al.* (2007), concerns the market for absence itself, characterised in the way introduced here in Chapter 4 by a set of isoprofit curves on the supply side and a set of workers' (or unions') indifference curves on the demand side. The second, by Lanfranchi and Treble (2010), deals with the market for sick pay. Dionne and Dostie (2007) also use linked employer–employee Canadian data to analyse absenteeism, but they do not estimate a properly specified market model, choosing instead to concentrate on an absence demand model.

Before describing what these papers show, it is perhaps worthwhile pointing out that, while they mark a break with the previous practice of estimating labour supply (or absence demand) curves, the data on which they are based are still not ideal, and there remain concerns that the number of data sets that actually enable meaningful analysis of absence and sick pay are few. The market aspects of the study of absence seem to us to deserve far more careful and detailed study than this one data set is able to support.

The waters are muddied in many economies by the existence of state regulation. If there were no state regulation then we could think of firms making their own arrangements with workers to supply different amounts of absence at, possibly, different prices. At one level, a completely regulated system takes away all discretion from the firm to decide on its supply behaviour on this margin, and recovering the supply schedule from data will simply recover the regulations relating to absence and reveal little about firms' behaviour at all. Such empirical work would not perhaps be very interesting, except to the extent that it may reveal something about the objectives (or success) of government regulators.

Many regulatory regimes for absence from work specify replacement rates for sick pay – that is, sick pay is expressed as some function of the normal wage of the worker, in which case the firm affects the amount it will pay in sick pay by setting the wage. The complexity of the relationship between the wage and the level of sick pay may vary substantially from a simple proportion (absent workers get half-pay, for instance) to situations in which there is quite sophisticated time dependence in eligibility for pay, as in the régime général of the French social security system, which we discuss in detail below.

These considerations are important when undertaking empirical work on the supply side of the market. If firms can set the cost or price of absence to individual workers independently then it will be logical for an empirical analyst to look at the relationship between absence and the supply price directly to recover the supply schedule. If a regulatory regime sits between the firm and the worker, the empirical analyst might more naturally consider the relationship between the wage rate and absence.

Studying the market for absence as a whole requires the careful choice of data, or, more realistically, the discovery of data that enables meaningful research to be carried out. As far as we know, there is only one extant source of data that enables simultaneous study of both sides of the market. This is a survey of French firms undertaken by the French statistical agency INSEE in 1992, which was called Enquête sur le Coût de la Main d'Oeuvre et la Structure des Salaires, or ECMOSS for short. A subset of the ECMOSS respondents were asked to respond to a second survey, called Enquête sur les Relations Professionnelles et les Négociations d'Entreprise (REPONSE). Together these two sources constitute a unique source for the study of the relationship between households, firms, labour contracts and absenteeism.

Sick pay in France is regulated by the social security law. This lays down minimum levels of provision, and a division of responsibility between the state and employing firms. The régime général specifies state payments at a replacement rate of 50 per cent for sixty days, following a three-day waiting period (the délai de

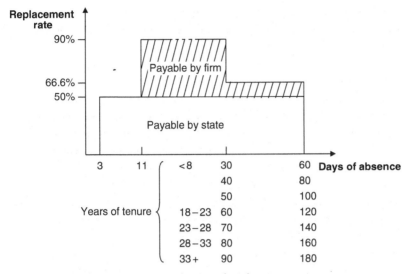

Figure 6.8 Replacement rates in the French sick pay system

carence). Qualifications for the state benefits imply that virtually all workers will be eligible.[6] In addition, employing firms must make complementary payments, of 40 per cent for the first thirty days of a spell of sickness and 16.66 per cent for the next thirty days. These payments are subject to a ten-day délai de carence and are payable only to workers with at least three years' tenure in their job. The system is illustrated in Figure 6.8. For workers with tenure in excess of eight years, the period over which sick pay is payable is extended according to the schedule shown in the horizontal scale. After the sixty days of entitlements are exhausted, other provisions of the French social security system are activated.

Complicating the picture is the fact that the régime général specifies minimum rates only for sick pay. Unions and employers frequently agree higher replacement rates than those specified by the law. It is also possible for employers not to follow the régime général if they are subject to special regulations. Among these employers are state-owned enterprises.

---

[6] Workers must have had at least 200 hours of work in the three months prior to the spell of sickness, or have been paid at least 1.015 times the minimum wage in the previous six months.

The ECMOSS survey constitutes a nationally representative cross-section of establishments with representative data on workers. It contains information on 15,858 establishments as well as an employer-reported description of the individual characteristics of 148,976 of their employees. The REPONSE sample is a subset of the ECMOSS population: 3,091 managers and union representatives of production units were interviewed, resulting in 2,998 usable questionnaires. Only two-thirds of the REPONSE respondents also responded to ECMOSS, though, resulting in attrition of the sample. Nonetheless, the final matched data set remains a representative sample of French establishments belonging to firms with at least fifty employees from the non-agricultural private sector.

The information about sick pay comes from the establishment questionnaire in ECMOSS. No information is available for firms that did not follow the régime général, which restricts the sample further to 1,690 productive units. This sample remains representative of the establishments in which the majority of the workforce was regulated by the régime général.

The data set includes details of any sick pay entitlements in excess of those specified by the law. Among the 1,690 sampled establishments, 205 offered the minimum replacement rates specified in the régime général. We regard these data as uniquely informative about the way in which the market for absence operates, since they include some information about both sides of the market. In particular, firms' technologies and work organisation are described in addition to their sick pay arrangements. Some characteristics of workers are available as well as a record of attendance behaviour. Coles *et al.* (2007) use this information to shed light on the relationships between wage rates and absenteeism, while Lanfranchi and Treble (2010) analyse patterns in the provision of sick pay.

The key to Coles *et al.*'s work is the identification argument. From Chapter 4, recall that the theory suggests that observed wage–absence rate pairs occur at tangencies between firms' isoprofit lines and workers' indifference curves. It follows that, if we can control for differences in isoprofit lines, leaving indifference curves to vary, the resulting data should trace out an isoprofit line. Alternatively, if we can control for differences in indifference curves, leaving isoprofit lines to vary, the resulting data should trace out an indifference curve. The argument is illustrated in Figures 6.9 and 6.10.

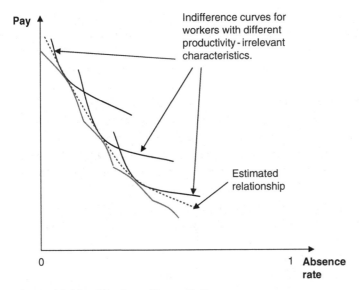

Figure 6.9 Identification of isoprofit line

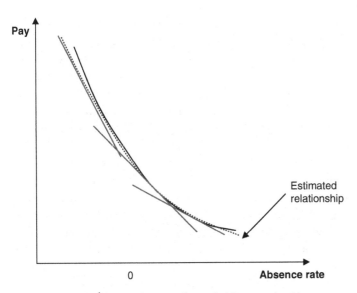

Note: Isoprofit lines are shown as linear, but they need not be.

Figure 6.10 Identification of indifference curve

In Figure 6.9, we show how the isoprofit line in wage–absence rate space may be identified by controlling for all relevant factors, but allowing the characteristics of workers (and, hence, their indifference curves) to vary so that different points on the isoprofit line are picked out (identification condition 1). In doing this, it is important to take care that worker characteristics that might affect their productivity at work are controlled for, since these will cause isoprofit lines to shift, as well as indifference curves. The statistical work done by Coles *et al.* (2007) thus attempts to distinguish productivity-relevant characteristics of workers from non-productivity-relevant ones. How convincingly this distinction is made readers can decide by referring to the arguments in the published paper.

Figure 6.10 shows the second case, in which isoprofit lines are allowed to vary, but all characteristics of workers, apart from their pay and absence rates are allowed to vary (identification condition 2). Both diagrams depict an ideal, since there are always unobserved or unobservable characteristics that cannot be controlled for. Nevertheless, the claim of the Coles *et al.* paper is that the data enable us to identify either the isoprofit line or the indifference curve, depending on what variables are controlled for.

Two wage–absence rate relationships are estimated, one for firms that say they use just-in-time techniques, the other for firms that do not. The focus on the just-in-time system is justified, because these production methods seek to minimise the use of inventories, which, as we argued in Chapter 2, are an important source of absence buffering. Firms that use just-in-time techniques do not use this method of buffering, and so will in general incur higher costs of absence, which may be controlled by setting a higher wage or by running a tighter absence control policy.

The theory predicts that the intercept of the wage equation for just-in-time establishments should be higher than the intercept for non-just-in-time establishments, and both should be positive. At the same time, the slope of the relationship between wage and absence rates in just-in-time establishments should be strictly negative, and steeper than the slope for non-just-in-time establishments, which should be non-positive.

Much of Coles *et al.*'s paper is devoted to a discussion of how their empirical technique handles three econometric issues that arise in estimating this system of equations. Interested readers are referred to that discussion, and we simply note here that the paper attempts to deal with omitted variable bias, selectivity bias and four potential sources of measurement error.

The main focus here is on the results, and their interpretation. We restrict our comments to the main set of results, which refer to blue-collar workers who are employed full-time during the entire year. The estimated slopes of the isoprofit lines are as the theory would predict, as are the estimated slopes of the indifference curves. However, the two sets of estimates, which should in theory be the same, are not. The isoprofit lines are almost certainly cleaner that the indifference curve estimates, though, because the data set enables firm fixed effects to be dealt with but not individual fixed effects.

It is to be expected that firms generally would pay no higher wages for a less reliable workforce than for a more reliable one, and this expectation is confirmed. More subtle is the rate at which remuneration should fall with increased unreliability. If, as the theory suggests, just-in-time technology implies that absence will be more expensive for firms using it, the loss of productivity when absence occurs will be greater for such firms than for others, and the wage premium for reliability should thus be higher for such firms. This is what Coles *et al.*'s analysis indeed shows.

What are the implications of these estimates? The slope of the equilibrium relationship between the wage rate and the absence rate can be interpreted as a measure of the loss due to increased absence. The estimates imply that non-just-in-time production is more robust to absenteeism than just-in-time production. The estimate of the slope of the efficient frontier for non-just-in-time firms is -0.1868. This implies that a 1 per cent increase in the absence rate (e.g. from 3.00 per cent to 3.03 per cent) could be condoned if wages were reduced by 0.56 centimes per hour – or about Fr4.77 per worker per annum. The equivalent calculation for just-in-time workers gives an estimate of about Fr8.79 per worker per annum. Applied across the entire French labour force, this amounts to about Fr152 million, or €23.2 million.[7] Given the doubts over the precision of both sets of estimates, comparison of this figure with Allen's (1983) estimates of a similar quantity reveals quite extraordinary agreement. Allen gives a range of gains associated with a one-day-per-worker reduction in absence. This

---

[7] Details of the calculation of these figures are provided by Coles *et al.* (2007).

translates roughly to $23.5 million to $137.5 million for a 1 per cent reduction. Thus the supply elasticity of absence appears to be about 100 for non-just-in-time firms and about 200 for just-in-time firms.

The estimate by the Confederation of British industry (CBI)[8] of the entire cost of absence for the British economy is around £13 billion for 2005 (€19 billion). Allen (1983) uses Steers and Rhodes' (1978) estimate of $26.4 billion as his comparator for the United States. The 'conventional' estimates are, of course, the answer to a different question from the one posed in our work. The CBI are trying to answer the question 'What would happen to costs and revenues, if firms could reduce absenteeism rates to zero without incurring any additional costs of absenteeism reduction?'. The approach taken by Allen (1983) and Coles *et al.* (2007) tries to answer the question 'How much would firms be prepared to pay to reduce absence at the margin taking account of the costs of absence reduction?'. From a practical point of view, we believe the latter question to be of more interest. Any manager knows that absence cannot be reduced without cost.

In a related piece of work, Lanfranchi and Treble (2010) use the same French data set to ask a different question: 'Is there any evidence to suggest that firms with high absence costs try to give workers better incentives for attendance than firms with low absence costs?'. Their answer is 'Yes', and it is based once again on a comparison of firms that have just-in-time technology installed with firms that do not. The measure of incentives is the generosity of sick pay, which, although it is regulated by the French state, does not provide 100 per cent replacement for all workers. Furthermore, the state system allows firms to negotiate regionally and locally to enhance the replacement rate to which workers are entitled. Lanfranchi and Treble's paper shows that firms using just-in-time methods are less generous in providing these enhancements than those that do not.

Summary

This chapter has presented several pieces of evidence about the market for absence. First, we review evidence about how absence rates vary between countries, regionally within Britain, and with age, gender and

---

[8] See the CBI's press release dated 15 May 2006, at www.cbi.org.uk/ndbs/press.nsf.

occupation. Then we review some empirical work in which absence is seen as the result of market interactions between firms and workers. First we go over work done by Allen, whose papers in the early 1980s used the idea of a hedonic market for deriving characteristics of labour contracts in order to interpret market data. We then look in some detail at two further papers, one of which attempts to take an equilibrium approach to the issue of how much absenteeism costs. It concludes that, at least in France, managers manage absenteeism rather well. The second paper looks at the relationship between the robustness of technology to absenteeism and firms' provision of sick pay. It appears that firms with low absence costs are more generous with their sick pay than firms with high absence costs.

7 | *The demand for absence: empirical evidence*

Buzzard and Shaw's study

The first study of the demand for absence was Buzzard and Shaw's (1952) analysis of ordnance factories in Britain. These researchers were in the fortunate position of being able to observe the introduction in 1948 of a sick pay scheme when none had existed previously – a situation rarely enjoyed by modern researchers, who have to rely on changes in schemes or the internal structure of schemes to identify behavioural effects. Buzzard and Shaw were able to obtain records of workers' absence behaviour for twelve months before and twenty-four months after the introduction of a sick pay scheme whereas previously there had been none, so that they were able to make a difference-in-differences interpretation of their results:

Under the scheme an employee who is absent from work because of illness receives his full flat rate of pay for as long as 13 weeks in any year. National Insurance benefit and any further allowances from other Government sources are deducted from this pay. All employees are entitled to receive sick pay once they have completed 26 weeks' Government service. If an employee has had five years' Government service, he is entitled to a further 13 weeks' absence on half pay. No one may receive more than one year's sick pay in any four years. Absences of three days only are not paid; absences of four days receive one day's pay, but if a man is absent for a period of five days or more he receives sick pay for the whole period of absence. A doctor's certificate is required as evidence of incapacity.

The data for Buzzard and Shaw's study was abstracted from the administrative records of the establishments involved. It was individual data containing a record from September 1947 to August 1950 of the sickness absence of each sampled worker. For each absence, the data indicate whether it was paid, unpaid or casual, and its cause. Job and personal characteristics were included: 'Industrial' or 'Non-industrial' job, location, gender and marital status (females only), date of birth, date of entry into job, date of discharge from job, whether registered disabled or not, job description ('Trade'), basic wage and type of bonus scheme (if any). Absence data were recorded separately for each of the three years of the study, as the total number of days lost and the total number of separate absence spells. In addition, the number of days lost was recorded for the six months before qualification for the sick pay scheme and the six months afterwards. If a worker had been discharged, the reason was sought.[1]

The sample design had two stages: establishments were sampled so as to be representative of the four government departments that ran them: the Admiralty, the War Office, the Air Ministry and the Ministry of Supply. The samples within each establishment were taken from the workforce employed at each establishment at the time of the researchers' visit. They did not therefore include workers who had left their employment between the start of the study and the date of sampling. Small establishments were over-sampled. The method of drawing names or numbers from the lists of employees is not described, but the resulting sample included 8,000 of them. The data were recorded on punched cards, which enabled some quality checks to be done with a card sorter. These appear crude by modern standards, but were probably state of the art in 1950.

In 1947/8, before the introduction of paid sick leave, 27 per cent of workers experienced some sickness absence. In 1949/50, after its introduction, the comparable figure was 46 per cent. The rules of the scheme allow for the replacement of 'full flat rate of pay', which allowed the analysis of a natural experiment, since the replacement rate implied by this phrase differed between two groups of workers – those who were paid entirely on a flat-rate or time-rate basis (about two-thirds of the total), and those whose pay included some kind of incentive element. This facilitates the use of what is today called a difference-in-differences approach to measuring the effect that differing replacement rates had on rates of absence.

While it is true that workers on incentive pay generally have lower absence rates than those who are not, and it is also true that the introduction of the sick pay scheme raised absence rates among both types of workers, the difference-in-differences calculation indicates

---

[1] We have made efforts to discover whether these data still exist. So far we have been unsuccessful.

that the increase in absence rates among flat-rate workers between 1947/8 and 1949/50 was from 45.7 to 73.0 absences per 100 workers, while for incentive-pay workers it was from 36.3 to 59.3. These increases are almost identical in percentage terms.

This is compelling evidence that the demand for absence slopes downwards, or that sick pay encourages workers to increase their sickness absence, despite the fact that the experiment is not entirely clean. The British National Health Service was initiated in 1948, and it could be that the measured increase in absence demanded is partially due to the greater ease of certification following this change. However, Buzzard and Shaw reject this as a plausible explanation for the entire effect. They also point out that the increase in absence was not necessarily a bad thing:

The introduction of a sick pay scheme of this kind will enable many people to be absent who ought to have been absent before. Many executive officials stressed this aspect to us, and commented on the number of cases before the scheme where men came to work who ought to have stayed at home. To this extent some increase in sick absence was to be expected although it is impossible to know how much. But one would expect the increase in 'necessary' absence to bear some constant relation to sick absence rate before the scheme was introduced. Where it is found that one group of workers has both a higher rate and a larger proportional increase than another, and where no explanation can be found in terms of age, conditions of work or other causes, we presume, tentatively, that there is unnecessary absence in the group with the higher rate. We use the term 'unnecessary absence' deliberately because the adjective implies no condemnation.

With this sick pay scheme a man may remain absent from work until he and his doctor decide that he is fully recovered from an illness. If there is a reasonable incentive to return to work he may well decide that he is fit enough to do so at a relatively early stage. But, if there is no such incentive to return to work, he may both feel and be unwell for a longer time, and many people will display the signs of illness. The patient may be totally unaware of the connexion between his continued ill-health and the lack of an incentive to get well. No amount of exhortation will convince him that his absence is unnecessary.

We regard Buzzard and Shaw's study as a model of good practice in the empirical study of absence. It is true that they had an unusually informative data set, but they deal with it well, and make no excessive claims. The availability of powerful computing machinery should have made it possible to build on the foundations set by this paper, but this is not the way that absenteeism studies have developed.

This chapter discusses the estimation of demand for absence. In particular, we discuss in some detail how administrative data from firms might be exploited to generate estimates of the slope of the demand curve for absence among a particular workforce. While the literature on absenteeism is large, there appear to be comparatively few studies that provide estimates of this last quantity. Instead, researchers have tended to concentrate on non-price determinants of demand.

Estimating the demand function for absence

Estimates of the slope of and shifts in the demand for absence are both potentially useful for human resources managers. A manager who understands that his workforce may be a bit less reliable than usual during a major sports event will be better placed to deal with the matter. The design of monitoring and incentive arrangements (including flexible working) and the provision of childcare facilities will be better if accurate information about the demand for absence is available. Clearly, if there are worker characteristics that are associated with high absence, managers may wish to avoid these in hiring, even though it may be illegal to do so.

Our main aim is to discuss what is known about absence demand functions, and the first point that we stress is that, whatever absence demand functions may look like, they are certainly not simple. The list of variables that have been proposed as determinants of absence is as long as the list of things that people might want to do rather than work: alcohol consumption, peer pressure, royal weddings and funerals, the weather, sports events, etc. In fact, these last two have been the focus of two recent studies. Connolly (2008) analyses time-use data and concludes that time spent at work falls when the weather is good. Her study is not specifically about absenteeism, but presumably some of the reductions in time spent at work that she identifies take that form. Thoursie (2004) finds that Swedish men reported sick more frequently when major cross-country skiing events were being shown on television. Studies such as these point clearly towards the idea that the demand for absence is not driven simply by financial considerations, but that it varies in accordance with opportunities for non-work uses of time. This implies that, whatever control employers may have over absence, it is unlikely to be perfect.

We now turn to the question that is most frequently asked about the demand for absence: how does it respond to those variables that are under the control of employers? There are essentially three modes of control that employers can use: hours, marginal pay and selection. These are not, of course, independent. For instance, changing work hours by seeking part-time workers is likely to attract workers with different responses to marginal pay rates. This is one reason why we place so much emphasis on identification. Ideally, we would like to know what the impact of raising the marginal cost to a worker of a day's absence is, when the cost is raised without changing hours or worker characteristics. We would like to know what the impact of changed work hours is when marginal pay is kept constant. We would also like to know about the impact of hiring policies on absence rates, but, given that we have no data sets with information about potential (as opposed to actual) hires, this must remain as a topic for future study. Finally, it is of interest to know how these different policies interact, but, if the ultimate goal is to understand worker responses to the full range of possible variations in contracts, it is important to understand how the different elements of a policy might work in isolation.

The arguments in the theoretical part of the book suggest that the absence we observe is the result of market interactions between firms setting contractual arrangements that determine the price to the worker of the absence he or she takes (or, put another way, a supply schedule for absence) and workers deciding how much absence they would wish to take at a given price (a demand schedule).

As we have already noted, Working (1927) outlines the issues that arise when looking at market data of this sort. Is the demand schedule alone shifting? In this case, the supply schedule is identified (case C, Figure 5.1). Is the supply schedule alone shifting, and thus identifying the demand schedule (case B, Figure 5.1)? Or are both schedules shifting? In this case, more elaborate modelling is required to identify demand or supply.

An absence demand schedule is a relationship between the price of an absence and the amount of absence taken, but what is the 'price' of absence? There will generally be a loss of earnings for the day, which could be calculated as any wage loss less sick pay entitlement.

There are also impacts of absence behaviour on career prospects. Furthermore, there might be indirect components to the price: workers may place some intrinsic value on their perceived reliability, or they may be concerned not to let their co-workers or employer down.

Demand schedules shift for a number of reasons. A theme in the macro literature is that workers will be more cautious in times of relatively high unemployment, because they don't want to lose their jobs, so if unemployment is high the demand for absence at any given price will fall; or, expressed in another way, the schedule will shift down. Doherty (1979) conducted a time series analysis of absence in the United Kingdom between 1954 and 1974, finding some evidence that absence is procyclical with respect to the business cycle, meaning that absence rates tend to fall as unemployment increases. However, Buzzard in an earlier, but very perceptive, piece (1954) points to the problems of disentangling effects, as high employment, he says, will be usually associated with increases in wages and 'less rigorous selection of workmen'. This selection idea has been returned to in more recent papers. Arai and Thoursie (2005), for example, examine two effects. One is that, in periods of higher unemployment, workers have more incentive not to report sick. The second is that in periods of higher unemployment it is the workers who have poorer attendance records who will be laid off first, so that the remaining labour pool consists, on average, of better attendees. They conclude that the incentive effect is the dominant one. Fahr and Frick (2007) find similar results using data from a natural experiment.

There have been several recent attempts to measure the impact of career concerns on absenteeism. These include studies of job protection rules, and one study of promotion prospects. In many countries[2] workers' jobs are particularly well protected, and their entitlements have been subject to reform. They also vary with tenure. Either kind of change can be used to identify the impact of job protection on absenteeism, and a number of recent papers have exploited these features.

Ichino and Riphahn (2005) use data from a large Italian bank, whose workers begin to be protected against firing only after the twelfth week of tenure. They were observed for one year. The authors

---

[2] It is hard to do this kind of study in Britain, since the law relies on a body of cases that together define the notion of 'reasonable cause' for dismissal. In many economies job protection law is codified more clearly, and subject to revision at clearly identifiable times.

show that – particularly for men – the number of days of absence per week increases significantly once employment protection is granted at the end of probation. This suggests that the provision of employment protection causes the increase in absenteeism. The authors reject other possibilities, such as career concerns or on learning about social norms, since these would predict a smooth relationship between absenteeism and tenure instead of the observed discrete jump. Riphahn and Thalmeier (2001) find similar results in an analysis of the impact of German employment protection on individual worker absence histories.

These two studies show that individual workers change their behaviour when rules change. Another approach is to compare two groups of workers for whom the rules are different. Scoppa (2010) adds to the Italian evidence with a study of the impact of a 1990 reform of the Italian job protection rules relating to small firms. Using a difference-in-differences estimator, he finds a 'strong increase' in absenteeism in small firms. Engellandt and Riphahn (2005) use Swiss data to compare a number of aspects of the behaviour of temporary workers (whose jobs are less well protected in Switzerland) with that of permanent workers. They find no measurable effect of temporary employment on absenteeism, but put this down to an apparently low level of opportunistic absence in Switzerland.[3] On the other hand, Bradley, Green and Leeves (2007), using data referring to the population of Australian public sector workers, find that, on average, workers on a temporary contract take less absence than if they were employed on a permanent contract. They also present evidence that increasing the opportunities for gaining a permanent contract reduces the absence of temporary workers who have limited employment protection.

Together, these papers indicate clearly that the threat of job loss is an effective means of absence control, and that the elasticity of absence with respect to increases in that threat is negative. However, they do not provide any neat method of calculating such an elasticity, since they generally show a difference in absenteeism between people whom we know have different incentives. The comparisons in all the papers are binary (protected or not protected, permanent or

---

[3] Swiss absence rates are certainly very low by international standards. Barmby, Ercolani and Treble (2002) give 1.78 per cent as the rate for 1997.

temporary), and these authors show simply that there is a difference in absence probabilities. In order to calculate an elasticity it would be necessary to develop a measure of the threat of job loss.

There is also one paper in which the impact of differing prospects of advancement are analysed. Audas, Barmby and Treble (2004) use data from a British financial services firm, which allows them to investigate the impact on absenteeism (which they interpret as an indicator of effort) of two aspects of promotion: the increase in income, or wage spread, that results from promotion, and the extent to which workers can affect the chances of promotion by varying their effort. In the tournament model on which their work is based, the second of these aspects is measured by the height of the distribution of 'luck' at its mean. The data enable the authors to calculate this quantity for each worker. They find that absence falls with increased wage spreads and also when the effect of luck on promotion chances is weaker – that is, when workers can be more certain that increased effort will yield a dividend in the form of an increased probability of promotion.

These papers consider the threat of job loss, and promotion prospects, as incentive mechanisms. The third element of incentives that we consider in detail is the immediate marginal cost of an absence. As we saw in Figure 6.4, Barmby, Ercolani and Treble (2004) show that, in Labour Force Survey data for the United Kingdom, absence falls with the hourly wage. This does not necessarily mean that higher wages would improve absence rates, since there is no clear causal relationship. It may be that higher wages cause lower absence because workers on higher wages lose more earnings when absent. On the other hand, it may be that higher absence causes lower wages. Although there is a clear relationship between low absence and high wages on the one hand and low wages and high absence on the other, it cannot be asserted that absenteeism would fall if wages were to rise. Figure 6.4 is computed for quarterly data over a period of ten years, between 1992.4 and 2002.4. If we could be sure that the demand schedule remained constant over this decade; that all that was varying was the supply schedules; and that the wage was capturing the 'price' of absence (which would be the case if there were no sick pay, or if sick pay was either a fixed proportion of wage or at a fixed level in 2000 prices and there were no disciplinary implications) then Figure 6.4 would show an estimated demand schedule.

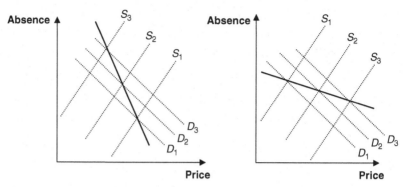

Figure 7.1 An identification problem?

These conditions are unlikely to hold. Over such an extended period, demand schedules will almost certainly have moved, and so we may be looking at something like panel C in Figure 5.1, where the supply schedule is identified. If, though, demand had been moving up over time from D_1 to D_3 while at the same time supply shifted *up* from S_1 to S_3 then we might pick out the heavy line in the left-hand panel of Figure 7.1. If supply shifted *down* from S_1 to S_3 then we might pick out the heavy line in the right-hand panel. The problem is that we have no way of knowing which.

Estimating absence demand using administrative data

Where else can suitable data be found, though? One possibility that we have pursued in our own work is to use data from individual firms. If a firm uses consistent HR policies that incorporate different prices for different workers, we can then argue that supply conditions are shifting but – given that we observe broadly the same workers for, say, a year – that demand conditions are the same. This situation potentially allows for estimation of the demand schedule.

While the use of data from individual firms may enable appropriate schedules to be identified more readily, it opens up the possible criticism that results might not be general – that is, that the relationships identified might be in some way specific to the firm in question. That, of course, is an empirical question. If results differ sharply between firms then careful analysis will reveal this. A priori, though, there is no obvious reason why the relationship linking an individual's demand

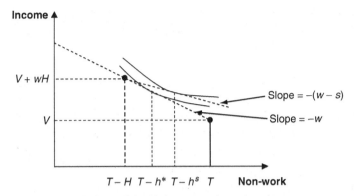

Figure 7.2 Simple model of labour supply with sick pay

for absence to the incentives that face them should be fundamentally different for someone working in a chicken processing plant from what it would be for someone working in a biscuit factory or a bank.

Figure 7.2 illustrates the simplest model of labour supply with sick pay. Without sick pay, an absent worker loses earnings at a rate equal to the wage rate. In such circumstances, the worker's desired hours are h^* hours, or, put another way, the quantity demanded of absence is $H - h^*$ hours. However, if sick pay is paid then the worker loses less income from each hour of absence and (unless non-work is an inferior good) 'desired' absence increases. The difference between wage and sick pay $(w - s)$ can be regarded as the cost of an hour's absence. If $w = s$, the replacement rate is one and the cost of absence is zero, so the worker always has the incentive to be absent.

A number of things can be said in this regard. First, if this were all, such contracts would never be offered in the market, as firms would continuously lose money on them. However, a cursory examination of what is seen in actual labour markets suggests that, although 100 per cent replacement of income is not uncommon, sick pay entitlement in such contracts is always time-limited. Time limitation may take the form of a reduction in the replacement rate (as in paid sick leave arrangements) or a mandatory change in the employment contract, either within the firm or outside it. This second possibility is usually the outcome of managerial intervention or, possibly, of a disciplinary proceeding. Until data and techniques can be found to separate out the impacts of such career concerns from the immediate impact of the marginal wage rate, studies of the latter are always likely to yield biased results.

What data are needed to enable this empirical investigation of the relationship between sick pay and absence? Ideally, we would look for a data set in which individual workers are observed over a short span of time, during which the rate of sick pay changes. It is not impossible to get data of this sort from the administrative records of firms, but even data sets that satisfy the basic criteria pose analytical challenges. Most of the rest of this chapter presents a case study of such a data set and the various issues that arise in its analysis. This data set incorporates endogenous variation in the rate of sick pay, which poses some analytical complications. We suggest a number of ways in which to deal with these.

In a sequence of papers starting with Barmby, Orme and Treble (1991), the present authors along with various co-authors have analysed data from a single firm in which the conditions described above are close to ideal. We observed individual workers' daily absence records over a number of years. The data set was provided by a firm in the 'fast-moving consumer goods' industry.[4] Its four plants all produce much the same consumption good, but local labour market conditions are quite different for each plant. Workers within the different factories face the same sick pay arrangements, and within these arrangements there is variation in the sick pay that workers face, generated by experience rating in the company's sick pay scheme.

This implies that variation in the sick pay is not exogenous. However, we developed an empirical approach that we argue can, in principle, be applied to *any* firm's data to recover an estimate of workers' absence demand schedule. Estimates can usually be improved by adding data from other sources. We give an example of how this can help below.

The FMCG firm's sick pay scheme defines the eligibility of workers to sick pay in excess of a minimum statutory sick pay (SSP). Eligibility is based on each individual worker's past attendance, and so the scheme is *experience-rated*. It is the operation of this sick pay scheme that generates substantial variations in the cost of a day's absence for different individual workers. Any experience-rated scheme has this effect, including the widespread paid sick leave arrangement, with the result that the techniques we use are applicable to those schemes as well.

---

[4] FMCG for short. No, these are not high-powered cars or motorbikes.

At the FMCG firm, a worker's attendance record includes a count of points accumulated. Points are given for 'unacceptable' absence days, each of which may attract one or two points.[5] Unacceptable absences include unexplained and self-certified absence (in the United Kingdom, workers can self-certify themselves sick for up to one week before having to obtain a medical certificate).

At the beginning of each year, workers' eligibility for sick pay is determined according to the points they have accumulated over the previous two years. Eligibility can be at one of three levels of generosity, A, B and C. If the average over the previous two years was less than ten points per year then the worker is assigned to grade A, which for most workers carries an entitlement to full replacement of normal earnings. Workers with a ten to twenty point average are assigned to grade B and allowed sick pay equal only to the basic component of their earnings. In the event of absence, these workers would lose any bonus earnings. Workers with more than twenty points on average over the previous two years are graded C and receive no company sick pay. A worker's sick pay entitlement is therefore determined by their sick pay grade, which is computed from their points score, which in turn is calculated from their absence record. Thus, each worker's absence history maps in a rather complicated way into their entitlement to sick pay.

Firms usually hold data on their workers' attendance for the purposes of accurately calculating correct payments to these workers, and, if necessary, to inform any disciplinary action that might be taken. Table 7.1 gives an idea of the structure of the data that we gathered from the FMCG firm. These are quite typical of the records usually held by commercial organisations, so we can claim some general applicability of the methods we have developed. What is unusual about the specific firm we studied is the use of varying sick pay replacement rates.

Table 7.1 illustrates a number of different contractual arrangements, and also illustrates turnover. There are four different symbols used to distinguish employed from non-employed days (–), among employed workers, contracted from non-contracted days (*) and, among contracted days, absent days (A) and days worked (W). Each

---

[5] The doubling of points occurs for days when sick pay costs are not recoverable from the government.

Table 7.1 *Hypothetical absence records for eight workers*

Time Worker	1	2	3	4	5	6	7	8	9	10	11	12	Absent Days	Absent Spells	Contracted
1	–	W	W	W	A	*	*	A	A	W	–	–	3	1	7
2	W	W	W	A	*	*	*	W	W	W	W	*	1	1	8
3	W	W	W	W	W	*	*	W	W	W	W	W	0	0	10
4	A	A	W	W	W	*	*	W	W	W	W	W	2	1	10
5	*	W	W	W	*	*	*	*	W	W	A	*	1	1	6
6	W	W	W	A	W	*	*	W	A	A	W	W	3	2	10
7	*	*	*	*	*	W	W	*	*	*	*	*	0	0	2
8	W	W	W	W	A	*	*	A	W	W	W	–	2	1	9
Days lost	2	2	1	3	3	0	0	3	2	1	1	0			
Number of workers	5	7	7	7	5	1	1	6	7	7	6	3			

Notes: W = attend work; A = absence; – = not employed at firm; * = employed but not contracted to work on that day.

of the twelve columns in Table 7.1 represents a day, so that the entire table covers two hypothetical weeks and the intervening weekend in periods 6 and 7. Thus worker 1 joined the firm on the first Tuesday, and left after working through Wednesday, except that the worker was not present on the Friday of the first week and the Monday and Tuesday of the second week. With the exception of worker 7, there are no workers contracted to work over the weekend, and worker 7 works only at the weekend.

Data such as these can be analysed in several different ways. One can look, for instance, at absence rates for individual workers. The last three columns of the table do this. The column headed 'Absent – Days' gives the total number of absent days for each worker. The column headed 'Contracted' gives the number of contracted days for each worker. Individual absence rates can be calculated simply by dividing the second of these numbers into the first. Some analyses are carried out by counting absence spells, by which is meant sequences of contiguous days absent. The number of spells for each of the eight workers in the table is given in the penultimate column. Alternatively, one can look at the daily patterns revealed by individual columns of the table. The number of contracted days varies each day, as does the number of absent days.

Our focus is on the incentive effects of pay and sick pay. For this, we think of the data in the table as sequences of daily events occurring at the individual worker level. Such a sequence is often referred to as an *event history*, and a set of such event histories (such as the one in Table 7.1) is called a *discrete panel*.[6]

An event history is a sequence of events observed over time, which in the present context are treated as binary – workers are either present or absent. We formulate a model for the probability that these events occur from time to time. We assume that workers have a contract with the firm, in the context of which their attendance decisions are made.

The utility that a worker attaches to each of the two available choices can be described by the linear system

$$U_{it}^W = \eta z_{it}^W + \delta c_i + \varepsilon_{it}^W \atop U_{it}^A = \gamma z_{it}^A + \theta c_i + \varepsilon_{it}^A \qquad i = 1, \ldots, N; \; t = 1, \ldots, T_i \qquad (7.1)$$

where η and γ are conformable row vectors describing the effect on the worker's utility of the characteristics z of the alternatives being chosen and δ and θ are conformable row vectors describing the effect of worker characteristics c on utility. The superscripts A and W label the dependence of job characteristics and utilities on the decision to be absent or to work, respectively. Thus z_{it}^W includes the wage, while z_{it}^A includes sick pay. The characteristics of individuals described in the vectors c do vary over alternatives, but may influence the utility of work and absence differently. If so, $\delta \neq \theta$. The probability of observing worker i absent at time t can be written

$$\begin{aligned}
P(D_{it} = 1) &= P(U_{it}^A > U_{it}^W) \\
&= P(\varepsilon_{it}^W - \varepsilon_{it}^A < \gamma z_{it}^A - \eta z_{it}^W + \theta c_i - \delta c_i) \\
&= P(\varepsilon_{it}^W - \varepsilon_{it}^A < \gamma z_{it}^A - \eta z_{it}^W + (\theta - \delta)c_i) \\
&= F(\beta x_{it})
\end{aligned} \qquad (7.2)$$

---

[6] The occurrence of weekends in panels creates a difficulty, which, for simplicity, we ignore in the present discussion. Nolan (2000) provides an exhaustive treatment of how weekends should be handled in these models.

where $\beta = \begin{pmatrix} \gamma \\ \theta - \delta \end{pmatrix}$, $x_{it} = \begin{pmatrix} z_{it}^A - z_{it}^W \\ c_i \end{pmatrix}$ and F is the cumulative distribution function of $\varepsilon_{it}^W - \varepsilon_{it}^A$. Since the z_{it}^A vector contains sick pay and the z_{it}^W vector earnings then, if increments of income affect utility equally no matter what their source ($\gamma = \eta$), the probability of absence is a function of the difference $z_{it}^A - z_{it}^W$, as we pointed out in the discussion of Figure 7.2. Since the characteristics of individuals do not vary over the alternatives, the estimated coefficient can be interpreted as the difference $\theta - \delta$. If a characteristic of an individual has an equal effect on the utility of two alternatives then knowledge of this characteristic cannot be informative with respect to the choice.

In building this empirical model to analyse absence data, it will be useful to consider how it relates to Figure 7.1 and Figure 7.2. Consider the utilities in equation (7.1) for a single worker on a given day. The i and t subscripts are now unnecessary, and the effect of individual characteristics irrelevant. The equation can therefore be written in a simplified form as

$$U^W = \delta^* + \eta z^W + \varepsilon^W$$
$$U^A = \theta^* + \eta z^A + \varepsilon^A \qquad (7.3)$$

Suppose further that z^W and z^A each have only two elements, representing income and hours. Including the individual's earnings for the day (w) and the amount of non-market time available if work is attended, ($T - h$), in z^W, and sick pay, s, and the greater non-market time available when not at work, T, in z^A, equation (7.3) becomes

$$U^W = \delta^* + \eta_1 w + \eta_2(T - h_c) + \varepsilon^W$$
$$U^A = \theta^* + \eta_1 s + \eta_2 T + \varepsilon^A \qquad (7.4)$$

or

$$U^W = \bar{U}^W + \varepsilon^W$$
$$U^A = \bar{U}^A + \varepsilon^A \qquad (7.5)$$

where $\bar{U}^W \equiv \delta^* + \eta_1 w + \eta_2(T - h_c)$ and $\bar{U}^A \equiv \theta^* + \eta_1 s + \eta_2 T$ are the systematic parts of utility yielded by working and not working, respectively. Equation (7.2) is now

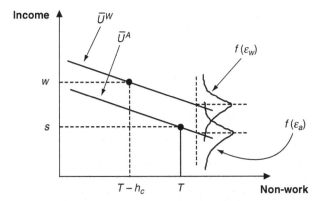

Figure 7.3 Binary choice model of absenteeism

$$P(D = 1) = P(U^A > U^W)$$
$$= P(\varepsilon^W - \varepsilon^A < \eta_0 - \eta_1(w - s) + \eta_2 h_c)$$
$$= F(\eta_0 - \eta_1(w - s) + \eta_2 h_c)$$
$$= F(x\beta)$$

(7.6)

The system in equation (7.5) is illustrated in Figure 7.3. The probability of an absence is generated by the realisations of the errors ε^W and ε^A, which are indicated as normal densities indicating the probabilities of deviations of utility from its mean in each of the two states – working and absent. Note particularly that a large realisation of ε^A relative to ε^W can result in an absence even though the systematic utility of work is greater than that of non-work. Note also that in this framework the marginal rate of substitution is constant, and can be estimated as MRS $= -\frac{\eta_2}{\eta_1}$.

If ε^W and ε^A are independently distributed as extreme value type 1 random variables then F is logistic and

$$P(Absence) = \frac{1}{1 + \exp(-x\beta)}$$

(7.7)

which is the well-known logit model. If ε^W and ε^A are normally distributed then we obtain the probit form for the probability of absence $P(Absence) = \Phi(x\beta)$, where Φ is a normal cumulative distribution function.

Absence can occur only on days when the worker is contracted to work. We define R_i to be the set of contracted days for worker i.

Table 7.2 *Notation for event histories*

Event	d_{it}	$P(D_{it} = d_{it})$
Absence	1	P_{it}
Work	0	$(1 - P_{it})$

The event histories in Table 7.1 can be described by sequences of dichotomous random variables D_{it}, which are defined in Table 7.2.

For example, for worker 1 in Table 7.1, the realisations of D_{1t} for days on which the event of absence was at risk of occurring would be $d_{1\{t \in R_1\}} = \{0001110\}$. Similarly, $d_{3\{t \in R_3\}} = \{0000000000\}$. The joint probability of $d_{i\{t \in R_i\}}$ for all workers $i = 1, \ldots, N$ can be written

$$P[\bigcap_{t \in R_i} (D_{it} = d_{it})] = \prod_{t \in R_i} P_{it}^{d_{it}} (1 - P_{it})^{(1 - d_{it})} \tag{7.8}$$

With an appropriate parameterisation of P_{it} such as that developed in equation (7.7), this can be used to form the likelihood for estimation:

$$L = \prod_{i=1}^{N} \prod_{t=1}^{T_i} P_{it}^{d_{it}} (1 - P_{it})^{1 - d_{it}} \tag{7.9}$$

as used by Barmby and Treble (1991) and Barmby, Orme and Treble (1991).

The likelihood function in equation (7.9) depends only on observable characteristics x_{it}. If the data source allows for an extensive regressor list, then many such characteristics may be included, but when data are gathered from firms' administrative records then this isn't ensured, and there are, of course, some characteristics that are intrinsically non-observable. Firms typically keep records of absence so as to ensure that workers are paid correctly and treated fairly. Many characteristics of workers and their households are unimportant in this regard, and gathering some kinds of information may be seen as unnecessarily obtrusive. This raises the real possibility that some factors that systematically affect the probability of absence will not appear in the regressor list.[7] As usual, the omission of relevant variables from an analysis can lead to bias in estimation.

---

[7] See Keynes (1939) for an early and particularly perceptive view regarding the problem of unobserved heterogeneity.

This issue can be handled in the following way. We acknowledge that there exist unobservable individual effects u_i that should be included in the regressor list – that is, we acknowledge that the probability of absence should be written as

$$P(D_{it} = 1) = p_{it}(u_i) = F(\beta x_{it} + u_i) \tag{7.10}$$

Consider two workers, one who has 'high' u_i and one who has 'low' u_i; despite the fact that their observed characteristics are identical, the first worker will persistently have a higher propensity to be absent than the second. Although this difference between workers is not observed, we can modify the model to incorporate a distribution of unobserved us in the population. In doing this, we are supposing that the observed sample is a set of draws from that population. So we assume that u is a random variable with density $f(u)$. The probability in equation (7.10) is now dependent on the random variable u, so it cannot be used directly to form a usable likelihood. However, it is possible to form a marginal likelihood in which the random variable is integrated out. Essentially, this procedure takes a weighted average of the possible values of $p_{it}(u_i)$, where the weights are derived from the supposed distribution of u:

$$L = \prod_{i=1}^{N} \left[\int \prod_{t=1}^{T_i} F(\beta x_{it} + u)^{d_{it}} (1 - F(\beta x_{it} + u))^{1-d_{it}} f(u) du \right] \tag{7.11}$$

where the range of integration is the support of $f(u)$. A common assumption for $f(u)$ is that it is normal.

The likelihood defined in (7.11) using daily data forms the main workhorse of our statistical analysis of absence using administrative data. Analysis based on the likelihood (7.11) is used by Barmby, Orme and Treble (1995) and Barmby, Bojke and Treble (1997), for a sample of data from 1988 for one factory in the FMCG group.[8] To illustrate the main findings of these studies, in Table 7.3 we report results calculated using a slightly simplified version of the model reported by Barmby, Bojke and Treble (1997). The results are very similar.

---

[8] Johansson and Palme (2002) use a similar likelihood estimated on daily data for a random sample of the Swedish workforce drawn from administrative data from the National Social Insurance Board.

Table 7.3 *Random-effects logistic regression of individual daily absences*

	Coefficient	Standard error	|t| statistic
Female	0.1573*	0.0579	2.72
Cost	−0.0152*	0.0067	2.27
Hours	0.0401*	0.0168	2.39
Grade B	0.3320*	0.0614	5.41
Grade C	0.6828*	0.1448	4.72
Monday	0.2743*	0.0666	4.12
Tuesday	0.0838	0.0659	1.27
Wednesday	0.0530	0.0662	0.80
Thursday	0.1074	0.0663	1.61
Lagged absence	5.1829*	0.0432	119.97
Total absence to date	0.0203*	0.0025	8.12
Constant	−5.2947*	0.1474	35.92
σ_u	0.2408*	0.0485	4.96

Notes: Number of observations = 13,2080; number of individuals = 615;
* = significant effects at 5 per cent level.

They show a clear influence of the cost of absence on its incidence. Much (but not all) of the variation in cost here is due to workers being assigned to different grades, and this assignment is itself determined by past absence behaviour. We defer further discussion of the results on cost until after the discussion of instrumental variables estimates contained in Table 7.6.

The positive coefficient on the dummy for gender, which takes the value of one for females, indicates that women have a higher probability of absence than men. That this is true is evident in the raw data illustrated in Figures 6.5 to 6.7. The estimates here are considerably more refined than the raw differences shown in those figures, though, since they show that the increased absence is not due to women being paid less or working different numbers of hours from men. These influences have been netted out by their inclusion in the regression. It would probably be helpful if we could include measures of household characteristics in the analysis, but this information was not reliably maintained by the firm. Recall, though, that the technique used to generate the estimates incorporated a method of controlling for the effect of unobserved heterogeneity, and the effect of gender persists.

The economic literature has been much concerned with gender differences in absence, as well as with the influence of the cost of absence. While all analysts agree that women's absence rates are higher than men's, the source of this difference is not a matter of agreement at all. This remains an area in which more research effort could be usefully applied, and the use of the administrative records of firms is likely to be an important part of this. More detailed data enable the elicitation of more detailed effects.

Early work on women and absence is summarised succinctly by Vistnes (1997): 'Previous research on gender differences in absenteeism has found that health status measures are more consistently important than economic factors in explaining absenteeism across genders (Paringer (1983) and Leigh (1983)).' Her own investigation finds a similar pattern. Note that this does not necessarily mean that men and women do not respond to economic factors; the claim is that there appears to be no difference in this response. This means that the widely observed difference in men and women's absence rates is unlikely to be due to differential responses to economic incentives. Differences in household circumstances, or in health, are almost certainly more important. Vistnes (1997) shows that there is little difference in absence behaviour between women and men with similar childcare responsibilities. Nonetheless, since women are more likely to have childcare responsibilities than men, this is clearly part of the explanation. Findings such as these cast doubt on VandenHeuvel and Wooden's (1995) suggestion that the study of men's and women's absence should be conducted separately. The fact that responses to both childcare and economic factors have been found to be similar suggests that joint estimations with an appropriate structure allowing for separate responses for men and women is likely to be a more efficient estimation approach.

On the question of health differences between women and men, Ichino and Moretti (2009) recently claimed to show that the menstrual cycle is implicated in women's absence. This difference between men and women accounts in their data for about 14 per cent of the gender wage differential. They use the personnel database of a large Italian bank, which contains the exact date and duration of every employee absence from work. They build their paper on the striking finding that the hazard of an absence due to illness increases significantly (relative to that for males) for females who are forty-five years old or younger, relative to males, twenty-eight days after the previous absence. There is no evidence of such a difference for older employees.

Absences with twenty-eight-day cycles are an important determinant of gender differences in sick days, explaining roughly a third of the overall gender gap in days of absence, and more than two-thirds of the overall gender gap in the number of absences.[9]

Ichino and Moretti (2009) also examine the effect of this additional absenteeism on women's earnings, using a model of statistical discrimination in which employers use observable worker characteristics – including absenteeism – to predict productivity and set wages. Since men do not suffer from the additional disruption of the menstrual cycle, absenteeism is a noisier signal of worker quality for females than for males. If this is the case, the signal extraction of underlying shirking rates based on absenteeism is more informative for men than for women. As a result, the relationship between earnings and absenteeism should be more negative for men.

A second implication is that this gender difference in the slope between earnings and absenteeism should decline with seniority. As employers learn more about a worker's true productivity, the importance of the signal should decline. These predictions are borne out in Ichino and Moretti's data. The relationship between earnings and cyclical absenteeism is negative for both genders, with the slope significantly steeper for men. However, this gender difference in slope is larger when an employee first joins the firm than it is for longer tenures. For those men and women with fifteen years' seniority, the negative relationship between earnings and absenteeism is the same.

---

[9] During the production of this book, Ichino and Moretti's findings have been challenged by Rockoff and Herrmann (2010), who are unable to find similar patterns among a group of US teachers. In addition, they reanalyse Ichino and Moretti's data, and argue that the claimed twenty-eight-day cycle is a statistical artefact.

Returning now to our analysis, the remaining variables listed in Table 7.3 give some information about the dynamic structure of absence. Absence has long been believed to vary through the week, with Monday traditionally notorious for low work attendance rates. This turns out still to be the case. Dummy variables indicating the other days of the week show that absence is higher on Mondays. The lagged absence regressor captures the effect of a spell in progress on the probability of absence on a given day. These show that a day absent is much more likely to be followed by another day absent. This does not mean that one-day absences are unlikely, since this variable is set to one for every day in a spell other than the first. We have not tried investigating longer lags, such as those concentrated on by Ichino and Moretti.

The dynamic structure of absence spells is the focus of two further papers, by Barmby (2002) and Barmby and Sibly (2004). They expand the model described in equation (7.11) to allow the effect of all regressors on the probability of being absent to be different depending on whether the previous day is an absent day or not. This investigation can be seen as relevant to the theory described in Chapter 4, although the empirical papers do not deal with the dynamics of incentives during spells in the same detail as the theory does. These two empirical papers differ mainly in the way in which the error structure is handled.

In both models, the conditional probabilities of absence at time t given the state occupied at time $(t-1)$ make up a Markov transition matrix of the form

$$T = \begin{bmatrix} P(D_{it} = 0 \mid D_{i,t-1} = 0) & P(D_{it} = 1 \mid D_{i,t-1} = 0) \\ P(D_{it} = 0 \mid D_{i,t-1} = 1) & P(D_{it} = 1 \mid D_{i,t-1} = 1) \end{bmatrix}$$

The transition matrix describes a stochastic process in which a worker, occupying one of two states at $(t-1)$, will either remain in that state or transition to the other state at time t. It also contains the relevant information for a personnel manager's decision when the two states being considered are work and absence. These are the quantities that are important to managers – that is, the probability that an absent worker will return to work in the next period and also that a non-absent worker will be absent in the next period. The model underlying (7.11) implies that these two quantities respond to regressors in the same way, but there is no reason to suppose that they do. The results of the enhanced model of Barmby and Sibly (2004) indicate that these doubts are well placed.

As before, the conditional probabilities defining the transition matrix can be written in logistic form:

$$P_0 = P(D_{it} = 1 \mid D_{i,t-1} = 0) = \frac{\exp(\beta_0' x_{it} + \alpha_0 e_i)}{1 + \exp(\beta_0' x_{it} + \alpha_0 e_i)}$$

$$P_1 = P(D_{it} = 1 \mid D_{i,t-1} = 1) = \frac{\exp(\beta_1' x_{it} + \alpha_1 e_i)}{1 + \exp(\beta_1' x_{it} + \alpha_1 e_i)} \tag{7.12}$$

where β_0' and β_1' are vectors of parameters describing the effect of regressors x_{it} (some of which may be time-invariant). The conditional probabilities are also written as functions of an unobservable individual specific term e_i, with coefficients α_0 and α_1 describing the variability of these components. The variance of the unobserved component in the above probabilities is $Var(\alpha_1 e_i) = a_j^2$, where j indicates whether the worker is absent or present. The unobserved components are drawn randomly from a distribution $f(e)$, which is assumed to have a standard normal distribution. These unobserved components can be regarded as nuisance parameters and integrated out to form a marginal likelihood. The ith worker's contribution to the marginal likelihood can therefore be written as

$$L_{it}(\beta_0, \beta_1, \alpha_0, \alpha_1) = \int \prod_{t=2}^{T_i} P_0^{d_{it}(1-d_{it-1})} (1 - P_1)^{(1-d_{it})d_{it-1}}$$

$$(1 - P_0)^{(1-d_{it})(1-d_{it-1})} P_1^{d_{it}(d_{it-1})} f(e) de$$

Barmby (2002) develops a similar model, but replaces the normally distributed error with a discrete alternative. The details of this reformulation can be found in his paper, but it amounts to replacing (7.12) with

$$P_0 = P(d_{it} = 1 \mid d_{i,t-1} = 0) = \frac{\exp(x_{it}\beta_0 + A_i^0)}{1 + \exp(x_{it}\beta_0 + A_i^0)}$$

$$P_1 = P(d_{it} = 1 \mid d_{i,t-1} = 1) = \frac{\exp(x_{it}\beta_1 + A_i^1)}{1 + \exp(x_{it}\beta_1 + A_i^1)} \tag{7.13}$$

where the unobservable individual specific terms (A_i^0, A_i^1) are found to have a bivariate discrete mass point distribution defined over 2×2 support points, $a = \{(a_1^0, a_1^1), (a_2^0, a_1^1), (a_1^0, a_2^1), (a_2^0, a_2^1)\}$ with probabilities attached to each pair of these, $\pi = \{\pi_{1,1}, \pi_{2,1}, \pi_{1,2}, \pi_{2,2}\}$.

The error terms are 'integrated out' to form a marginal likelihood, although the integration here is a weighted sum because the distribution is discrete. The ith worker's contribution to the marginal likelihood is

$$L_i(\beta, a, \pi) = \sum_{a_i^0=1}^{M_0} \sum_{a_i^1=1}^{M_1} \prod_{t=2}^{T_i} P_0^{d_{it}(1-d_{it-1})} (1 - P_1)^{(1-d_{it})d_{it-1}} \qquad (7.14)$$

$$(1 - P_0)^{(1-d_{it})(1-d_{it-1})} P_1^{d_{it}(d_{it-1})} \pi_{a_i^0, a_i^1}$$

The results are reproduced in Table 7.4. A key finding is that, for workers who have not already started an absence spell, the effect of the cost of absence is negative but insignificant. The impact of cost on starting spells is estimated here as insignificantly different from zero. On the other hand, workers who have already started an absence spell are significantly affected by cost. The greater the incentive to return to work, the more likely they are to do so. According to these estimates, an HR policy in which the cost of absence to the worker is increased will successfully reduce the absence rate. It does this by reducing the duration of absence spells rather than by reducing the incidence of newly started spells. This result fits well with the theoretical prediction of the random utility model described in Chapter 3, where Figure 3.7 indicates clearly that the incentives in a (different) experience-rated scheme are stronger for workers in an ongoing spell than they are for those who are not.

Contracted hours have a positive effect on absence when the worker is at work, so workers with high contracted hours are more likely to *initiate* a spell of absence, but the expected length of the spell is not affected by the number of contracted hours.

The estimates of the distribution of errors are given in Table 7.5. The first row and first column are the location of the mass points; the body of the sub-table consists of the probabilities, with estimated standard errors in parentheses. The implied mean errors are $E(A_0) = -5.6763$ and $E(A_1) = -0.0224$.

A number of further empirical refinements would be interesting to explore in the context of this model. One of these is the relationship between absence and tenure. In the likelihood (7.11), the time at risk for a worker is T_i, which are the contracted days for worker i with the firm, or the tenure of the worker with the firm is not a fixed quantity.

Table 7.4 *Maximum likelihood model of worker absence*

Variable (mean)	State 0 (work)		State 1 (absence)	
	Estimate	Standard error	Estimate	Standard error
Gender (0.7)	−0.0626	0.0772	0.4885*	0.1002
Contracted hours (7.42)	0.0785*	0.0239	0.0394	0.0347
Cost (£5.27)	−0.0085	0.0088	−0.0399*	0.0142
Grade B (0.37)	0.6367*	0.0829	0.0827	0.1236
Grade C (0.20)	0.9109*	0.1887	0.7247*	0.3039
Monday	1.4214*	0.0795	−2.0793*	0.1339
Tuesday	0.3808*	0.0973	−0.1047	0.1123
Wednesday	−0.0315	0.1020	0.2485*	0.1208
Thursday	−0.0765	0.1131	0.5159*	0.1300
Sum of days (4.75)	0.1436*	0.0246	0.2085*	0.0361

Note: *=significant effects at 5 per cent level.
Source: New estimates following Barmby (2002).

Table 7.5 *Estimate of mass point distribution* ($M_0 = M_1 = 2$)

		A^0	
		−6.0111	−4.3456
		(0.2111)	(0.4285)
	−0.3598	0.6064	0.0064
A^1	(0.3173)	(0.0482)	(0.0046)
	1.9080	0.3804	0.0068
	(0.2692)	(0.0482)	−

Note: The standard error in the bottom right-hand cell cannot be estimated, because the sum of the estimates is constrained to unity.
Source: New estimates following Barmby (2002).

A number of studies have proposed that a link may exist between absence and turnover (which will of course be reflected in T_i). Empirically, there has been little examination of this link. However, it can be incorporated into the model by supposing that the likelihood in (7.11) is conditional on T_i:

$$L(\beta | T_i = t_i) = \prod_{i=1}^{n} \prod_{j=1}^{t_i} p_{ij}^{d_{ij}} (1 - p_{ij})^{(1-d_{ij})} \tag{7.15}$$

Making the simplest assumption, that workers leave the firm with probability θ_i in each time period, a worker's tenure with the firm follows the geometric law

$$P(T_i = t_i) = (1 - \theta_i)^{(t_i-1)} \theta_i \tag{7.16}$$

The likelihood then becomes

$$
\begin{aligned}
L(\beta) &= L(\beta | T_i = t_i) P(T_i = t_i) \\
&= \prod_{i=1}^{n} \prod_{j=1}^{t_i} p_{ij}^{d_{ij}} (1 - p_{ij})^{(1-d_{ij})} (1 - \theta_i)^{(t_i-1)} \theta_i
\end{aligned}
\tag{7.17}
$$

which weights the likelihood contribution by the probability of an event history of the observed length.

Another possible line of enquiry concerns the autocorrelation structure of the error in the latent variable model that lies behind equation (7.10). This will have two components: an unobserved individual-specific component (which will itself induce an autocorrelated structure in the composite error); and an individual time-varying error representing the worker's state of health (or household emergencies). This may itself have an autocorrelated structure. The simulated maximum likelihood models used by Stewart (2006) could, we think, be applied in this context. Another alternative is to use the random utility model described in Chapter 3. We argued there that the notion that the marginal rate of substitution of workers will vary according to some probability law (which might also be autocorrelated) was very persuasive in its description of how workers make decisions about absence. We contrasted this with the Dunn and Youngblood (1986) model, in which the MRS is some characteristic of the worker that will predict average behaviour, so workers with a high MRS would be more likely to be absent than those with a low one.

If we look at equations (7.1) we can see that the MRS will be constant for workers of given characteristics. This comes from the linear structure of the utility equations. Since the error term is additive it doesn't affect the ratio of the derivatives. What the random utility model gives us is a model in which the stochastic structure is built into

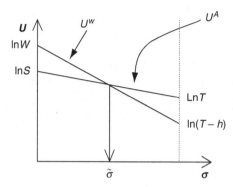

Figure 7.4 Reservation morbidity

the daily decision,[10] in a way that alters the MRS. The random utility model can be motivated by the common idea that a worker's health state varies from day to day.

Suppose that the parameter $\sigma \in [0,1]$ represents the worker's health state, with higher values representing greater morbidity. Write the utility function in Cobb–Douglas form, as in (3.6). The implied marginal rate of substitution is $-\frac{\sigma}{1-\sigma}$. As σ increases, the value of the marginal non-work hour increases.

Under quite general conditions, a 'reservation sickness level', $\tilde{\sigma}$, exists such that the utilities from work and absence are equalised: $U^A(\tilde{\sigma}) = U^W(\tilde{\sigma})$. The worker's behaviour can be characterised in a very natural way. The worker will decide to attend work if $\sigma_{it} < \tilde{\sigma}$ and go absent from work otherwise. This argument is illustrated in Figure 7.4.

Barmby, Sessions and Treble (1994) use this framework in the context of analysing absence, although there is, of course, a prior literature. Viscusi and Evans (1990) characterise behaviour as individuals maximising expected utility, with the expectations being taken over health states. The formulation developed here can be thought of in this way, since, so long as there is support for realisations of σ in the neighbourhood of $\tilde{\sigma}$ using the decision rule defined above, it will maximise expected utility.[11]

---

[10] This idea is drawn directly from search models of unemployment, in which it is now part of the accepted wisdom. The econometric implications were first described by Lancaster (1979).

[11] To see this, consider another 'reservation' level, $\tilde{\tilde{\sigma}} > \tilde{\sigma}$. So long as there is some probability of a health realisation in the interval $(\tilde{\sigma}, \tilde{\tilde{\sigma}})$ then expected utility will be smaller, since $U^W < U^A$ in this interval.

Let σ have distribution $F(\sigma)$; then the probability of an absence is $1 - F(\tilde{\sigma})$, or, using the notation of equation (7.2),

$$P(D_{it} = 1) = \int_{\tilde{\sigma}}^{1} f(\sigma)d\sigma \tag{7.18}$$

This can be used to construct a likelihood for the data that will be a function of both preference parameters and parameters of the morbidity distribution, F.

An instrumental variable approach

We now turn to the key coefficient in the absence demand schedule, namely the coefficient on cost. In the specification that we estimated using equation (7.11), we cannot be confident that the measure of the effect of cost is unbiased. As we have noted beforehand, the cleanest way to measure the effect of variation in the cost of absence on an individual worker's behaviour is to exploit some *exogenous* change in the circumstances the worker faces and observe the effect on behaviour. Here, because the cost to the worker is largely determined by the grade they are in in a given year, and because the grade a worker is in is due to their behaviour in the previous two years, the cost that the worker faces is *endogenous*. As we explained in Chapter 5, the appropriate estimation procedure in this case is an IV approach, in which the expected cost is predicted by an instrumenting equation, and then the expected (or predicted) cost is included as a regressor in place of the cost itself.

In what follows, we report a new analysis that uses health data to achieve this identification. This means that we are departing from the strict use of administrative data by augmenting the data set with publicly available data. We had hoped to use the incidence of influenza as our health variable. Unfortunately, detailed regional data on flu incidence is not easily obtained in the United Kingdom, but data on mortality resulting from pneumonia is available on a regional basis, and is correlated with the incidence of flu (see Denoeud *et al.*, 2007), so we use this as our instrument for cost. If there were a higher incidence of flu, a worker would have a higher probability of contracting flu and being absent from work. Under the experience-rated sick pay rules, they may then face a higher cost of absence the following

Table 7.6 *Regression for full-time male employees from three factories*

	Cost not instrumented		Cost instrumented with health data	
	Coefficient	|t| statistic	Coefficient	|t| statistic
Constant	0.0309	7.83	0.0309	7.27
Grade B	0.0104	1.46	0.0137	1.96
Grade C	0.0186	0.88	0.0527	2.52
Cost	−0.0009	0.95	−0.0027	2.29

Notes: $N = 715$ in 1988; dependent variable = individual worker absence rate for the year.

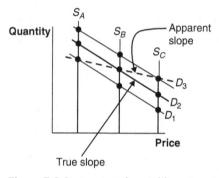

Figure 7.5 Instrumental variable estimation

year, but the incidence of flu in a previous year would not affect the workers' absence choice directly the following year.[12]

Table 7.6 reports the results of our analysis for three of the FMCG factories, one in Scotland, the others in England. The estimated effect of cost becomes larger, and significantly different from zero. Within the FMCG firm, absence is supplied at three 'prices' according to whether the worker is in sick pay grade A, B or C. If the worker were randomly allocated to face one of these prices then variations in cost would be exogenous. Each of the heavy black dots in Figure 7.5 would occur with equal probability and the estimate would give an accurate impression of the middle demand curve, D_2. However, if workers with demand D_3 are more likely to be in grade C and workers with demand

---

[12] Barmby and Larguem (2009) attempt to analyse illness transmission within firms.

D_1 are more likely to be in grade C, something closer to the dotted line will be picked out. To the extent that the IV methodology takes account of this selection, it will generate an estimated curve with a different slope.

Finally, how might we interpret the effect of the variables we have discussed as being important to the absence rate? The conventional way of measuring this is to use an elasticity. An elasticity is the ratio of the percentage change in one variable (the absence rate) to the variable that theory suggests it is related to (wage). The elasticity of the absence rate R with respect to cost C can be computed[13] as

$$\eta_{RC} = \frac{dR}{dC} \cdot \frac{C}{R} \tag{7.19}$$

For the IV estimates reported in Table 7.6, this elasticity is -0.1825.

Table 7.7 provides a comparison of wage (rather than cost) elasticities derived from studies over the last six decades. We are forced, rather than choosing, to compare these rather than cost elasticities, because more studies use the wage than try to construct a true measure of cost. The relationship between cost and wage elasticities is discussed in the Appendix to this chapter. The relationship between the two elasticities is straightforward. In particular, if sick pay is directly proportional to wages, they are the same. If sick pay is fixed (and less than the wage) then the cost elasticity is less than the wage elasticity, as equation (A7.5) in the Appendix shows. Sadly, the wage and sick pay tend to be related in more complicated ways than either of these simple extremes allow, and there is probably no general way of converting one elasticity to the other, or even of assessing whether the wage elasticity is an over- or an underestimate.

The one case for which we are fairly confident that the cost elasticity can be calculated accurately is Buzzard and Shaw's (1952) study. Here the cost change is essentially exogenous. Buzzard and Shaw do not themselves report a cost elasticity, but we have deduced an approximate value of such an elasticity from information in their paper.

The first thing to note is that the sick pay introduced by the British government for their industrial workers was, for a significant proportion of the workforce, a substantial increase. For those workers who had completed twenty-six weeks' service this represented a cost

---

[13] Some aspects of the problem of recovering comparable elasticities from existing studies are discussed more fully in the Appendix to this Chapter.

Table 7.7 *The wage elasticity of absence rate* $\eta_{a,w}$ *computed from various studies*

Study	$\eta_{a,w}$	Type of study	Notes
Allen (1981a)	[−0.48, −0.35]	US Quarterly Employment Survey 1972–3	As reported by author, p. 82.
Allen (1981b)	−1.2	Data from US paper industry	
Leslie (1982)	−0.39	Data from records of UK National Coal Board 1974–9	As reported by author, p. 108.
Allen (1983)	−0.21		
Kenyon and Dawkins (1989)	[−2.98, −2.04]	Australian quarterly time series 1966.3–1984.4	
Barmby, Orme and Treble (1995)	[−0.84, −0.41]	UK manufacturing firm data 1988	Daily earnings included as regressor; elasticity taken with respect to estimated daily probability of absence.
Barmby, Bojke and Treble (1997)	−0.46	UK manufacturing firm data 1988	Daily cost of absence included as regressor.
Barmby, Ercolani and Treble (2004)	−0.48	UK time series (LFS) 1993–2004	

reduction of essentially 100 per cent, as prior to the scheme being introduced they would have lost all their earnings by not reporting for work. Now they would receive their full basic pay. For workers who earned incentive pay or piece rate the cost reduction would be less than 100 per cent, as they reverted to basic pay for their sick pay entitlement, but the cost reduction was still substantial.

Buzzard and Shaw report the increase in absence in a number of ways, but the average increase in the number of days lost was 171 per cent which, if the number of contracted days remained the same, indicates an increase in the absence rate of the same percentage. These two quantities taken together, and the average reduction of cost of something approaching 100 per cent corresponding to an increase of absence of 171 per cent, suggest an elasticity in excess of 1.71. This makes our IV estimate seem modest.

The wage elasticity estimates in Table 7.7 are nonetheless informative. The first thing to note is that they are all negative. They vary considerably in size, with Kenyon and Dawkins' (1989) time series estimate for Australia leading the pack at somewhere between −2 and −3.

Summary

This chapter has discussed critically some of the evidence on the demand for absence, and laid out in detail how administrative data from firms can be used. The main advantages of administrative data are that the supply conditions facing workers are more homogeneous, and the costs of an absence can be more clearly described. However, administrative data may need to be augmented with information from other sources to enable identification. We provide an illustration of how this may be done using health data.

Appendix: Computing elasticities for absenteeism

The measure used to compare what the empirical studies say on the effect of wage on absence in Chapter 7 is the elasticity of the absence rate, R, with respect to wage, W, or η_{RW}. It is the percentage change in the absence rate divided by the percentage change in wage, or

$$\eta_{RW} = \frac{\frac{dR}{R} \cdot 100}{\frac{dw}{w} \cdot 100} = \frac{dR}{dw} \cdot \frac{w}{R} \tag{A7.1}$$

Ensuring that elasticities calculated from estimates in different studies are comparable sometimes requires a certain amount of work. Researchers do not all use the same empirical model, and, even if they do, the exact specifications of their models can be different. For a simple example: what if the researcher had entered the logarithm of the wage rate in their equation in place of the wage itself? In this case, since $\frac{d \ln w}{dw} = \frac{1}{w}$, equation (A7.1) becomes

$$\eta_{RW} = \frac{\frac{dR}{R} \cdot 100}{\frac{dw}{w} \cdot 100} = \frac{dR}{wd \ln w} \cdot \frac{w}{R} = \frac{dR}{d \ln w} \cdot \frac{1}{R} \tag{A7.2}$$

For instance, in Figure 6.4, as ln (*wage*) varies between one and four the absence rate falls at a reasonably constant rate from about 0.045 to about 0.01, implying a rate of change $\frac{dR}{d \ln w} \approx -0.012$. The mean absence rate is around 0.03, so the elasticity of the absence rate with respect to the wage is about –0.4.

Barmby, Orme and Treble (1995) use daily earnings instead of hourly wage as their explanatory variable. So long as contractual daily hours are constant at, say, h_c, this creates no problem. In fact, under these circumstances, the elasticity with respect to daily earnings is the same as the elasticity with respect to the hourly wage:

$$\eta_{RE} = \frac{dR}{dh_c w} \cdot \frac{h_c w}{R} = \frac{dR}{h_c dw} \cdot \frac{h_c w}{R} = \frac{dR}{dw} \cdot \frac{w}{R} = \eta_{RW} \tag{A7.3}$$

Contractual hours may vary for different workers. When this is the case, it is because different workers will have agreed to different given h_cs in the light of the wage rates offered. Of course, individual workers will have a labour supply function, $h^* = h(w)$, where h^* is their desired hours. Perhaps on account of search costs (as has been discussed in Chapter 3), h^* is not necessarily equal to h_c; we could think of $h_c = h^* + \varepsilon$, where, if $\varepsilon > 0$, the worker has accepted a job with contracted hours in excess of their desired hours. Assuming that h^* is a function of w but ε is not, then $\frac{dh_c}{dw} = \frac{dh^*}{dw} = h'_c$. Therefore, the analogue of (A7.3) when h_c may change as w changes is

$$\begin{aligned} \eta_{RE} &= \frac{dR}{dE} \cdot \frac{E}{R} = \frac{dR}{dw} \cdot \frac{dw}{dE} \cdot \frac{E}{R} \\ &= \frac{dR}{dw} \cdot \frac{h_c}{(h_c + wh'_c)} \cdot \frac{w}{R} \\ &= \frac{h_c}{(h_c + wh'_c)} \cdot \eta_{RW} \end{aligned} \qquad (A7.4)$$

This follows since $dE = \frac{\partial E}{\partial w} dw + \frac{\partial E}{\partial h} dh = \left(h + w\frac{dh}{dw}\right) dw$. So elasticities taken with respect to earnings when hours may be sensitive to wage changes may *understate* the wage elasticity.

As we have seen, some studies are able to enter the cost of absence, $C = (w - s)$. This should still allow the recovery of a wage elasticity if the sick pay rate is fixed such that $s < w$, since

$$\eta_{RC} = \frac{dR}{dC} \cdot \frac{C}{R} = \frac{dR}{dw} \cdot \frac{dw}{dC} \cdot \frac{C}{R} = \frac{C}{w} \cdot \frac{dR}{dw} \cdot \frac{w}{R} = \frac{C}{w} \cdot \eta_{RW} \qquad (A7.5)$$

Many studies, such as those by Delgado and Kniesner (1997) and Barmby, Nolan and Winkelmann (2001), report estimates of models in which the dependent variable is the number of days' absence during a period of time, T. These models are called *count data models* (see Winkelmann, 1996, 2008). Estimates from a count data model can also be used to recover the elasticity of the absence rate with respect to the wage, by observing that the expected number of days of absence in, say, the Poisson count data model is

$$E(N_i) = \hat{\theta} = e^{x_i \hat{\beta}} \qquad (A7.6)$$

where θ is the average arrival rate of absences. It follows that $\theta = pT$ or $p = \theta/T$, where p is the probability of absence. If this can be measured as the observed individual worker absence rate, it follows from (A7.6) that

$$\eta_{RW} = \frac{dp}{dw} \cdot \frac{w}{p} = \frac{d\theta}{dw} \cdot \frac{w}{Tp} \qquad\qquad \text{(A7.7)}$$

8 | *Policy implications for firms*

In this chapter, we try to bring out the practical implications of the work that economists have done in recent years. However, this is not a manual of absence control for human resources managers. The lessons to be learned from these studies are more strategic than tactical in nature, and we hope that those who are charged with the development of strategic approaches to absenteeism control will find something of use in them.

Setting the target rate of absence

The first lesson (and possibly the most important) is that the idea of 'minimising absence' or 'zero tolerance' should have no place in an absenteeism strategist's mind. The fact that all workers are human, and most of them have some kind of life outside their work, implies that their attendance will never be 100 per cent, even though for many workers it is not much less than this. Add in the incidence of minor and major illness, and it is clear that trying to push absence too low is inconsistent with profit maximisation.

Given this basic fact, there are two sets of actions that a manager can take: one can try to manage absence itself, or one can try to manage its impact on operations and costs. Most managers (and certainly most firms) probably do both these things, and advice from organisations such as the Chartered Institute of Personnel Development[1] in Britain recognises this. What that advice misses, though, is the idea that absence can be too low. This is the CIPD advice on choosing a target for absence rates:

---

[1] See, for example, the CIPD's publication by Evans and Walters (2002) and the advice given in the 'absence management toolkit'. See also footnote 16, Chapter 2, page 45.

Benchmarking is important because it tells you how well your organisation is performing compared with competitors and the world at large, highlighting areas for improvement, and helping to set performance standards.

The CIPD and the Confederation of British Industry (CBI) publish regular reports providing the latest data for benchmarking purposes. Both are surveys of employers. The information in the surveys includes the overall absence rate, and breakdowns by region, sector, and organisation size . . .

The CBI and the CIPD are important sources of general information on absence levels. But you might want something less general and more specific to your needs, such as absence levels in your locality or sector, or for particular occupations. Options for gathering this kind of information include setting up a club of employers who agree to provide their absence rates, or using, say, an existing pay club survey to gather absence details. Another possibility is to seek the help of local employer bodies, such as Chambers of Commerce, or your own industry body, both of whom may already be collecting absence data.

When you've found benchmarking data that meets your needs, remember that your target shouldn't be just to match your absence rate with the average. This might be your immediate objective, but being among the best 25% makes a better longer-term aim and will help to keep managing absence firmly on your organisation's agenda.

The research discussed in this book suggests a rather different approach to this admittedly difficult problem. Specifically, while it might be the case that competitors, either in the local labour market or in the product market, are using similar technologies, it should not be taken as given that they are. Second, the idea of a benchmark rate *for an organisation* is not obviously the profit-maximising approach. As we have argued, it is the presence of complementarities in the production function that drives the costs of absence, and these are unlikely to be uniform across all jobs in a single organisation.

If pushing absence too low is undesirable, how can one know what 'too low' is? Zero is certainly too low. It is literally impossible to hire perfectly honest workers with no susceptibility to illness, and without household or transport difficulties or interests that sometimes compete for time with work commitments. Beyond the observation that the optimal absence rate is not zero, there is no general answer to the question 'How low is too low?', since, as Coles and Treble (1996) point out, what in equilibrium is too low for one firm (or job) may be just right for another.

However, it may not matter too much exactly what benchmark rate is chosen. Firms can *choose* what their optimal level of absenteeism is, so long as compensating adjustments are made in other aspects of jobs, especially the wage rate. In the competitive equilibrium analysed by Coles and Treble (1996), and by Coles *et al.* (2007), the optimal rate of absence for each firm depends not just on its choice of technology, which determines the shape and location of its isoprofit map, but also on the characteristics of the local labour market. These latter are summarised in the indifference map of workers who are attracted to work at that firm. In practical terms this means that, if a firm makes a particular choice of absence rate, it must accept the consequences of this for the wages it offers: if a low wage is offered, the firm will get a more unreliable workforce, leading to higher non-wage costs; if a high wage is offered, the resulting more reliable workforce will enable the firm to economise on covering workers, production rescheduling and all the other management issues that accompany unreliability. What the appropriate choices are for any particular firm depends on the wide range of factors described in previous chapters: the nature of the local labour market, the production technologies available and the nature of the competition.

While economists' models are not able to give specific guidance as to what a firm's target absence rate should be, they do suggest what job characteristics may be associated with high or low absenteeism. Once again, there are elements of choice here, but the basic argument is that the rate of absence will be associated with characteristics of firms' technology and work organisation and the labour available in the local labour market. The key concept here is *complementarity.* This is a measure of the extent to which the various inputs of a production process work together to produce output. In some workplaces, the production of output is individual. Thus, for instance, each piece produced by a bespoke furniture workshop may be the work of a single worker. In other workplaces, workers may be linked through the mechanism of work being organised in teams, or in a production line arrangement, so that each contributes only a part of the labour necessary for the generation of the output. If a worker's output is individual then absenteeism is not a problem. Pay the worker a piece rate, and absence implies that, so long as the marginal value product of the worker is no greater than the wage, the firm loses nothing. The difficulty arises when the input of the worker is complementary to some other input, either other workers or a machine. The simple example given by Coles and Treble (1996) is of teamwork in which no output at all is produced if there is a worker missing. There are plenty of other, more complicated, circumstances in which complementarity occurs. For instance, not all output may be lost. Production lines in frozen chicken plants begin with live chickens being hung on the line by chicken hangers. Suppose the capacity of the line at normal working speed requires four chicken hangers to be present. If there are only three, output need not drop by the full 25 per cent, since the three attenders may be able to work a bit more quickly, or more efficiently than usual. Nonetheless, the fact that the productivity of all the workers further down the line is diminished implies that the cost to the firm of the absent worker is likely to be greater than just that worker's productivity, so that it would be difficult to provide appropriate incentives using a simple piece rate.

A special case worth highlighting is education, in which sector complementarity arises in a rather different form. Running a class successfully requires the attendance both of a producer's representative (a teacher) and consumers (pupils). Absence on the part of a teacher is potentially very expensive, since the education of all pupils is affected. The absence of a pupil will clearly affect the education of that pupil, but the loss to the entire class may well be ameliorated, since more teacher time will be available for other pupils.[2]

The idea that complementarity is at the root of absence costs has a second implication for strategic thinking about absenteeism. Different jobs within the same firm may have different degrees of complementarity. Workers on a production line depend for their productivity on other workers upstream, but secretarial or clerical work in the same firm may be more individualistic. This raises the question of whether a single absence control policy should be applied to all workers.

---

[2] Despite this asymmetry, the literature on the absence of teachers seems to be smaller than the literature on the absence of pupils. Ehrenberg *et al.* (1991), using data from schools in New York state, find that teacher absenteeism is not associated with students' academic performance, although student absenteeism is associated with poor performance on a set of standardised tests. Kremer *et al.* (2005, 2006) suggest that teacher absenteeism is a serious barrier to development in many countries, including India, where teacher absence rates are about 25 per cent, according to their survey. These very high rates of absence do not apparently have a great impact on student performance. Neither of the two Kremer *et al.* papers has anything to say about the use of cover arrangements.

The idea that complementarity is intimately related to the holding of inventories of semi-finished goods may be less than obvious. In fact, it is possible to imagine circumstances in which they are exactly the same thing.[3] To see the connection, think of a production line. A downstream worker is able to work only if there is a flow of semi-finished output from an upstream worker; but a stock of semi-finished output that had been generated earlier may be a good substitute for a flow of newly produced output. The extent to which they are good substitutes depends on two things: storage costs and durability. It is expensive to keep semi-finished automobiles because they are large. It is expensive to keep semi-processed chickens because they decompose rapidly. This implies that absenteeism will be more expensive for production processes for which inventories of semi-finished goods are costly to maintain.

The link between the production process, inventory holdings and the cost of absence has important implications for managing absence, because it makes clear the fact that reducing the costs of absence to a firm is not necessarily an issue for the HR department alone. Using the language introduced in this book, costs can be effectively reduced either by changing the demand for absence or by changing its supply. The first of these has to do with human resources, since the two main ways in which the demand for absence can be managed are by means of the remuneration system (including the provision of sick pay) and the firm's hiring policy.

Changing the supply of absence involves making choices about production technology, and so is more likely to be in the domain of the production department. An extreme example of the kind of action that may be required is provided by the recent experience of one of Germany's leading dairy producers, which on acquiring a new plant in Russia decided that absence was a sufficiently serious problem for it to re-equip the entire plant in such a way as to reduce the impact of poor attendance on production.[4]

It is probably no accident that action of this kind, at the extreme end of the organisation of production, should have been deemed necessary in an economy in which the state control of sick pay arrangements is

---

[3] Coles *et al.* (2007) include a simple example in which an assembly-line technology and a particular system of inventory holding give rise to an equivalent formal representation of the production function.

[4] Fritz Summer, personal communication.

very rigorous. Actions taken to control the supply of absence and those taken to control its demand are substitutes, so that, if it is impossible to control demand for absence because of state regulation, the more extensive use of supply-side methods may be expected.[5]

In the last three or four decades many firms have chosen to introduce so-called 'lean' production methods. These were once widely claimed to reduce absenteeism by changing the behaviour or attitudes of workers, specifically by 'empowering' them. Our work suggests a different explanation, namely that the reductions in absenteeism associated with lean production are the consequence of changed managerial behaviour.[6] Lean production involves reducing inventory, which makes the production process less robust to absenteeism, which in turn makes effective control of absence more desirable. Absence falls in firms that use lean production methods, because managers have incentives to manage it better.[7] So far as we know, there are no studies that try to disentangle cause from effect in this matter, but there are a number of studies that confirm the association, such as those by Coles *et al.* (2007), Heywood and Jirjahn (2004) and Heywood, Jirjahn and Wei (2006). There is also one study that shows that lean production methods in the form of just-in-time production (which concentrates specifically on the reduction of inventories of semi-finished goods) are associated with less generous sick pay provision: that by Lanfranchi and Treble (2010). At the moment investigation of the relationship between production methods, work organisation, remuneration structures and absence rates is in its earliest stages. The currently available information for meaningful study of these issues is very meagre.

We have argued that the 'choice' of what absence rate to try to enforce is to some extent a matter of taste, in that what is lost on the swings of absent workers can be gained on the roundabouts of absence control and the use of buffer stocks. The choice should be informed by consideration of the nature of production, and, especially, the extent of complementarities and the nature of the local labour market.

---

[5] The idea that supply- and demand-side measures are substitutes is, in principle, testable, but we know of no published attempts to test it.

[6] Some recent management studies have come to a similar conclusion by a different route. See, for example, Oliver *et al.* (2005).

[7] Lean production reduces the supply of absence, but an increasing number of studies claim that at the same time it increases stress at work, and may increase absence demand through its effects on worker health. See, for example, Landsbergis, Cahill and Schnall (1999).

The importance of responding appropriately to the local labour market can be illustrated by an interview that we once had with the manager of one of the 'fast-moving consumer goods' plants that we studied. All the plants had similar contracts on offer, and absence control in particular was organised in accordance with quite strict centralised guidelines. Nevertheless, this particular manager was pleased if seven out of every eight of his workers turned up. We asked him how he managed with such a high absence rate, and it appeared that the most effective tool he used was the employment of a buffer stock of workers. When he was asked why he thought his workers were absent so much, his reply was: "The people around here are Scots!"[8]

Enforcing acceptable absence

Once the acceptable absence rate has been decided it needs to be enforced. There is little we have to add to existing advice on this matter. Enforcement requires communication with employees (who, ultimately, are the ones deciding whether or not they are going to turn up to work). It requires knowing what the absence rate is from time to time, and it requires letting employees know what the policy is and how it is being enforced.

There is nothing magic about keeping records. Since the calculation of pay usually requires knowledge of which workers worked when, any system that will enable a record similar to that shown in Table 7.1 aids the calculation both of pay and of absence rates. Computer software that does this is readily available. As Table 7.1 shows, with such a record it is straightforward both to calculate time lost day by day and to check the record over weeks, months or years in terms of individual workers or groups of workers. Both kinds of summary statistics are useful.

With a target absence rate set, the first thing to be checked is the extent to which actual absence rates differ from it. This one would do by looking at absence rates per unit of time. A good place to start is probably the annual absence rate. Take all the contracted days during the year and all the absent days (non-contracted) and divide the latter by the former. This gives the annual absence rate. If this is a lot higher than your target, something needs to be done to reduce it. The first

---

[8] Barmby, Ercolani and Treble (1999) show that Scots are actually not especially prone to high absence rates. We must suppose that the manager had a more local phenomenon in mind.

thing to look for is patterns, because, if there is a pattern to absence, there is almost certainly a policy that can be introduced to alter it. For instance, since there are sometimes weekly patterns to absence, it is worthwhile looking at absences on each day of the week. To do this, take all the Mondays in a quarter, add up the number of absences and the number of contracted days and divide the first number by the second. This gives the absence rate for Monday during the quarter. The same calculation can be done for years to give the absence rate for Monday during the year. Doing the same for all other days of the week will give a picture of how the absence rate varies through the week.

It may be the case that the weekly pattern is due to the activities of just a few individuals, in which case it is probably a good idea to look at the records of individuals such as are given in the rows of Table 7.1. A complication here is that a manager may view very differently two workers one of whom has, say, one ten-day absence while the other has ten one-day absences. This means that, as well as individual absence rates, one may wish to look at the number of separate spells of absence that make up that rate. The Bradford factor (BF) is one way of doing this, but it does not seem to us to be a very useful tool, except to the extent that it encourages careful interpretation of data.

The Bradford factor

The origins of the Bradford factor are shrouded in mystery, but it has attained a place in British human resources management practice that it barely justifies, on the basis of the little evidence that we have been able to find. The BF seems to be a uniquely British idea. Despite the fact that managements the world over are all trying to manage absenteeism, the only managers who seem to find the Bradford factor useful are British ones, and it has now spread into the highest reaches of government in Britain. In November 2004 the report produced jointly by the Ministerial Task Force for Health, Safety and Productivity and the Cabinet Office entitled *Managing Sickness Absence in the Public Sector*[9] included the following description of the BF, which it introduces as a 'sophisticated tool':

For many organisations, the cost and disruption of recurrent short spells of absence can be greater than for occasional, longer periods of absence which

[9] The review is available at www.hse.gov.uk/gse/sickness.pdf.

can be planned for. In the private sector this is true for many retailers. In the public sector it is true for many front line roles: nurses, prison officers, teachers, police. To address this problem, some organisations make use of an approach often referred to as the 'Bradford Formula'. The formula measures an employee's irregularity of attendance.

The calculation is:

S × S × D = Bradford points score

S is the number of occasions of absence in the last 52 weeks and

D is the total number of days' absence in the last 52 weeks.

So for example, employees with 14 days' absence in one rolling 52-week period, distributed differently, the score can vary enormously.

- one absence with 14 days is 14 points (1 × 1 × 14)
- seven absences of two days is 686 points (7 × 7 × 14)
- 14 absences of one day each is 2,744 points (14 × 14 × 14)

This system is used in the Prison Service (where it is known as the 'attendance score'), tied to a sliding scale of management action: 51 points in 6 months leads to a verbal warning; 201 points to a written warning and 401 points for a final warning. This also provides a clear framework for tackling persistent short term absence – a member of staff with an attendance score of 601 points in 12 months with a final warning may be dismissed on grounds of unsatisfactory attendance. 300 staff have been dismissed for all categories of sickness absence on these grounds in the prison service in 2003–04.

This approach has had a significant effect in reducing short term absence by an average of 0.4 days per person. The strength of the system seems to be that it requires line managers to issue mandatory warnings in all cases where trigger points are reached, without local discretion. This ensures that all staff know that poor attendance will be tackled. The mandatory management warnings are supported by sound local and corporate data, strong monitoring arrangements driven through the line by operational directors and an auditing system to ensure compliance.

Far from being a 'sophisticated tool', the BF adds nothing to the information carried in the two numbers from which it is calculated. To see this, note that of the three numbers involved – S, the number of spells; D, the total number of days; and B, the Bradford factor – any one can be calculated from the other two. B is calculated from S and D using the instructions above: $B = S^2 D$. If you know B and S, though, you can figure out that $D = B / S^2$; and, if you know B and D, you can figure out that $S = \left| \sqrt{\frac{B}{D}} \right|$. Any two of these numbers carry exactly the same information as all three of them.

The BF therefore, is a statistic calculated from two others: the total number of days that a person has had off sick during some period of time and the number of distinct spells. Whenever two numbers are replaced by one, a loss of information is involved. Let us see what kind of information may be lost in the calculation of the Bradford factor. Someone with a BF of 125 may have had six months off work continuously. Under the Prison Service scheme described above, this would earn them a verbal warning. Equally, they may have had five separate days off, earning them two or more verbal warnings (assuming the five spells are evenly spread over a year). These two cases hardly belong in the same category. How do we know? Because we know the numbers that underlie them. Neither do they necessarily warrant any sort of management action. The first case may be of a person who has contracted some protracted illness or injury, while the second could be someone who, on average, gets a migraine every ten weeks.

The argument that is used to justify the use of the BF is that a total absence count does not distinguish between someone who has lots of short absences and someone who has a few long ones, but, as we have just shown, neither does the Bradford factor. If you want to distinguish these two cases you need to know something about the actual length of the absences, not hide this information in a 'sophisticated' formula. A claim that is often made for the use of BF is that it highlights people with many short absences, but this can more readily be done by looking at the mean lengths of absences and the number of absences. If the first number is small and the second is large, you have identified the people you want without doing any further arithmetic.

However, just because calculating this statistic is not a lot of use does not necessarily mean that it does no harm. The BF attempts and fails to make one number do the job of two. Its problems do not end there, though, because, like any other statistic, when it is used as a target it creates incentives. For this particular statistic, the behaviour that it is likely to generate is not what HR managers generally seek in their workers.

The Bradford factor clearly generates incentives for taking longer absences rather than shorter ones. To see why, consider a worker with two spells of absence, one on Monday, the other on Thursday. Such a person can halve their Bradford factor (from eight to four) by doubling their absence from two days to four days. To do this, they simply take Tuesday and Wednesday off as well.

That absenteeism rates respond to incentives is by now well established. As we have seen in Chapter 7, people tend to go absent more frequently when the weather outside is good, when there is something tempting on the television and when their absence doesn't cost them much. So far as we are aware, there are no carefully constructed empirical studies of the Bradford factor's impact on absence rates, only a rather vivid folklore, and a much-copied source that we have been unable to identify.[10] The case study of the Prison Service above is an example of the folklore: it presents a raw statistic, '0.4 days reduction', and attributes it entirely to the operation of the Bradford factor, and none of it apparently to the fact that, when a company introduces a new policy or procedures for absenteeism, it also usually introduces a reporting system, which employees will know all about. Often such changes are accompanied by changes in disciplinary arrangements as well. How much of the impact of the Prison Service's new policy is due to the detail· of the Bradford factor, and how much to the fact that workers suddenly realise that they are being watched, or are going to be punished more severely than they were in the past? If collecting data alone has a large impact, why bother doing anything with the information other than collect it and record it?

The one advantage that the Bradford factor might have is that it encourages managers to collect the data in the first place and to look at them critically. At its introduction, it may also have the effect of impressing on workers that they are being watched. However, it is not a magic formula. It creates incentives by itself that are not obviously the ones that someone managing absenteeism would want to create. Linked to an explicit set of actions, in the way that the Prison Service apparently does, it seems to us to have much potential for injustice. Finally, whatever else it might be, it is not 'a formula for measuring an employee's irregularity of absence'. This remark shows deep misunderstanding on the part of whoever originally wrote it, and a lack of critical faculties in those who have copied it. Neither the number of

---

[10] This seems to be the source for the Ministerial Task Force's remarks referred to above, which reproduce some of the source's errors. These have been independently copied or recopied in many other places, including one of the authors' (John Treble's) own past employer's absence management policy (see www.swan.ac.uk/media/Media,7128,en.pdf), which includes the words: 'The Bradford factor uses a formula for measuring an employee's irregularity of absence.'

spells nor the total number of days carry any information about irregularity. In order to do that one would need a measure of dispersion. The Bradford factor does not include one. It includes no information other than the spell count and the absent days count that goes into it. Intelligent and sensitive interpretation of these two pieces of information is far preferable to muddying the water by calculating a third number.

Incentives

A manager who is collecting accurate information about absence, is keeping an eye on the overall absence rate and on the behaviour of individual workers, and is alive to the vagaries of the local labour market may still have an absence rate that is above target. What can be done then? It is at this point that managers should start to consider the incentives that their workers face. What we mean by this is not just any disciplinary procedures that they may have in place – these are always unwieldy and expensive to operate – but a properly designed incentive scheme, which can be a comparatively cheap add-on to existing personnel systems for recording attendance and calculating pay.

It is useful to distinguish between two types of incentive scheme: group incentives and individual incentives. Group incentives are generally harder to analyse than individual incentives. They are also harder to set up successfully. This is partly because there are opportunities for collusion, explicit or implicit, between workers arising in group schemes that do not arise in individual schemes. Evans and Walters (2002) recount a story concerning the truck division of Iveco Ford, which introduced a group scheme under which sick pay was more generous for everyone if overall absence fell below some threshold. This appeared to work, but had the unanticipated side effect of inducing a cycle of rising and falling absence rates. When the aggregate absence rate was below the threshold, sick pay entitlement rose, and absence rose; when it was above, sick pay entitlement fell, and absence fell. Evans and Walters suggest that switching to an individual rather than a group scheme may be a solution to this 'problem'. A second story concerns Canadian air traffic controllers.[11] An air

---

[11] Rick Audas, personal communication.

traffic control centre must always be fully manned, so absence policies include the requirement that any absence has to be covered. Covering staff were paid an overtime premium in Canada, with the result that establishing an informal rota of absences implied that wage payments could be boosted for everyone. In this situation, there was no intention to create group incentives, as they arose from the interaction of the absence policy with the overtime policy, and could have been avoided by ensuring that the loss of pay when absent was greater than the gain from overtime.

In Chapter 4 we argued that a remuneration scheme could be structured in order to attract workers with a particular demand for absence, and to avoid the moral hazard that arises once a contract with sick pay is signed. In addition, we argued that it was better if firms were left to determine their own sick pay scheme: first, because of the advantage that they have in monitoring; and, second, because the optimal design of sick pay scheme depends on job-specific factors that are hard for third parties to measure.

An optimal sick pay arrangement, we argued, is experience-rated, so that its terms depend on the claims made on it by each worker individually. The main reason this is helpful is that enables control of absence by way of fixed incentives. It does this in two ways. In the first place, it has a *selection* role. So long as the structure of the experience rating is set up correctly, only workers who believe that they are able to abide by its terms will find it worthwhile to take the job in the first place. Second, it encourages *truth-telling*. Once again, with the proviso that the structure must be well designed, workers should not take absences in excess of whatever rate has been built in to the system design.

One design that is feasible in the United States but not in the United Kingdom (or most of the rest of Europe) provides 100 per cent replacement for a limited period of time, after which no replacement is available. This arrangement is commonly called paid sick leave. According to the argument of Chapter 4, the effectiveness of the scheme in keeping absence within acceptable bounds relies on the period over which sick pay is payable, which should be set having regard to two things: the degree of complementarity in the job, and an allowance that falls as a contract proceeds.

Finally, a note on the recent development of very short, but regular and contracted, hours of work. This development is known as 'slivers of time' in Britain.[12] Whatever its other virtues may be, this approach can clearly be seen as a defence against absenteeism, since a worker who is employed only on Thursday afternoons can be absent only on Thursday afternoon. However, the problems of managing complementary workers and equipment with very short time contracts are likely to be substantial, and will undoubtedly be an important limiting factor in the use of this approach.

We observed earlier that there has been a recent trend in the United States to merge vacation time with sick leave to create 'personal time off'. Under such schemes, workers are given a total allowance of paid days, which they can use either as vacation or as sick days. A key feature of optimal paid sick leave is that firms can control their absence costs by setting the terms of the scheme. This ensures the adherence of workers to the absence rate that is acceptable to the firm. Allowing workers to substitute vacation time for sick leave, and vice versa, has the effect of blunting that control, and may therefore not be as positive a move as it appears. However, administrative costs and equity considerations may be important in determining the shape of attendance policies, and it may be that the trade-off between these costs and the loss of control implied by personal time off justifies the introduction of the latter. This can be confirmed only by an accurate calculation of costs, though.

The number of firms that structure sick pay in an optimal way is probably zero. There are three main barriers: state regulation; the expense of separate assessment of the absence costs associated with different jobs; and the difficulty of explaining to workers why one group is eligible for more generous sick pay than another. The last of these is perhaps less serious than it may seem. Examples of differential treatment abound, although they tend to be based on observable characteristics of workers, such as length of service, childcare responsibilities and blue-collar and white-collar status. Buzzard and Shaw's classic account of the introduction of sick pay into British ordnance factories (1952) is given great depth by the presence of two groups of workers: those who were paid a time rate only, and those whose pay was dominated by piece rates. Since the latter group's piece rate earnings were regarded as a 'bonus', they were not subject to

---

[12] See, for instance, www.slivers.com and www.guardian.co.uk/politics/2010/nov/ 14/welfare-reform-working-slivers-of-time.

replacement under the terms of the sick pay scheme, and overall replacement rates for this groups were lower than for the time-rate workers. Unequal treatment is a common feature of sick pay arrangements, but the idea of complementarity would probably be hard to introduce into contract negotiations, let alone contracts. It may well be, though, that some of the existing examples of different treatment constitute a way of distinguishing jobs with differing complementarity characteristics.

The assessment of the costs of absence associated with different jobs is something that conscientious managers probably do already. Official advice in Britain certainly suggests that they consider this. The element in this book that may be a novelty is the idea of complementarity, which determines how much of the output of workers other than those who are themselves absent is lost when an absence occurs. As the discussion in Chapter 4 makes clear, this loss is determined largely by the extent to which people work together in teams and by the extent to which inventories of semi-finished goods are held while production proceeds. Ordering jobs according to the absence costs they are likely to create is, therefore, a matter of assessing these two factors. Actually measuring the sizes of those costs is more difficult, and would almost certainly require some rather sophisticated data analysis.

Finally, we come to the question of state regulation. We discuss the implications of our ideas for state policy in the following chapter. In many economies, HR managers are severely limited in the extent to which they can create incentives in the remuneration system, since many governments control what can be done both in the structure and the actual rates of sick pay provided. British managers are comparatively unfettered, but they still have to abide by the regulations on statutory sick pay, which prevents them, for instance, from introducing paid sick leave designed according to the prescription above. Experience rating can be created in other ways, though. The firm that we studied in Barmby, Orme and Treble (1991) and subsequent papers varied the replacement rate in a similar way, but instead of withdrawing sick pay altogether for workers who made the largest claims on the system, they reduced it to the statutory minimum rate. US firms are probably in the best position to structure incentives in the way we propose here, since the right to sick leave is enshrined in federal law. Many firms do provide paid sick leave as well, but we doubt if the usual calculation of how much sick leave should be remunerated is often done according to the principles that we describe here.

Our evidence from France suggests that managers there actually control absence rather well, within the system that exists in that country. If this is also true in other countries (and we have no reason to suppose that it is not) then further progress in reducing the costs of absence to firms can be made only by liberalisation of the regulation of sick pay and job protection – a task that can be undertaken only by states. The next chapter considers their role in the markets for absence and sick pay.

Summary

Setting optimal absence rates as targets for firm performance is a more subtle problem than official advice suggests. Enforcement of whatever rates are set is very important. Incentive schemes need to be designed with care, but can be very effective in controlling absence behaviour.

9 | *Policy implications for states*

What should governments do about worker absence and sick pay? Governments have two roles to play, since they are employers themselves as well as being able to regulate. The last chapter dealt with the interests of employers generally, and applies equally to governments in their role as employers. This chapter deals with the regulatory role.

Why should governments intervene?

The discussion is guided by the idea, advanced in Chapter 4, that there is no obvious economic reason for government intervention in this market, which raises the question of what purpose the widespread adoption of state-regulated and -administered sick pay serves, and what its costs might be. Such schemes are almost universal in European economies. An important exception is the United Kingdom, where state intervention is minimal. At present, there is no sign of any widespread dissatisfaction with the sick pay that employers provide. In North America, too, there is little intervention, but there is considerable dissatisfaction with the system as it is, with a vocal movement for reform enjoying some success in encouraging city governments (notably that of San Francisco) to enact local legislation requiring employers to provide sick pay. On the other hand, the sick pay arrangements in place in Sweden have been the subject of a long and extensive debate on reform, with a number of reforms having being made in recent years.

The argument of Chapter 4 was that, although the market for insurance against loss of income due to sickness is an insurance market just like any other, there are special reasons for supposing that employers themselves have an advantage in bundling up this insurance with the rest of the job package. In particular, unlike third parties, they have an interest in monitoring and controlling claims. It is also cheaper for an employer actually to undertake monitoring and control roles. Monitoring involves collecting and analysing data on absence, and control is exerted by the operation of disciplinary procedures or of an incentive scheme of some kind.

The fact that firms are well placed both to understand and to influence their own workers' absence suggests that any third party, be it a commercial insurer or a government agency, would find it hard to provide a better service to the workers of any particular firm than the firm itself.

The Great Divide

How do modern economies provide this insurance? There are three possible providers: governments, employing firms and workers themselves. Practice varies widely both between and within economies. In order to tease out the various dimensions in which these variations occur, we begin with what we regard as the Great Divide between North America,[1] where the dominant model is private provision, and Europe, where state regulation, and often provision, are used. Ever since Bismarck's social reforms in late nineteenth-century Germany, European economies have adopted an insurance model in which premiums are paid into a general fund, and then disbursed when claims are made upon it by qualifying workers.[2] The early twentieth century saw a debate in the United States as to whether similar arrangements should be adopted there, which proponents of the European-style government-mandated insurance model lost to those who favoured private provision. The debate has been chronicled by Murray (2007), who summarises his book as follows:

This book … proposes that the sickness insurance funds that workers and their employers organized were stable and capable institutions. [. . .] Industrial sickness funds provided the service that workers most desired – paid sick leave – and skimped on provision of medical care that at best was ineffective and at worst was a cover for coercing sick workers to return to their posts prematurely. It was the success, not the incompetence, of the sickness funds that led to the failure of Progressive reform efforts.

[1] The North American model applies in Australia as well: see www.actu.asn.au/ public/library/linentideasaug1995.html.
[2] Within Europe, a further distinction is made between the Bismarck and Beveridge systems. These are both insurance-based, but have different financing models. See CESifo (2008).

On both sides of the Atlantic, the schemes that are the basis of current arrangements (except perhaps in Britain) were put in place as the result of hard-won political debates. The Great Divide is therefore not the result of historical accident, but of deliberate and sometimes hotly contested choices. The fact that the schemes have remained controversial bears witness to the nicety of the issues that are involved in their design. The issues boil down to two: coverage and the usual bugbears of insurance – adverse selection and moral hazard. Much of the recent US debate has been driven by the large proportion of workers who apparently are not covered, while much of the Swedish debate has been encouraged by the persistently high rates of absence in the Swedish economy. Agell (1996) puts the case succinctly:

In the imperfect world of human beings, it is hard to see how a social insurer can manage without a stick which discourages misuse. A suggestive example is the Swedish system of sickness insurance. Since the early 1960s it became increasingly generous. According to the rules in place by the end of the 1980s, employees were entitled to a 90% compensation level from the first day of reporting sick. Due to supplementary insurance agreements in the labour market, however, many employees had a compensation level of 100%. For the first seven days of sickness leave, a physician's certificate was not required. If individuals ever respond to economic incentives, work absenteeism ought to be widespread in Sweden.

Calls for wider coverage in the United States have been heeded to some extent. Indeed, five states operate European-style insurance-based arrangements. Murray's (2007) account finishes around the beginning of World War II, during which Rhode Island adopted a state temporary disability insurance scheme. Rhode Island's lead was followed after the war by New York state, New Jersey, California and Hawaii. In addition, workers in the US railroad industry are covered by a federal scheme. Some idea of the relative sizes of these can be gained from table Bf864–874 in the second volume of Carter *et al.* (2006). In 1994 $19 billion was paid to private sector workers, in the forms of paid sick leave ($14 billion) or cash sickness insurance ($5 billion). Approximately a half of the insurance-based payments came from publicly operated sources, the other half being private insurance provided by employing firms or self-insurance by workers. Paid sick leave for government workers amounted to about $14 billion. More recent statistics do not seem to be publicly available.

On both sides of the Great Divide, the arrangements in place have been the subject of almost continual modification and development, and systems are being actively debated and redesigned, particularly in the United States, Sweden and Germany. In North America, systems are largely, but not entirely, unregulated. In the United States, state intervention takes several forms. First, at the federal level, the Family and Medical Leave Act of 1993 (FMLA)[3] provides that qualifying employees must be allowed up to twelve weeks of leave annually. Second, states are employers themselves and can make provision that can influence private sector behaviour, to the extent that the two sectors compete in the same labour markets. Third, some states, at least one city and the railroad industry have enacted European-style insurance-based sick pay arrangements.

The main force of the FMLA is to make it illegal for an employer to fire or demote an employee because they have taken leave. It is a job protection measure, but it has created a legal background against which employees are entitled to take days off.[4] Two consequences arise. (1) Employers are not required to pay workers while they take their sick days, but many do, thus providing a form of insurance against loss of income. The idea of sick leave has therefore led to a particular structure for such insurance, in which income replacement is at 100 per cent until the sick leave entitlement is exhausted, when it drops to zero. (2) Entitlements are valuable, and, if they are not exercised by their owners, may be tradable.

This last fact explains why certain recent developments in US sick leave have occurred. The legal entitlement to a specified number of sick days each year has created a limited market in these days. Thus there are institutional arrangements in place in most states that enable workers to pay unused sick days into a 'sick leave bank'. The bank can give, or lend, these sick days to other workers who may have exhausted their sick day entitlement. Some workers can also borrow against future entitlements. The extent to which sick days are the subject of trades outside these formal banking arrangements does not seem to have been studied, although they can certainly attract a cash value. Many employers are prepared to cash in unused sick pay

---

[3] Current information about the FMLA can be found at http://www.dol.gov/esa/whd/fmla and is provided by Guerin and England (2007).

[4] Of course, many employers, particularly in the public sector, granted this entitlement before the FMLA passed into law.

on retirement. It is probably only a matter of time before other cash arrangements emerge, and perhaps even the use of an interest rate on loans of sick days.

On the European side of the Great Divide there is another bewildering array of interventions, ranging from an almost complete lack of state control in Britain to almost total state-administered insurance coverage in Sweden. We give three examples, chosen to enable the main dimensions of variation in these arrangements to be understood.

(1) The British state sick pay scheme was initiated in the 1940s as part of the National Insurance system and Great Britain's welfare state. By the middle of the 1980s the system had become extremely complex, but since then it has been gradually dismantled.[5] The remaining vestige of the scheme is a system of statutory sick pay that is now purely regulatory in nature. SSP provisions apply to anyone who has a contract of service with an employer and who is unable to work because of sickness for at least four days in a row. At £72.55 per week,[6] SSP is equivalent to about one-third of the national adult minimum wage;[7] slightly less than 15 per cent of the median earnings of full-time male employees; or slightly more than 18 per cent of the corresponding statistic for women.[8] Not surprisingly, the company sick pay offered by many firms to their employees often exceeds the statutory minimum. Furthermore, many British firms have proved to be inventive in developing and implementing sick pay arrangements intended to manage the moral hazard arising in the provision of sick pay.

(2) France has a system of sick pay regulated by laws that specify a structure of replacement rates, called the régime général. These are 0 per cent for the first three days of a spell, 50 per cent for the next eight days and 90 per cent until the total spell length exceeds some

---

[5] We have been unable to track down any carefully researched history of the development of sick pay in Britain. Even Timmins' (2001) seemingly exhaustive account of the development of the welfare state in Britain has very little to say about it. Dilnot, Kay and Morris (1984) describe the system as it was in the early 1980s and conclude (100): 'This dreadful mess is a tribute to the havoc which politicians' over-zealous response to interest group pressures can create.' Russell (1991) includes a partial, but unsystematic, account of policy developments.

[6] April 2007 revision.

[7] October 2007 revision.

[8] These deliberately vague statements are based on earnings distributions reported in the 2006 Annual Survey of Hours and Earnings, updated for subsequent earnings growth using http://www.statistics.gov.uk/cci/nugget.asp?id=285.

length between thirty and ninety days according to the worker's tenure in the job. The rate then drops again to 50 per cent for a further period of the same length, unless the worker has responsibility for the care of children, in which case the rate is enhanced. A spell of absence longer than the ninety to 180 days provided for by the sick pay scheme triggers a reconsideration of the worker's contract. Many firms replace income at rates greater than the mandatory minimums, but these supplementary schemes tend to retain the structure of the mandatory scheme (Lanfranchi and Treble, 2010, give details). What is surprising about the French scheme is that its already quite generous mandated replacement rates are exceeded by a large proportion of the firms that are subject to it. Calculations based on a 1997 French establishment survey suggest that 77 per cent of such firms have some scheme supplementary to the régime générale. Some of these are, inevitably, more ambitious than others. A measure of generosity has been calculated and is reported by Lanfranchi and Treble (2010).

(3) Sweden currently has the most elaborate and generous system of state-administered sick pay in Europe.[9] It is so extensive that some economists have suggested that it is implicated in the low rates of unemployment that Sweden enjoyed during the 1980s and 1990s.[10] The argument is that the scheme leads to rates of absence so high that it acts as a kind of job-sharing scheme, with firms hiring additional workers in an effort to manage their high absenteeism. Thoursie (2004) describes the system as a

> mandatory and government-financed sickness insurance system that covers all employed and self-employed. The insurance provides compensation for forgone labour earnings to individuals who due to illness

---

[9] This statement is correct unless Russia is counted as part of Europe. Mikhalev (1996) describes the Russian system of sick pay as follows: 'Sick pay is available to every employee without any contribution or previous work conditions. The level of benefit is equal to 100% of the individual's previous wage for employees with eight or more years of service, to parents of three or more children, to war veterans and to Chernobyl victims; 80% for individuals with five to eight years of service and 60% for those with less than five years of service. Sick pay is generally provided until recovery unless an invalidity pension is granted. An individual caring for a sick family member may also be eligible for a benefit. It is of the same level as sick pay, though the duration is limited to three days if caring for an adult and to 14 days if caring for a child.'

[10] Richard Freeman, personal communication.

have a temporary reduced work capacity. In 2003, the compensation rate which is received from the second day of absenteeism was 80% up to a cap of 7.5 times the 'basic amount' (about SEK 24,000 or USD 3000 a month). In addition to this public system, a supplementary sickness benefit of 10% for certain sick spells (mostly longer) is provided as a result of negotiations between the employers and trade unions. These agreements cover in principle all employers in Sweden. A doctor's certificate is required from the eighth day absent from work. Even if the local insurance office is responsible for controlling potential abuse, it is in practice very difficult to perform an investigation of the individual's work capacity and the monitoring is very light for the first seven days. The system has been reformed a great number of times. For example, until December 1987 there was one waiting day which was reintroduced in 1993. From 1974 to 1991, the compensation rate from the government-financed system was 90% but lowered in 1991 to 65% during the first three days.

These arrangements bear the hallmarks of ordinary insurance contracts, and include many of the features that can be adopted to make them work, such as co-insurance (*jours de carence* or waiting days) and monitoring (or, in Sweden's case, the lack of it). Some of them also allow for screening (France's use of tenure as a determinant of replacement rates might be interpreted this way.)

The design of sick pay and sick leave schemes

The model described in Chapter 4 provides an explanation as to why firms can provide this insurance better than third-party insurance companies or the state. It also suggests a structure for the insurance contract, which avoids both adverse selection and moral hazard. Since a system designed along the lines analysed in Chapter 4 is available, there seems to be no good reason why a government would get involved in this market at all, except perhaps to enforce (or encourage the adoption of) a system that does the trick. The generally non-invasive policies adopted by US and British governments would seem to be justified, and recent attempts in the United States to widen the scope of state-sponsored sick pay along European lines are probably mistaken.

However, the US and UK governments both intervene in this market in ways that influence the form that sick pay arrangements take.

Because of the FMLA, which requires sick leave provision (but not necessarily paid sick leave), most US sick pay is structured as paid sick leave. This structure is the same as the structure derived theoretically by Radner (1981) and the subsequent literature (see Chapter 4). Whether or not the thresholds and triggers are set optimally is a question that has not been investigated. The theory described in Chapter 2 proposes that it is job rather than firm characteristics that should determine the number of days of paid sick leave, which suggests that sick pay provision should vary between jobs within a single firm, as well as between firms. The FMLA's minimum sick leave provision imposes no constraint on the extent to which paid sick leave can be varied between either jobs or firms, since there is no reason why some days of the mandatory sick pay should be paid while others remain unpaid.

Another recent US development is the idea of sick leave as a tradable commodity, which has given rise to sick leave banks and other institutions.[11] It might seem strange for an economist to object to the creation of a market where one has not previously existed. The economist's usual complaint is that the world doesn't work well because there are missing markets. The issue here, though, is that the working of the labour market may be adversely affected by the tradability of sick leave. One of the functions of the sick leave allowance in the model is to signal to workers what an acceptable rate of absence is. Another is to eliminate moral hazard. Both these functions can be jeopardised if sick leave is traded.

Turning to Europe, it is clear that state provision or regulation of sick pay that constrains firms to make uniform provision is inefficient. This is a consequence of the theoretical argument, and is also suggested by the voluntary provision by firms in Britain and France (and even Sweden) of sickness insurance over and above state-mandated provision. The problem is that these constraints prevent firms from signalling to the market, by their offers of sick pay, what their acceptable absence rate is. This is true even in the British system, in which much flexibility is allowed, but the flexibility to drop replacement rates to zero after a period of 100 per cent replacement is not available.

---

[11] Sick leave banks are now making an appearance in British organisations in which sick leave (rather than sick pay) is provided. See, for instance, www.eastdorsetdc.gov.uk/democracy/docstore/0506/050606165141-3e78226f-9aa3-401e-98ae-3f8c8434738d.pdf.

However, it is interesting to note that some British firms have adopted experience rating as a method of absence control. A notable example is the firm studied by Barmby, Orme and Treble (1991), in which, each year end, the absence for the previous two years forms the basis for the calculation of the following year's sick pay replacement rate.

Finally, the idea that there exists an optimal scheme has been developed in a largely static context, and it assumes that no externalities arise in each worker's contract with their employer. That absence is associated with macroeconomic fluctuations has been claimed by several commentators,[12] and there exists a mechanism in the model described here by which this might come about. If the labour market tightens, the average match between workers and jobs is likely to worsen, since the cost of non-optimal absence rates will become lower relative to the cost of moving jobs. Of course, the opposite will occur as the labour market becomes less tight. The issue of externalities is difficult to assess. HR professionals frequently express their belief in peer group pressure as a means of absence control, and some of them try to reinforce this kind of mechanism with group incentive schemes. Issues such as fairness and equity are probably important considerations when attendance control policies are being negotiated. These, and the cost of administration, probably account for the fact that sick pay arrangements are usually uniform across firms, rather than being job-specific, as the efficient arrangements described above suggest they should be. The job of constructing a model in which workers are members of three social groups (firm, household and work group) rather than just two, as here, seems daunting, and we can only suggest that it be the subject of later research.

The arguments here and in Chapter 4 suggest to us that the role of the state in the provision of insurance against loss of income due to sickness should be limited. The main reason for supposing that state provision is inefficient is that state agencies do not have the detailed information about the costs and control of absence that firms have. This does not mean that the state should have no role at all. It seems that the reluctance of some firms to provide sick pay was a major motivation behind the current arrangements both in the

---

[12] The well-known Shapiro–Stiglitz (1984) shirking argument can be interpreted as referring to absenteeism. For a search equilibrium approach to absenteeism, see Engström and Holmlund (2007).

United States and in Europe, so that some encouragement to do so would be a welcome intervention. Nonetheless, that intervention should be limited to the state providing well-structured sick pay provision to its own employees, and possibly decreeing that all firms should provide experience-rated sick pay (or, equivalently, paid sick leave) as part of their employment packages.

Summary

Since experience-rated sick pay schemes (such as paid sick leave) can be designed in such a way as to avoid moral hazard and adverse selection, state intervention has little role to play in sick pay markets, other than to enable the implementation of such schemes.

10 | *Conclusion*

In this book, we treat absenteeism as a labour market phenomenon. Work contracts may or may not specify hours of work. If they do, absenteeism may arise. It will arise if workers' desired hours are fewer than (or possibly just different from) the hours specified in their contract. There are at least two ways in which such a circumstance might arise: it may be that workers sign contracts that they do not mean to keep; or it may be that their desired hours vary from time to time in some unpredictable fashion. In the latter view, contracts are signed with the intention that they be kept to, unless circumstances imply low desired hours.

The extant literature is not very clear as to which of these models is being used. Implicitly, the hedonic pricing model adopted by Allen and used by him to great effect takes the latter view. It is contrary to the idea of equilibrium in an hedonic pricing model for workers to want to sign a contract that does not reflect their desired hours. A better deal can be obtained by not doing so. Absenteeism in this model is part of the deal. Workers demand, and employers are prepared to supply, some flexibility in the contract, which will enable workers to be absent from time to time. How can this flexibility be modelled?

Consistency can be achieved only by supposing that the deviations of desired from contractual hours are the result of random variation in desired hours. If variation were predictable then it would be advantageous to build it into the contract, so that it need not give rise to contractual violations. In some occupations, random variation can be accommodated by allowing flexibility in work schedules so as to permit employees to match their changing desired hours to the demands of their employers. In these arrangements, accounts are kept of the hours attended, and employees are expected to bring their accounts into balance at regular intervals (usually weekly). Even these arrangements will not eliminate absenteeism completely though. If a random shock is experienced that is larger than can be accommodated within a week, contractual violations can still occur.

The extent to which employers are able to tolerate the consequent uncertainty in their operations depends, in turn, on how robust their production techniques are to variation in inputs. The substitutability of labour for labour and of labour for capital is then important, and these characteristics depend on the nature of the production technology and work organisation. Technologies and modes of organisation that encourage complementarity between inputs make absence more expensive for employers.

This view of absenteeism as an outcome of an equilibrium in an economy in which labour supply is subject to random shocks contrasts sharply with the alternative, which requires us to believe in persistent errors in bargains that are struck. In this view, employers and employees consistently strike bargains in which workers agree to supply an amount of labour that they, and their employers, know will not be forthcoming. In what Dunn and Youngblood (1986) describe as a 'non-optimal equilibrium', workers seek to deviate from the number of hours for which they have signed up. Their paper attempts to demonstrate that workers' marginal rates of substitution at their desired hours are different from those implied by the wage rates they have accepted. This suggests that absence is somehow premeditated, and that illness has no part in it. Their idea could be rejected on these grounds alone, but there are other reasons to object to it. Not only is the idea of an equilibrium in which one of the agents is not optimising a strange one, but, if absence were really always the result of a calculus of this kind, it could always be unmasked by employers as such, and used as evidence for disciplinary action. The reason is that in the Dunn–Youngblood model there is no opportunity for dissembling on the part of workers. If they are absent, they are absent because they intend to be absent. It is part of their plan. There is no veil behind which they can conceal their malfeasance. Any employer for whom absence is costly would therefore have good reason to object, and, equally importantly, the evidence to make their objection credible.

Things are different in the random utility model. Here both parties understand that absence will occur occasionally for most workers. Indeed, it is not unusual for employers to provide insurance for their employees against the risk of income loss from absence. Modelling the market for this insurance jointly with the market for absence is a novel feature of this book, which is desirable for two reasons. First, it is a fact that free market provision of sick pay occurs, even in heavily regulated economies. This is a curiosity that invites attempts to explain it. Second, the model of the absence market developed in Chapters 2 and 3 is incomplete, in that it models a market for jobs, each of which is a package of wages and an absenteeism probability. The question arises as to how a probability can be enforced in a contract. One answer to this question is developed in the optimal insurance literature. Chapter 4 exploits this idea of experience rating as a way of ameliorating the problem of moral hazard in this market. Allied with the assignment of workers to jobs generated by the Coles–Treble model, the classic problems of insurance markets can both be solved.

In the empirical work inspired by these ideas we have tried to do two things: first, to discover what credibility rests with the view of the world based on random utility; and, second, to develop empirical models that will aid in the understanding of the structure of absence demand. Neither task can be regarded as complete. Coles *et al.* (2007) take care over identification in their work, but the data set that they used was far from perfect, and required the use of several econometric tricks that may not convince everyone. It also referred only to France, and what is true of France may not be true of other economies.

Even more incomplete is our development of the random utility model as a vehicle for the study of absence demand. The theory outlined in Chapter 3 suggests several features that are borne out by our empirical studies. Especially striking is Barmby, Orme and Treble's (1995) finding that financial incentives impact more heavily on the ends of absence spells than on their beginnings. Although their econometric technique is not directly based on the theory described by Treble (2009b), the empirical finding is echoed strongly in the predictions generated by his theoretical model.

There are many opportunities for further work using the approach that we describe here. One of the main barriers to progress is the availability of suitable data. Of course, much useful information exists. Most, if not all, firms maintain a database with detailed records of absence and pay. If, in addition, they operate an experience-rated sick pay scheme, there will also be endogenous variation in the cost of absence to individual workers. We have shown how the bias arising from the endogeneity can be handled using instrumental variable techniques. Potentially, then, any firm that operates an experience-rated sick pay scheme of some kind (including firms that offer paid sick leave) is a source of data that can be used to study absence demand.

Other characteristics of the market are harder to study. Using survey data in which workers have different employers is problematic, because of the identification problem. Conflating the responses of workers with different employers almost certainly leads to misleading estimates. We have long had an ambition to study absence markets using labour force survey data from a range of different economies. This would enable us, for instance, to get a handle on the impact of different regulatory regimes; the effect of differences in industrial and occupational structures; and the impact of gender ratios on absence rates. Unfortunately, although the labour force surveys are supposedly designed in such a way as to enable just such investigations, proposals to use the individual data in international comparisons create difficulties for national statistical agencies. Apparently, there are attempts under way to resolve these problems, but, until they are resolved, this approach will have to remain as a proposal. In the meantime, this gap is being partially filled by the studies based on the European Working Conditions Surveys.

We hope that the work outlined in this book will prove useful to future researchers. There is certainly much still to be done, and we believe that adopting the models that we describe here will enable faster and greater progress with the understanding of the markets for absenteeism and sick pay than alternative approaches have yielded.

References

Agell, J. (1996): 'Why Sweden's welfare state needed reform', *Economic Journal*, 106, 1760–71.

Allen, R. G. D. (1938): *Mathematical Analysis for Economists*, London: Macmillan.

Allen, S. G. (1981a): 'An empirical model of work attendance', *Review of Economics and Statistics*, 63(1), 77–87.

(1981b): 'Compensation, safety, and absenteeism: evidence from the paper industry', *Industrial and Labor Relations Review*, 34(2), 207–18.

(1983): 'How much does absenteeism cost?', *Journal of Human Resources*, 18(3), 379–93.

(1984): 'Trade unions, absenteeism and exit-voice', *Industrial and Labor Relations Review*, 37(2), 331–45.

Aoki, M. (1988): *Information, Incentives, and Bargaining in the Japanese Economy*, Cambridge University Press.

Arai, M., and P. S. Thoursie (2005): 'Incentives and selection in cyclical absenteeism', *Labour Economics*, 12(2), 269–80.

Audas, R., T. Barmby and J. G. Treble (2004): 'Luck, effort and reward in an organizational hierarchy', *Journal of Labor Economics*, 22(2), 379–95.

Barmby, T. (2002): 'Worker absenteeism: a discrete hazard model with bivariate heterogeneity', *Labour Economics*, 9(4), 469–76.

Barmby, T., C. Bojke and J. G. Treble (1997): 'Worker absenteeism: a note on the effect of contract structure', *Australian Journal of Labour Economics*, 1(2), 97–102.

Barmby, T., M. G. Ercolani and J. G. Treble (1999): 'Sickness absence in Great Britain: new quarterly and annual series from the GHS and LFS 1971–1997', *Labour Market Trends*, 107(8), 405–15.

(2002): 'Sickness absence: an international comparison', *Economic Journal*, 112, F315–F331.

(2004): 'Sickness absence in the UK 1984–2002', *Swedish Economic Policy Review*, 11(1), 65–88.

Barmby, T., and M. Larguem (2009): 'Coughs and sneezes spread diseases: a study of infectious illness and absence', *Journal of Health Economics*, 28(5), 1012–17.

Barmby, T., M. A. Nolan and R. Winkelmann (2001): 'Contracted workdays and absence', *Manchester School*, 69(3), 269–75.

Barmby, T., C. Orme and J. G. Treble (1991): 'Worker absenteeism: an analysis using microdata', *Economic Journal*, 101, 214–29.

(1995): 'Worker absence histories: a panel data study', *Labour Economics*, 2(1), 53–65.

Barmby, T., J. Sessions and J. G. Treble (1994): 'Absenteeism, efficiency wages and shirking', *Scandinavian Journal of Economics*, 96(4), 561–6.

Barmby, T., and S. Sibly (2004): 'Analysing absence behaviour using event history models', *Managerial and Decision Economics*, 25(3), 141–5.

Barmby, T., and G. Stephan (2000): 'Worker absenteeism: why firm size may matter', *Manchester School*, 68(5), 568–77.

Barmby, T., and J. G. Treble (1991): 'An analysis of the incidence of absence from work', *Labour Economics and Productivity*, 3(2), 163–7.

Barzel, Y. (1973): 'The determination of daily hours and wages', *Quarterly Journal of Economics*, 87(2), 220–38.

Becker, G. (1965): 'A theory of the allocation of time', *Economic Journal*, 75, 493–517.

(1993): *A Treatise on the Family*, enlarged edn., Cambridge, MA: Harvard University Press.

Benge, E. J. (1923): 'The effect of prohibition on industry from the viewpoint of an employment manager', *Annals of the American Academy of Political and Social Science*, 109(1), 110–20.

Bishop, E. (2006): *The Sick Day Handbook*, San Francisico: Conari Press.

Bliksvær, T., and A. Helliesen (1997): 'Sickness absence: a study of 11 LES countries', working paper, NOVA – Norwegian Social Research Institute, Oslo.

Blundell, R., M. Brewer and M. Francesconi (2008): 'Job changes and hours changes: understanding the path of labor supply adjustment', *Journal of Labor Economics*, 26(3), 421–53.

Bradley, S., C. Green and G. Leeves (2007): 'Employment protection, threat and incentive effects on worker effort', Working Paper no. 2007/026, Lancaster University Management School.

Brown, S. (1999): 'Worker absenteeism and overtime bans', *Applied Economics*, 31(2), 65–74.

Bryson, B. (2007): *Shakespeare*, New York: HarperCollins.

Butler, R. J., B. D. Gardner and H. H. Gardner (1998): 'More than cost shifting: moral hazard lowers productivity', *Journal of Risk and Insurance*, 65(4), 671–88.

Buzzard, R. B. (1954): 'Attendance and absence in industry: the nature of the evidence', *British Journal of Sociology*, 5(3), 238–52.

Buzzard, R. B., and W. J. Shaw (1952): 'An analysis of absence under a scheme of paid sick leave', *British Journal of Industrial Medicine*, 9(4), 282–95.

Cahuc, P., and A. Zylberberg (2001): *Labor Economics*, Cambridge, MA: MIT Press.

Camerer, C., L. Babcock, G. Loewenstein and R. Thaler (1997): 'Labor supply of New York City cabdrivers: one day at a time', *Quarterly Journal of Economics*, 112(2), 407–41.

Carter, S. B., S. S. Gartner, M. R. Haines, A. L. Olmstead, R. Sutch and G. Wright (2006): *Historical Statistics of the United States*, millennial edn., Cambridge University Press.

CESifo (2008): 'Bismarck versus Beveridge: social insurance systems in Europe', in CESifo, *DICE [Database for Institutional Comparisons in Europe] Report no. 4/2008*, Munich: CESifo, 69–71.

Chadwick-Jones, J. K. (1981): 'Renegotiating absence levels', *Journal of Occupational Behaviour*, 2(4), 255–66.

Chatterji, M., and C. Tilley (2002): 'Sickness, absenteeism, presenteeism, and sick pay', *Oxford Economic Papers*, 54(4), 669–87.

 (2003): 'Theoretical approaches to managing sickness absenteeism', Working Paper no. 143, Department of Economic Studies, University of Dundee.

Chemin, M., and E. Wasmer (2009): 'Using Alsace– Moselle local laws to build a difference-in-differences estimation strategy of the employment effects of the 35-hour workweek regulation in France', *Journal of Labor Economics*, 27(4), 487–524.

Coles, M. G., and J. G. Treble (1993): 'The price of worker reliability', *Economics Letters*, 41(2), 149–55.

 (1996): 'Calculating the cost of worker reliability', *Labour Economics*, 3(2), 169–88.

Coles, M. G., J. Lanfranchi, A. Skalli and J. G. Treble (2007): 'Pay, technology and the cost of absence', *Economic Inquiry*, 45(2), 268–85.

Connolly, M. (2008): 'Here comes the rain again: weather and the intertemporal substitution of leisure', *Journal of Labor Economics*, 26(1), 73–100.

Cooper, R., and B. Hayes (1987): 'Multi-period insurance contracts', *International Journal of Industrial Organization*, 5(2), 211–31.

Cox, J., and R. L. Oaxaca (1999): 'Can supply and demand parameters be recovered from data generated by market institutions?', *Journal of Business and Economic Statistics*, 17(3), 285–97.

Deardorff, A. V., and F. P. Shafford (1976): 'Compensation of cooperating factors', *Econometrica*, 44(4), 671–84.

Delgado, M. A., and T. J. Kniesner (1997): 'Count data models with variance of unknown form: an application to a hedonic model of works absenteeism', *Review of Economics and Statistics*, **79**(1), 41–9.

Denoeud, L., C. Turbelin, S. Ansart, A. -J. Valleron, A. Flahault and F. Carrat (2007): 'Predicting pneumonia and influenza mortality from morbidity data' *PLoS ONE*, **2**(5), e464.

Dilnot, A. J., J. Kay and C. Morris (1984): *The Reform of Social Security*, Oxford University Press.

Dionne, G., and B. Dostie (2007): 'New evidence on the determinants of absenteeism using employer–employee data', *Industrial and Labor Relations Review*, **61**(1), 108–20.

Dionne, G., and P. Lasserre (1985): 'Adverse selection, repeated insurance contracts and announcement strategy', *Review of Economic Studies*, **52** (4), 719–23.

(1987): 'Adverse selection and finite-horizon insurance contracts', *European Economic Review*, **31**(4), 843–61.

Doherty N. A. (1979): 'National Insurance and absence from work', *Economic Journal*, **89**, 50–65.

Douglas, P. H. (1919): 'Absenteeism in labor', *Political Science Quarterly*, **34**(4), 591–608.

Dunn, L. F. (1990): 'An empirical study of labor market equilibrium under working hours constraints', *Review of Economics and Statistics*, **72**(2), 250–58.

Dunn, L. F., and S. A. Youngblood (1986): 'Absenteeism as a mechanism for approaching an optimal labor market equilibrium: an empirical study', *Review of Economics and Statistics*, **68**(4), 668–74.

Ehrenberg, R. G., R. A. Ehrenberg, D. I. Rees and E. L. Ehrenberg (1991) 'School district leave policies, teacher absenteeism, and student achievement', *Journal of Human Resources*, **26**(1), 72–105.

Ekeland, I., J. J. Heckman and L. Nesheim (2004): 'Identification and estimation of hedonic models', *Journal of Political Economy*, **112**(1, part 2), S60–S109.

Engellandt, A., and R. Riphahn (2005): 'Temporary contracts and employee effort', *Labour Economics*, **12**(3), 281–99.

Engström, P., and B. Holmlund (2007): 'Worker absenteeism in search equilibrium', *Scandinavian Journal of Economics*, **109**(3), 439–67.

Evans, A., and M. Walters (2002): *From Absence to Attendance* (2nd edn.), London: CIPD.

Fahr, R., and B. Frick (2007): 'On the inverse relationship between unemployment and absenteeism: evidence from natural experiments and worker heterogeneity', Discussion Paper no. 3171, Institute for the Study of Labor (Institut zur Zukunft des Arbeit), Bonn.

Farber, H. S. (2005): 'Is tomorrow another day? The labor supply of New York City cabdrivers', *Journal of Political Economy*, 113(1), 46–82.

Fehr, E., and L. Goette (2007): 'Do workers work more if wages are high? Evidence from a randomised field experiment', *American Economic Review*, 97(1), 298–317.

Frick, B., and M. A. Malo (2008): 'Labor market institutions and individual absenteeism in the European Union: the relative importance of sickness benefit systems and employment protection legislation', *Industrial Relations*, 4(4), 505–29.

Gardiner, R. C. (1992): 'Tracking and controlling absenteeism', *Public Productivity and Management Review*, 15(3), 289–307.

Gimeno, D., F. G. Benavides, J. Benach and B. C. Amick (2004): 'Distribution of sickness absence in the European Union countries', *Occupational and Environmental Medicine*, 61(10), 867–9.

Guerin, L., and D. C. England (2007): *The Essential Guide to Family and Medical Leave*, New York: Nolo.

Hall, R. E., and D. M. Lilien (1979): 'Efficient wage bargains under uncertain supply and demand', *American Economic Review*, 69(5), 868–79.

Hamermesh, D. S. (1993): *Labor Demand*, Princeton University Press.

Harrison, D. A., and J. J. Martocchio (1998): 'Time for absence: a 20-year review of origins, offshoots and outcomes', *Journal of Management*, 24 (3), 305–50.

Hassink, W. H. J., and P. Koning (2009): 'Do financial bonuses reduce employee absenteeism? Evidence from a lottery', *Industrial and Labor Relations Review*, 62(3), 327–42.

Heywood, J., and U. Jirjahn (2004): 'Teams, teamwork and absence', *Scandinavian Journal of Economics.*, 106(4), 765–82.

Heywood, J., U. Jirjahn and X. Wei (2006): 'Teams, monitoring, absence and productivity', *Journal of Economic Behavior and Organization*, 68 (3–4), 676–90.

Hicks, J. R. (1932): *The Theory of Wages*, London: Macmillan.

Holt, C. A., and S. K. Laury (2002): 'Risk aversion and incentive effects', *American Economic Review*, 92(5), 1644–55.

(2005): 'Risk aversion and incentives: new data without order effects', *American Economic Review*, 95(3), 902–12.

Ichino, A., and E. Moretti (2009): 'Biological gender differences, absenteeism and the earnings gap', *American Economic Journal: Applied Economics*, 1(1), 183–218.

Ichino, A., and R. Riphahn (2005): 'The effect of employment protection on worker effort: a comparison of absenteeism during and after probation', *Journal of the European Economic Association*, 3(1), 120–43.

Jacobson, S. L. (1989): 'The effects of pay incentives on teacher absenteeism', *Journal of Human Resources*, 24(2), 280–6.

Johannsson, E., P. Böckerman and A. Uutela (2009): 'Alcohol consumption and sickness absence: evidence from microdata', *European Journal of Public Health*, 19(1), 19–22.

Johansson, P., and M. Palme (2002): 'Assessing the effect of public policy on worker absenteeism', *Journal of Human Resources*, 37(2), 381–409.

Katz, L. F. (1986): 'Efficiency wage theories: a partial evaluation', *NBER Macroeconomics Annual*, vol. I, Cambridge, MA: NBER Books, 235–76.

Kenyon, P., and P. Dawkins (1989): 'A time series analysis of labour absence in Australia', *Review of Economics and Statistics*, 71(2) 232–9.

Keynes, J. M. (1939): 'Professor Tinbergen's method', *Economic Journal*, 49, 558–77.

Killingsworth, M. R. (1983): *Labor Supply*, New York: Cambridge University Press.

Kremer, M. (1993): 'The O-ring theory of economic development', *Quarterly Journal of Economics*, 108(3), 551–75.

Kremer, M., K. Muralidharan, N. Chaudhury, J. Hammer and F. Halsey Rogers (2005): 'Teacher absence in India: a snapshot', *Journal of the European Economic Association*, 3 (2–3), 658–67.

(2006): 'Missing in action: teacher and health worker absence in developing countries', *Journal of Economic Perspectives*, 20(1), 91–116.

Krueger, A. B., and L. H. Summers (1988): 'Efficiency wages and the inter-industry wage structure', *Econometrica*, 56(2), 259–93.

Laffont, J.-J., and D. Martimort (2001): *The Theory of Incentives: The Principal–Agent Model*, Princeton University Press.

Lancaster T. (1979): 'Econometric methods for the duration of unemployment', *Econometrica*, 47(4), 939–56.

Landsbergis, P. A., J. Cahill and P. Schnall (1999): 'The impact of lean production and related new systems of work organization on worker health', *Journal of Occupational Health Psychology*, 4(2), 108–30.

Lanfranchi, J., and J. G. Treble (2010): 'Just-in-time production, work organisation and absence control', *Manchester School*, 78(5), 460–83.

Lazear, E. P. (2000): 'Performance, pay and productivity', *American Economic Review*, 90(5), 1346–61.

Leigh, J. P. (1983): 'Sex differences in absenteeism', *Industrial Relations*, 22 (3), 349–61.

Leontief, W. (1946): 'The pure theory of the guaranteed annual wage contract', *Journal of Political Economy*, 54(1), 76–9.

Leslie, D. (1982): 'Absenteeism in the UK labour market', in M. Artis, C. J. Green, D. Leslie and G. W. Smith (eds.), *Demand Management, Supply Constraints and Inflation*, Manchester University Press, 97–110.

Lindbeck, A., and M. Persson (2006): 'A model of income insurance and social norms', Working Paper no. 659, Research Institute of Industrial Economics, Stockholm.

Lindeboom, M., and M. Kerkhofs (2000): 'Multistate models for clustered duration data: an application to workplace effects on individual sickness absenteeism', *Review of Economics and Statistics*, **82**(4), 668–84.

Lundberg, S. (1985): 'Tied wage–hours offers and the endogeneity of wages', *Review of Economics and Statistics*, **67**(3), 405–10.

Malueg, D. A. (1988): 'Repeated insurance contracts with differential learning', *Review of Economic Studies*, **55**(1), 177–81.

Manski, C. F. (2007): *Identification for Prediction and Decision*, Cambridge, MA: Harvard University Press.

McCabe, K. (2003): 'Neuroeconomics', in L. Nadel (ed.), *Encyclopedia of Cognitive Science*, vol. III, New York: Nature Publishing, 294–8.

McCall, J. J. (1970): 'Economics of information and job search', *Quarterly Journal of Economics*, **84**(1), 113–26.

McFadden, D. (1981): 'Econometric models of probabilistic choice', in C. Manski and D. McFadden (eds.), *Structural Analysis of Discrete Data with Econometric Applications*, Cambridge, MA: MIT Press, 198–272.

Mikhalev, V. (1996): 'Social security in Russia under economic transformation', *Europe–Asia Studies*, **48**(1), 5–25.

Moore, H. L. (1914): *Economic Cycles: Their Law and Cause*, New York: Macmillan.

Murray, J. E. (2007): *Origins of American Health Insurance: A History of Industrial Sickness Funds*, New Haven, CT: Yale University Press.

Nolan, M. A. (2000): 'Spell durations and the impact of censoring', *Empirical Economics*, **25**(4), 699–714.

O'Hara, K., C. M. Johnson and T. A. Beehr (1985): 'Organizational behavior management in the private sector: a review of empirical research and recommendations for further investigation', *Academy of Management Review*, **10**(4), 848–64.

Oliver, N., R. Delbridge, D. Jones and J. Lowe (2005): 'World-class manufacturing: further evidence in the lean production debate', *British Journal of Management*, Special Issue **5**(1), S53–S63.

Paringer, L. (1983): 'Women and absenteeism: health or economics', *American Economic Review*, **73**(2), 123–7.

Pedalino, E., and V. U. Gamboa (1974): 'Behavior modification and absenteeism: intervention in one industrial setting', *Journal of Applied Psychology*, **59**(6), 694–8.

Radner, R. (1981): 'Monitoring cooperative agreements in a repeated principal–agent relationship', *Econometrica*, **49**(5), 1127–48.

Reza, A. M. (1975): 'Labour supply and demand, absenteeism and union behaviour', *Review of Economic Studies*, 42(2), 237–47.

Riphahn, R., and A. Thalmeier (2001): 'Behavioral effects of probation periods: an analysis of worker absenteeism', *Journal of Economics and Statistics* (*Jahrbücher für Nationalökonomie und Statistik*), 221(2), 179–201.

Robbins, L. (1930): 'On the elasticity of demand for income in terms of effort', *Economica*, 10, 123–9.

Rockoff, J. E., and M. A. Hermann (2010): 'Does menstruation explain gender gaps in work absenteeism', Working Paper no. 16523, National Bureau of Economic Research, Cambridge, MA.

Rosen S. (1974): 'Hedonic prices and implicit markets', *Journal of Political Economy*, 82(1), 34–55.

Rotemberg, J. J. (1994): 'Human relations in the workplace', *Journal of Political Economy*, 102(4), 684–717.

Rothschild, M. (1974): 'Searching for the lowest price when the distribution of prices is unknown', *Journal of Political Economy*, 82(4), 689–711.

Rothschild, M., and G. J. Werden (1979): 'Returns to scale from random factor services: existence and scope', *Bell Journal of Economics*, 10(1), 329–35.

Russell, A. (1991): *The Growth of Occupational Welfare in Britain*, Aldershot: Gower.

Sandmo, A. (1971): 'On the theory of the firm under uncertainty', *American Economic Review*, 61(1), 65–73.

Scoppa, V. (2010): 'Shirking and employment protection legislation: evidence from a natural experiment', *Economics Letters*, 107(2), 276–80.

Shapiro, C., and J. E. Stiglitz (1984): 'Equilibrium unemployment as a worker discipline device', *American Economic Review*, 74(3), 433–44.

Shearer, B. (1996): 'Piece rates, principal–agent models, and productivity profiles: parametric and semi-parametric evidence from payroll records', *Journal of Human Resources*, 31(2), 275–303.

(2004): 'Piece rates, fixed wages and incentives: evidence from a field experiment', *Review of Economic Studies*, 71(2), 513–34.

Skåtun, D. R., and J. D. Skåtun (2004): 'The impact of turnout on turning up: the complementarity of attendance among co-workers', *Journal of Economics*, 83(3), 225–42.

Skåtun, J. D. (2003): 'Take some days off, why don't you?: Endogenous sick leave and pay', *Journal of Health Economics*, 22(3), 379–402.

Skinner, B. F. (1973): 'A conversation with B. F. Skinner', *Organizational Dynamics*, 1(3), 31–40.

Smith, A. (1776): *An Inquiry into the Nature and Causes of the Wealth of Nations*, London: W. Strahan and T. Cadell.

Sorauren, I. F. (2008): 'New light on the Robbinsian theory of work supply', *Scottish Journal of Political Economy*, 57(4), 375–403.

Steel, R. P., J. R. Rentsch and J. R. Van Scotter (2007): 'Timeframes and absence frameworks: a test of Steers and Rhodes' (1978) model of attendance', *Journal of Management*, 33(2), 180–95.

Steers, R. M., and S. R. Rhodes (1978): 'Major influences on employee attendance: a process model', *Journal of Applied Psychology*, 63(4), 391–407.

Stewart, M. B. (2006): 'Maximum simulated likelihood estimation of random effects dynamic probit models with autocorrelated errors', *Stata Journal*, 6(2), 256–72.

Stone, L. (1950): 'An Elizabethan coalmine', *Economic History Review*, 3 (1), 97–106.

Thoursie, P. S. (2004): 'Reporting sick: are sporting events contagious?', *Journal of Applied Economics*, 19(6), 809–23.

Timmins, N. (2001): *The Five Giants: A Biography of the Welfare State*, 2nd edn., London: HarperCollins.

Treble, J. G. (2003): 'Intertemporal substitution of effort: some empirical evidence', *Economica*, 70, 579–95.

(2009a): 'A tale of two continents: insuring workers against loss of income due to sickness in North America and Europe', *National Institute Economic Review*, 209(1), 116–25.

(2009b): 'Evaluating experience-rated incentive schemes', working paper, School of Business and Economics, Swansea University.

Treble, J. G., and S. J. R. Vicary (1993): 'Equity, efficiency and insurance: explaining the structure of miners' wage payments in Victorian County Durham', *Economic Journal*, 103, 481–93.

Turner, C. A. (1982): 'A well pay incentive program', *Public Productivity Review*, 6(1–2), 127–30.

Umiker, W. O. (1988): 'Control of absenteeism: quick fixes vs. cures', *Medical Laboratory Observer*, 20(8), 47–50.

VandenHeuvel, A., and M. Wooden (1995): 'Do explanations of absenteeism differ for men and women?', *Human Relations*, 48(11), 1309–29.

Vernon, H. M. (1921): *Industrial Fatigue and Efficiency*, London: Routledge (replica edn. pub. 2005, Boston: Elibron Classics).

Viscusi, W. K., and W. N. Evans (1990): 'Utility functions that depend on health status: estimates and economic implications', *American Economic Review*, 80(3), 353–74.

Vistnes, J. (1997): 'Gender differences in days lost from work due to illness', *Industrial and Labor Relations Review*, 50(2), 304–23.

Winkelmann, R. (1996): 'Markov Chain Monte Carlo analysis of under-reported count data with an application to worker absenteeism', *Empirical Economics*, 21(4), 575–87.

(2008): *Econometric Analysis of Count Data*, 5th edn., New York: Springer.

Working, E. J. (1927): 'What do statistical "demand curves" show?', *Quarterly Journal of Economics*, **41**(2), 212–35.

Zame, W. R. (2007): 'Incentives, contracts and markets: a general equilibrium theory of firms', *Econometrica*, **75**(5), 1453–500.

Zerubavel, E. (1985): *The Seven Day Circle: The History and Meaning of the Week*, New York: Free Press.

Index

Printed in the United States
by Baker & Taylor Publisher Services